Drupal 7 Module Development

Create your own Drupal 7 modules from scratch

Matt Butcher
Greg Dunlap
Matt Farina
Larry Garfield
Ken Rickard
John Albin Wilkins

[PACKT] open source ✽
PUBLISHING   community experience distilled

BIRMINGHAM - MUMBAI

Drupal 7 Module Development

First published: December 2010

Production Reference: 1301110

Published by Packt Publishing Ltd.
32 Lincoln Road
Olton
Birmingham, B27 6PA, UK.

ISBN 978-1-849511-16-2

www.packtpub.com

Cover Image by Vinayak Chittar (vinayak.chittar@gmail.com)

Credits

Authors
Matt Butcher
Greg Dunlap
Matt Farina
Larry Garfield
Ken Rickard
John Albin Wilkins

Reviewers
Davy Van Den Bremt
Dave Myburgh
Jojodae Ganesh Sivaji

Acquisition Editor
Sarah Cullington

Development Editors
Mayuri Kokate
Susmita Panda

Technical Editors
Vanjeet D'souza
Harshit Shah

Copy Editor
Neha Shetty

Editorial Team Leader
Akshara Aware

Project Team Leader
Priya Mukherji

Project Coordinator
Srimoyee Ghoshal

Proofreader
Aaron Nash

Indexers
Tejal Daruwale
Hemangini Bari

Graphics
Nilesh R. Mohite

Production Coordinator
Aparna Bhagat

Cover Work
Aparna Bhagat

Foreword

Drupal has its roots in the humble hobby project of Dries Buytaert, Drupal project lead, then a university student. He originally created a small news site and web board so that he and his friends could stay in touch. When it was time for graduation, this small script was put on the public web, and a small but vibrant community of developers, hackers, tinkerers, and innovators started to gather there. The script powering the website was open sourced as "Drupal" in January, 2001, and attracted attention due to its extensibility and modular architecture.

Since then, both the Drupal project and its community have exploded in growth. The community now consists of over 700,000 people all over the world. Drupal also now powers over 1% of the web, including the websites of household names such as whitehouse.gov and grammy.com.

My current position in the Drupal community is that of the Release Manager for the latest release of Drupal, version 7. Dries Buytaert and I work together with the core contributor team to help prioritize initiatives, encourage people attacking similar problems to work together, act as final quality assurance reviewers on patches, and ultimately commit changes to the project once they're ready.

Drupal 7 represents a tremendous leap forward from previous releases. The core contributor team together took a very serious look at Drupal's limitations, from almost all angles. Usability testing research was done at several universities, highlighting long-standing problems with Drupal's user interface, and a usability team emerged to tackle the problems. Engineers collaborated together to identify and dissect severe API limitations that had plagued previous releases. The quality assurance team put tremendous efforts behind integrating automated testing into our development workflow, vastly improving our ability to refactor parts of the system. Drupal's designer community stepped up and became vocal about Drupal's limitations on the theming side that cause them to go flocking to other frameworks. An accessibility team emerged, not only pushing patches forward to improve Drupal's WCAG compliance, but also educating the members of the community about accessibility. Drupal 7 is a remarkable release for a number of reasons, but particularly for the diversity of the team involved in creating it.

As a result of all of this effort, however, there is very little in Drupal 7 that hasn't changed over previous releases. The database abstraction layer has been completely re-written and is now based on the PHP Data Objects (PDO) library, which introduces a new object-oriented syntax to queries. In addition to forms and certain content, such as node and user data, in Drupal 7 the entirety of the page is built on renderable arrays, which has tremendous (and exciting) implications for themes. Adding metadata fields to various system entities is now possible through Drupal 7's integrated field and entity API, which previously required an additional module, and was limited to only being able to expand content. There are literally hundreds of other under-the-hood improvements.

The Drupal 7 Module Development book offers a project-based approach that walks readers through the most important, new, and changed concepts in-depth, allowing you to put these into practice. The authors of this edition of the book have much more than "merely" a deep understanding of Drupal 7's internals — in many cases, they literally wrote the very patches that put those internals into place. Larry Garfield is the chief architect behind Drupal 7's new object-oriented database abstraction layer, and Drupal core's database system maintainer. John Wilkins engineered much of the improvements to template files and theme system internals in Drupal 7, based largely on his cutting-edge work on the Zen theme. Ken Rickard spear-headed numerous improvements to Drupal 7's node access system after exploring its outer limits in his contributed Domain Access and Menu Access modules. Matt Farina assisted with numerous core JavaScript improvements, including alterability of CSS and JavaScript, and front-end performance. Greg Dunlap's work with core API documentation has many times ferreted out particularly hard-to-find bugs.

It's my sincere hope that this book finds many eager readers who are able to not only extend Drupal 7 to meet their specific needs, but also join our vibrant development community to contribute back what they learn and help make Drupal even better.

Angela Byron

Drupal 7 Core Maintainer

Drupal Association Secretary

About the Authors

Matt Butcher is a web developer and author. He has written five other books for Packt, including *Drupal 6 JavaScript and jQuery* and *Learning Drupal 6 Module Development*. Matt is a Senior Developer at ConsumerSearch.com (a New York Times/About.Com company), where he works on one of the largest Drupal sites in the world. Matt is active in the Drupal community, managing several modules. He also leads a couple of Open Source projects including QueryPath.

I would like to thank Larry, Ken, Sam, Matt, Greg, and John for working with me on the book. They are a fantastic group of people to work with. I'd also like to thank the technical reviewers of this book, all of whom contributed to making this a better work.

I'd also like to thank Austin Smith, Brian Tully, Chachi Kruel, Marc McDougall, Theresa Summa, and the rest of the ConsumerSearch. com team for their support. The folks at Palantir.net were instrumental in getting this book off the ground, and I am always grateful for their support. Finally, Angie, Anna, Claire, and Katherine have sacrificed some weekends and evenings with me for the benefit of this book. To them, I owe the biggest debt of gratitude.

Greg Dunlap is a software engineer based in Stockholm, Sweden. Over the past 15 years, Greg has been involved in a wide variety of projects, including desktop database applications, kiosks, embedded software for pinball and slot machines, and websites in over a dozen programming languages. Greg has been heavily involved with Drupal for three years, and is the maintainer of the Deploy and Services modules as well as a frequent speaker at Drupal conferences. Greg is currently a Principal Software Developer at NodeOne.

Several people played crucial roles in my development as a Drupal contributor, providing support and encouragement just when I needed it most. My deepest gratitude to Gary Love, Jeff Eaton, Boris Mann, Angie Byron, and Ken Rickard for helping me kick it up a notch. Extra special thanks to the lovely Roya Naini for putting up with lost nights and weekends in the service of finishing my chapters.

Matt Farina has been a Drupal developer since 2005. He is a senior front-end developer, engineer, and technical lead for Palantir.net, where he works on a wide variety of projects ranging from museums to large interactive sites. He is a contributor to Drupal core as well as a maintainer of multiple contributed Drupal modules.

Matt wrote his first computer program when he was in the 5th grade. Since then he has programmed in over a dozen languages. He holds a BS in Electrical Engineering from Michigan State University.

Larry Garfield is a Senior Architect and Engineer at Palantir.net, a leading Drupal development firm based in Chicago. He has been building websites since he was 16, which is longer than he'd like to admit, and has been working in PHP since 1999. He found Drupal in 2005, when Drupal 4.6 was still new and cool, and never really left. He is the principle architect and maintainer of the Drupal database subsystem among various other core initiatives and contributed modules.

Previously, Larry was a Palm OS developer and a journalist covering the mobile electronics sector and was the technical editor for *Building Powerful and Robust Websites with Drupal 6*, also from *Packt*. He holds a Bachelors and Masters Degree in Computer Science from DePaul University.

If I were to thank all of the people who made this book possible it would take several pages, as the Drupal 7 contributor list was well over 700 people, the last time I checked. Instead I will simply say thank you to the entire community for being so vibrant, supportive, and all-around amazing that it still brings a tear to my eye at times even after half a decade.

Extra special thanks go to Dries Buytaert, not just for being our project lead, but for sitting down on the floor next to me at DrupalCon Sunnyvale and encouraging me to run with this crazy idea I had, about using this "PDO" thing for Drupal's database layer. I doubt he realized how much trouble I'd cause him over the next several years.

Of course to my parents, who instilled in me not only a love of learning but a level of pedantry and stubbornness without which I would never have been able to get this far in Drupal, to say nothing of this book.

Ken Rickard is a senior programmer at Palantir.net, a Chicago-based firm specializing in developing Drupal websites. He is a frequent contributor to the Drupal project, and is the maintainer of the Domain Access, MySite, and Menu Node API modules. At Palantir, he architects and builds large-scale websites for a diverse range of customers, including Foreign Affairs magazine, NASCAR, and the University of Chicago.

From 1998 through 2008, Ken worked in the newspaper industry, beginning his career managing websites and later becoming a researcher and consultant for Morris DigitalWorks. At Morris, Ken helped launch BlufftonToday.com, the first newspaper website launched on the Drupal platform. He later led the Drupal development team for SavannahNOW.com. He co-founded the Newspapers on Drupal group (`http://groups.drupal.org/newspapers-on-drupal`) and is a frequent advisor to the newspaper and publishing industries.

In 2008, Ken helped start the Knight Drupal Initiative, an open grant process for Drupal development, funded by the John L. and James S. Knight Foundation. He is also a member of the advisory board of PBS Engage, a Knight Foundation project to bring social media to the Public Broadcasting Service.

Prior to this book, Ken was a technical reviewer for *Packt Publishing's Drupal 6 Site Blueprints* by *Timi Ogunjobi*.

I must thank the entire staff at Palantir, the Drupal community, and, most of all, my lovely and patient wife Amy, without whom none of this would be possible.

John Albin Wilkins has been a web developer for a long time. In April 1993, he was one of the lucky few to use the very first graphical web browser, Mosaic 1.0, and he's been doing web development professionally since 1994. In 2005, John finally learned how idiotic it was to build your own web application framework, and discovered the power of Drupal; he never looked back.

In the Drupal community, he is best known as JohnAlbin, one of the top 20 contributors to Drupal 7 and the maintainer of the Zen theme, which is a highly-documented, feature-rich "starter" theme with a powerfully flexible CSS framework. He has also written several front-end-oriented utility modules, such as the Menu Block module. John currently works with a bunch of really cool Drupal developers, designers, and themers at Palantir.net.

His occasional musings, videos, and podcasts can be found at
`http://john.albin.net`.

I'd to thank the entire Drupal community for its wonderful support, friendship, aggravation, snark, and inspiration; just like a family. I'd also like to thank my real family, my wife and two kids, Jenny, Owen and Ella, for making me want to be a better person. I love you all.

About the Reviewers

Davy Van Den Bremt has been developing Drupal websites for about four years. He lives in Ghent, Belgium, and works as a Senior Drupal developer at Krimson.

He studied Computer Science at the University of Ghent but rolled into web as a designer and client side developer. He became a full time Drupal developer while working at VRT, the Flemisch public broadcasting company and has since developed websites for most major Belgian media companies, advertising agencies, and government institutions.

He maintains a blog at `drupalcoder.com` where he keeps notes of all things Drupal that he discovers during his work and wants to share with other Drupal users.

He has written some patches for Drupal 7 and maintains a few modules like Administration Theme and E-mail Marketing Framework.

Dave Myburgh has been involved with computers even before the web existed. He studied to become a molecular biologist, but discovered that he liked working with computers more than bacteria. He had his own computer business in South Africa, (where he grew up) doing technical support and sales. He even created a few static websites for clients during that time.

After moving to Canada, he got sucked into the world of Drupal a few years ago, when a friend wanted a site for a local historical society. Since then he has once again started his own company and now builds websites exclusively in Drupal (he doesn't "do static" anymore). There is no lack of work in the Drupal world and he now balances his time between work and family. He has reviewed several Drupal books including Drupal 5 Themes, and Drupal 6 Themes.

> I would like to thank my family for being so supportive of me and what I do. Working from home can be a mixed blessing sometimes, but having the opportunity to watch my son grow up makes it all worthwhile.

Jojodae Ganesh Sivaji has been involved with the Drupal community for more than two years. Sivaji is an active member; he has contributed to the community in terms of writing patches to `core` and `contrib` modules. He was involved in Google Summer of Code 2009. There he worked for the Drupal organization on quiz module features enhancement and bug fixing project with Matt Butcher and other Drupal developers. The project was completed successfully under the guidance of mentors, Matt Butcher and Shyamala.

He has developed and maintains a few contributed modules and themes on `drupal.org`. Sivaji's Drupal user account page can be found at `http://drupal.org/user/328724`.

He is currently the lead web developer and programmer at SG E-ndicus InfoTech Pvt Ltd, Chennai. At E-ndicus, he is responsible for requirement analysis, arriving at and providing solutions, building and maintaining websites, primarily on Drupal and Joomla.

I would like to extend my sincere thanks to my mentor, Matt Butcher, for giving me the time and continuous encouragement to pursue Drupal, including, reviewing this book.

Also, I would like to thank Mr. Vikram Vijayaragavan, Mrs. Shyamala, Mr. Sri Ramadoss, ILUGC, and the entire Drupal community (especially the Drupal Chennai community) for their support with my continual Drupal evangelism.

www.PacktPub.com

Support files, eBooks, discount offers and more

You might want to visit www.PacktPub.com for support files and downloads related to your book.

Did you know that Packt offers eBook versions of every book published, with PDF and ePub files available? You can upgrade to the eBook version at www.PacktPub.com and as a print book customer, you are entitled to a discount on the eBook copy. Get in touch with us at service@packtpub.com for more details.

At www.PacktPub.com, you can also read a collection of free technical articles, sign up for a range of free newsletters and receive exclusive discounts and offers on Packt books and eBooks.

http://PacktLib.PacktPub.com

Do you need instant solutions to your IT questions? PacktLib is Packt's online digital book library. Here, you can access, read and search across Packt's entire library of books.

Why Subscribe?

- Fully searchable across every book published by Packt
- Copy & paste, print and bookmark content
- On demand and accessible via web browser

Free Access for Packt account holders

If you have an account with Packt at www.PacktPub.com, you can use this to access PacktLib today and view nine entirely free books. Simply use your login credentials for immediate access.

Table of Contents

Preface

Drupal is an award-winning open-source Content Management System. It's a modular system, with an elegant hook-based architecture, and great code. Modules are plugins for Drupal that extend, build or enhance Drupal core functionality. In Drupal 7 Module development book, six professional Drupal developers use a practical, example-based approach to introduce PHP developers to the powerful new Drupal 7 tools, APIs, and strategies for writing custom Drupal code.

These tools not only make management and maintenance of websites much easier, but they are also great fun to play around with and amazingly easy to use.

What this book covers

Chapter 1, Introduction to Drupal Module Development gives a introduction to the scope of Drupal as a web-based Content Management System. It dwells on basic aspects such as the technologies that drive Drupal and the architectural layout of Drupal. A brief idea of the components (subsystems) of Drupal and the tools that may be used to develop it, completes the basic picture of Drupal.

Chapter 2, A First Module, gets things into action, by describing how to start building our first module in Drupal. That done, it will tell us how Block API can be used to create our custom code for Drupal. Finally, there is a word or two on how to test our code by writing Automated tests.

Chapter 3, Drupal Themes, is all about the Theme Layer in Drupal. It starts with ways to theme, and then proceeds to aspects associated with Theming. It talks about 'Render Elements' and concludes by getting us familiar with 'Theme Registry'.

Chapter 4, Theming a Module uses the concepts we saw in the previous chapter to theme modules in Drupal. It acquaints us with the concept of re-using a default theme implementation, and teaches us to build a theme implementation for real-life situations.

Chapter 5, Building an Admin Interface will show us how to go about building a module, complete with an administrative interface. While doing this, basic concepts of modules discussed in *Chapter 2* will be useful. A 'User Warn' module is developed as an illustration, in the chapter.

Chapter 6, Working with Content lays emphasis on managing content. Creation of entity, controller class, integrating our entity with the Field API, and displaying confirmation forms are some of the things that we come across in this chapter.

Chapter 7, Creating New Fields, will take a look into creating new Fields. Further, it teaches us how to use corresponding Widgets to allow users to edit the Fields. Finally, to ensure that data is displayed as desired, the role of Formatters is discussed in the chapter.

Chapter 8, Module Permissions and Security is all about access control and security. It talks about Permissions, which help users to gain access (or be denied access) to specific features. Also, the chapter talks about how to manage roles programmatically. One of the most crucial areas of website security, Form handling, is detailed here.

Chapter 9, Node Access deals with node access, which is one of the most powerful tools in the Drupal API. It sheds light on how access to a node is determined and on major operations controlled by the Node Access API, among other things.

Chapter 10, JavaScript in Drupal provides the fundamental knowledge required to work with JavaScript within Drupal. This helps to create powerful features such as the overlay, auto complete, drag and drop, and so on.

Chapter 11, Working with Files and Images talks about how management and maintenance can be made much easier by using File and Image APIs in Drupal 7. Also, the chapter tells us about various image processing techniques involved in working with images, making things more colorful and fun.

Chapter 12, Installation Profiles outlines the process of working with 'Distributions' and 'Installation Profiles' in Drupal. They help to make the developer's job easier.

Appendix A, Database Access, offers helpful insights regarding the developer's ability to take advantage of the Database Layer of Drupal 7, in order to make powerful cross-database queries.

Appendix B, Security, emphasizes the need to develop a practice to bear the security aspect in mind while writing the code. It deals with two ways of dealing with potentially insecure data, namely, 'filtering' and 'escaping'.

Who this book is for

If you are a PHP developer or a Drupal user looking to dive into Drupal development, then you will find this book an excellent introduction to coding within Drupal. Those with some Drupal experience will also find this an invaluable tool for updating their knowledge about the powerful new features of Drupal 7. Theme developers looking to extend their abilities will find this an accessible introduction to PHP coding within the Drupal environment.

This book assumes that you are familiar with basic PHP programming, along with HTML and CSS. No experience in programming Drupal is required, although it is also a handy way for experienced Drupal developers to get up to speed with Drupal 7.

Conventions

In this book, you will find a number of styles of text that distinguish between different kinds of information. Here are some examples of these styles, and an explanation of their meaning.

Code words in text are shown as follows: " The third argument specifies what `file_save_data()` should do when a file already exists with the same name as the file we're trying to save."

A block of code is set as follows:

```
$contents = ";
$handle = fopen("/var/www/htdocs/images/xyzzy.jpg", "rb");
while (!feof($handle)) {
  $contents .= fread($handle, 8192);

}

fclose($handle);
```

When we wish to draw your attention to a particular part of a code block, the relevant lines or items are set in bold:

```
$items['user/%/warn'] = array(
    'title' => 'Warn',
    'description' => 'Send e-mail to a user about improper site
                      behavior.',
    'page callback' => 'drupal_get_form',
```

New terms and **important words** are shown in bold.

The system for handling this is collectively called the **theme system**.

Words that you see on the screen, in menus, or dialog boxes for example, appear in the text like this: " In the screenshot above, you can see the grouping package **Core** in the upper-left corner."

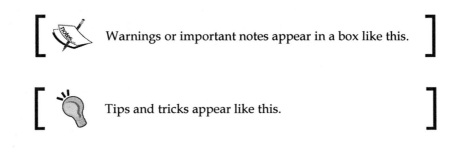

Warnings or important notes appear in a box like this.

Tips and tricks appear like this.

Reader feedback

Feedback from our readers is always welcome. Let us know what you think about this book—what you liked or may have disliked. Reader feedback is important for us to develop titles that you really get the most out of.

To send us general feedback, simply send an e-mail to feedback@packtpub.com, and mention the book title via the subject of your message.

If there is a book that you need and would like to see us publish, please send us a note in the **SUGGEST A TITLE** form on www.packtpub.com or e-mail suggest@packtpub.com.

If there is a topic that you have expertise in and you are interested in either writing or contributing to a book, see our author guide on www.packtpub.com/authors.

Customer support

Now that you are the proud owner of a Packt book, we have a number of things to help you to get the most from your purchase.

Downloading the example code for this book

You can download the example code files for all Packt books you have purchased from your account at http://www.PacktPub.com. If you purchased this book elsewhere, you can visit http://www.PacktPub.com/support and register to have the files e-mailed directly to you.

Errata

Although we have taken every care to ensure the accuracy of our content, mistakes do happen. If you find a mistake in one of our books—maybe a mistake in the text or the code—we would be grateful if you would report it to us. By doing so, you can save other readers from frustration and help us improve subsequent versions of this book. If you find any errata, please report them by visiting http://www.packtpub.com/support, selecting your book, clicking on the **errata submission form** link, and entering the details of your errata. Once your errata are verified, your submission will be accepted and the errata will be uploaded on our website, or added to any list of existing errata, under the Errata section of that title. Any existing errata can be viewed by selecting your title from http://www.packtpub.com/support.

Piracy

Piracy of copyright material on the Internet is an ongoing problem across all media. At Packt, we take the protection of our copyright and licenses very seriously. If you come across any illegal copies of our works, in any form, on the Internet, please provide us with the location address or website name immediately so that we can pursue a remedy.

Please contact us at copyright@packtpub.com with a link to the suspected pirated material.

We appreciate your help in protecting our authors, and our ability to bring you valuable content.

Questions

You can contact us at questions@packtpub.com if you are having a problem with any aspect of the book, and we will do our best to address it.

1
Developing for Drupal 7

Drupal is a web-based content management system (CMS) and social media platform. While it is useful out of the box, it is designed with developers in mind. The purpose of this book is to explain how Drupal can be extended in many ways and for many purposes. This chapter introduces the terminology, tools, and processes for developing Drupal 7. While subsequent chapters focus on code, this chapter focuses on concepts. We'll talk about the architecture of Drupal, and how you can hook into Drupal at strategic places to extend it for accomplishing new tasks.

The following are the major things we will be covering in this chapter:

- An introduction to Drupal development
- The architecture of Drupal
- Nodes, Fields, Users, and other major subsystems
- Tools for developing in Drupal

By the end of this chapter, you will understand the architectural aspects of Drupal and be ready to start writing code.

Introducing Drupal (for developers)

Out of the box, Drupal 7 performs all of the standard functions of a web-based content management system. Visitors can view published information on the site, navigate through menus, and view individual pages, complete with images. Users can create accounts and leave comments. Administrators can manage the site configuration and control the permissions levels of users. Editors can create content, preview it, and then publish it when it is ready. Content can be syndicated to RSS, where feed readers can pick up new articles as they are published. With several built-in themes, even the look and feel of the site can easily be changed.

As fantastic as these features are, they will certainly not satisfy the needs of all users. To that end, Drupal's capabilities can be easily extended with modules, themes, and installation profiles. Take a look at Drupal's main website, `http://drupal.org`, and you will find thousands of modules that provide new features, and thousands of themes that transform the look and feel of the site.

The fact that almost all aspects of Drupal's behavior can be intercepted and transformed through the module and theme mechanisms has lead many to claim that Drupal isn't just a Content Management *System (CMS)*, but a Content Management *Framework (CMF)* capable of being re-tooled to specific needs and functional requirements.

Whether or not Drupal is rightly called a CMS or a CMF is beyond our present interests, but it is certain that Drupal's most tremendous asset is its extensibility. Want to use a directory server for authentication? There's a Drupal module for that. Want to export data to CSV (Comma Separated Version) files? There are several modules for that (depending on what data you want to export). Interested in Facebook support, integration with Twitter, or adding a **Share This** button? Yup, there are modules for all of these too—all of which are available at `http://drupal.org/`.

Want to integrate Drupal with that custom tool you wrote to solve your specific business needs? There may not be a module for that, but with a little bit of code, you can write your own. In fact, that is the subject of this book.

The purpose of this book is to get you ramped up (as quickly as possible) for Drupal development. As we move chapter by chapter through this book, we cover the APIs and tools that you will use to build custom Drupal sites, and we don't stick to theory. Each chapter provides working, practically-oriented example code designed to show you how to build code. We follow Drupal coding conventions and we utilize Drupal design patterns in an effort to illustrate the correct way to write code. While we certainly can't write the exact code to meet your needs, our hope is that the code mentioned in this chapter can serve as a foundation for your bigger and better applications.

So let's get started with a few preliminary matters.

Technologies that drive Drupal

Many books of this ilk will begin with a chapter on installing the platform. We have decided not to follow this pattern for a few reasons. First of all, Drupal is incredibly well documented in this regard. The README file included with Drupal's download should meet your needs. Secondly, our experience has been that such chapters are unnecessary. Software developers rarely need step-by-step guides to installing a system as simple as Drupal.

However, what we do want to start with, is a quick overview of the technologies utilized in Drupal.

PHP

Drupal is written in the **PHP programming language** (http://php.net). PHP is a widely supported, multi-platform, web-centric scripting language. Since Drupal is written in PHP, this book is largely focused on PHP development.

One specific piece of information should be made explicit: As of Drupal 7, the minimum PHP version is PHP 5.2 (as of this writing, the current version of PHP is 5.3.3). Prior versions of Drupal included PHP 4.x support, but this is no longer the case.

Another thing worth mentioning is the *style of PHP coding* that Drupal uses. While many PHP applications are now written using **Object Oriented Programming**, Drupal does not follow suit. For many reasons, some historical, some practical, Drupal is largely written using **procedural programming**. Rather than relying strongly on classes and interfaces, Drupal modules are composed of collections of functions.

Before anyone jumps to conclusions, though, we would like to make a few qualifications on what we've just said:

- Drupal frequently uses objects
- Drupal does have certain subsystems that are object-oriented
- Many Drupal modules are substantially object-oriented
- Drupal makes frequent use of design patterns, for it is certainly the case that procedural code can use design patterns too

While the majority of this book uses procedural coding strategies, you will encounter OOP here and there. If you are not familiar with object oriented conventions and coding styles, don't worry. We will explain these pieces as we go.

Databases and MySQL

In the past, Drupal has supported two databases: MySQL and PostgreSQL. Drupal 7 has moved beyond this. Drupal now uses the powerful PDO (PHP Data Objects) library that is standard in PHP 5. This library is an abstraction layer that allows developers to support numerous databases including MySQL, PostgreSQL, SQLite, MariaDB, and many, many others. While Drupal does testing on only a few specific databases (namely, MySQL, PostgreSQL, and now SQLite), it is possible to move beyond these to SQL Server, Oracle, DB2, and others.

However, for the sake of size and readability, we have focused our examples on MySQL. We believe that our SQL should run on MariaDB, PostgreSQL, and SQLite without modification, but we have not made any attempt to test against other databases. If you find a bug, we'd appreciate hearing about it. Packt Publishing tracks errata on their website (`http://packtpub.com`), and you can submit errors that you find through the form you find there.

Drupal provides a database API along with some SQL coding conventions (such as "don't use `LIMIT` in your SQL"). The intent of these is to combine code and convention to make it as easy as possible to write portable code. Thus, we not only illustrate the API throughout this book, but we also focus on writing SQL statements that comply with standard Drupal conventions.

HTML, CSS, and JavaScript

The *de facto* web data format is HTML (HyperText Markup Language) styled with CSS (Cascading Style Sheets). Client-side interactive components are scripted with JavaScript. As Drupal developers, we will encounter all three of these technologies in this book. While you needn't be a JavaScript ninja to understand the code here, you will get the most from this book if you are comfortable with these three technologies.

Other technologies

The Internet thrives on change, it seems, and there are many other web technologies that have become common. Here and there, we will mention technologies such as RSS (Really Simple Syndication), XML (eXtensible Markup Language), XML-RPC, and others. However, these are all of secondary importance to us. While Drupal offers support for many of these things, using them is not integral to module or theme development.

The web server

Apache has long been the predominant web server, but it is by no means the only server. While Drupal was originally written with Apache in mind, many other web servers (including IIS, LigHTTPD, and nginx) can run Drupal.

We do not explicitly cover the web server layer anywhere here, primarily because development rarely requires working at that low level. However, Drupal expects a fair amount of processing from the web server layer, including handling of URL rewriting.

The Operating System

 Windows, Linux, Mac OS, BSD. These are terms that spark modern online holy wars. However, we don't care to take part in the argument. Drupal will run on most (if not all) popular server operating systems, including Windows and many UNIX/Linux variants.

In the interest of full disclosure, the authors of this book work primarily on Linux and Mac OS X systems. However, our code should run on any Drupal system. Again, if you find examples where our code does not run because of the operating system, submit an erratum on Packt Publishing's website. Drupal strives to be cross-platform, and so do we.

With these preliminaries behind us, let's move on to Drupal's architecture.

Drupal architecture

In the preceding section, we introduced the technologies that drive Drupal. However, how do they all fit together? In this section, we provide an overview of Drupal's architecture.

Let's begin with a visual representation. The following diagram sketches Drupal's main components:

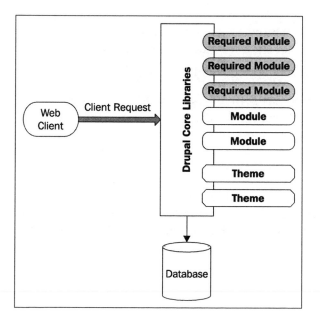

The preceding figure represents, in a roughshod way, how Drupal is structured. It also indicates how Drupal handles a request. We will talk about the components in the remainder of this section. As a first approach, though, let's walk through a simplified example of a typical request as it is handled on a Drupal website:

- A user enters the URL `http://example.com/node/123` in a web browser and hits *Enter*
- The browser contacts the web server at `example.com` and requests the resource at `/node/123`
- The web server recognizes that the request must be handled by PHP, and starts up (or contacts) a PHP environment to handle the request
- PHP executes Drupal's `index.php` file, handing it the path `/node/123`
- The **Drupal core** undergoes a **bootstrap** process, initializing resources, and then uses the **menu system** to find out how to handle `/node/123`
- The **node system** responds to the request for `/node/123` by loading the node (piece of content) with the ID `123`. This data is typically loaded from a database
- The **theme system** takes the node information and applies formatting and style information to it, essentially transforming data into chunks of HTML with associated CSS
- The **Drupal core** completes all processing (giving many other subsystems the opportunity to handle various bits of data processing) and then returns the data to the client
- The client web browser transforms the HTML and CSS into a visual presentation for the user, running any necessary JavaScript along the way
- The user views the document

While this illustration hasn't hit every technical detail, it does provide a glimpse into the way Drupal functions on the web. In the following section, we will spend some time looking at the big Drupal subsystems—nodes, themes, menus, and so on. However, in the present section, we are more concerned with the general way in which these systems work together.

Earlier, we saw that under normal conditions, PHP loads Drupal's `index.php` file to handle a Drupal request. This short script is responsible for starting up the Drupal environment, and it is part of what we typically call the **Drupal core**.

Drupal core is the foundational layer of Drupal which ships with a handful of **core libraries** along with over a dozen **core modules**. The index file loads the libraries and then initializes Drupal, a process called **bootstrapping**.

Drupal core libraries

The core libraries provide the functions and services used throughout Drupal. Facilities for interacting with the database, translating between languages, sanitizing user data, building forms, and encoding data are all found in Drupal's core libraries. These tools are what we might call utilities: They facilitate effective data processing, but are not responsible for handling the lifecycle of a request. The lifecycle is handled by modules.

Once Drupal has loaded core libraries and initialized the database, it loads the enabled modules and themes, and then it begins a systematic, step-by-step process of handling the request. This process is what I call the lifecycle of a request. It works as follows.

Drupal steps through a number of pre-determined operations. It checks to see if any modules need to be initialized. It looks up what code is responsible for handling the given URL. It checks whether the current user has access to the requested resource. It checks to see if some data can be retrieved from cache. It continues stepping through such operations until the request is complete.

However, the most important thing about this step-by-step process is the way Drupal does it.

Drupal hooks

The Drupal core doesn't attempt to *do the processing* for each of these steps. Instead, after each step, it *offers one or more modules the opportunity to handle that step*. Put in Drupal parlance, it offers opportunities for modules to hook into the lifecycle.

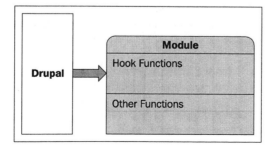

For example, we noted that Drupal checks to see if any module needs to be initialized. What it actually does, is look to see if any modules *implement a hook* for initialization. How does it do this? It scans the loaded modules to see if any of them implement the function `hook_init()`. To implement a hook in Drupal is to declare a function that follows the hook naming pattern. For a fictional module named `hello` to implement `hook_init()`, it would merely need to declare a function named `hello_init()` (replacing the word `hook` with the name of the module).

 Developers with a background in OOP or with strong knowledge of design patterns might recognize this as being similar to the event handling paradigm, captured in the Passive Observer pattern. When some particular event occurs, Drupal allows modules the opportunity to respond to that event.

Through this `hook_init()` hook, Drupal provides modules the ability to initialize themselves or their own resources right at the beginning of the request. Once all of these modules have been initialized, Drupal moves on to the next step. As it progresses through the request, it calls hook after hook, giving modules the opportunity to do their thing. Finally, it makes one last call for modules that implement `hook_exit()`, and then it returns any remaining data to the client and terminates the request.

Drupal's hook system is perhaps the single most important aspect of Drupal programming. Most (if not all) modules are nothing more than a collection of hook implementations that Drupal automatically calls as it works its way through the request lifecycle. It's not just the Drupal core that declares and calls hooks. Any module can declare and call its own hook. Many modules do in fact declare their own hooks, offering other modules the opportunity to integrate deeply with their services.

Drupal core modules

As noted earlier, Drupal provides several **core modules**. These modules cannot be disabled, as their capabilities are integral to the standard functioning of Drupal. Just like other modules (including the ones we will be writing), core modules function by implementing Drupal hooks.

As Drupal invokes these hooks, each core module will respond as necessary, performing crucial functions at specific times during the course of a request.

In the following section, we will discuss several core modules in more detail, explaining what purposes these modules serve.

The database

We have taken a brisk walk through a typical Drupal request, and we have learned a little about modules and libraries. However, what about the database?

Unlike many architectures, for Drupal the database doesn't stand front and center. The database layer is not a module, nor do modules need to declare a specific relationship with the database. In fact, many Drupal modules do not ever interact directly with the database.

> Unlike Model-View-Controller (MVC) frameworks, Drupal does not require that modules follow an MVC pattern. For that reason, a module can exist, yet not have any database structures (models), a central controller, or even any user-centered theming (view).

Instead of treating the database as a central architectural component, Drupal merely provides an API for working with the database. In Drupal, the database is just a place to store data. Need custom tables? Drupal provides a system for declaring them. Need to get data out of the database, or insert or update new data? Drupal provides functions and an OO library for doing so. However, if you don't need such features for your code, you needn't work with the database at all. In fact, in the next chapter we will write our first module without writing a single SQL query.

Later in this book, we will see how to interact with the database using Drupal's robust database tools.

> **More than just data**
>
> The Drupal database does not store just application data (or content), but also configuration, caches, metadata (data about data), structural information, and sometimes even PHP code.

While Drupal may not be database centric, it most certainly requires a database. During initialization, Drupal will connect to a database and retrieve certain configuration data. Later, as many of the core modules load, they too, contact the database to retrieve or update information. For most Drupal modules, the database is the location for data storage.

The theme system

The final component from our initial architectural diagram is the theme system. Drupal separates the look-and-feel components of the system from the rest of Drupal, and provides a programmatic way for theming data. The system for handling this is collectively called the **theme system**.

Some of the theme system resides in the Drupal core libraries. This part is responsible for initializing themes and locating what theme functions and templates should be applied under certain circumstances.

However, the majority of the theme code resides in themes and modules.

A **theme** is a structured bundle of code (like a module) that provides tools for transforming raw data into formatted output. Sites use at least one theme to apply a consistent and custom look-and-feel to all of the pages on the site.

However, Not all theme code resides inside of a theme. One of the distinct advantages offered by Drupal is the capability to define default theming inside modules, and then provide mechanisms by which the theme layer can selectively override those themes. In other words, a module might declare a rough layout for a component, but Drupal provides the structure for a theme developer to later modify the theme (not the module) to re-layout that component in a different way.

If this all sounds conceptually difficult, don't worry. *Chapter 3* and *Chapter 4* of this book are dedicated to working with the theming system.

Now that we've had a quick architectural overview, let's change perspectives and quickly peruse the major subsystems offered by Drupal.

Drupal's major subsystems

In the previous section we took a birds-eye view of Drupal's architecture. Now we are going to refine our perspective a bit. We are going to walk through the major subsystems that Drupal 7 has to offer.

Themes

The theme subsystem was introduced above, and since *Chapter 3* and *Chapter 4* will cover it, we won't dwell too much on it here. However, there are a few details that should be mentioned at the outset.

The responsibility of theming a given piece of data is spread out over the Drupal core, the modules, and the applied theme itself. While we don't modify the Drupal core code, it is important for developers to be able to understand that both module code and theme code can manipulate the look and feel of data.

In this book, our focus will be on the module perspective. We work primarily with theming functions and templates that are defined within the module. Typically, it is the best practice to work this way first—to ensure that every module has the ability to theme it's own data.

Menus

Drupal not only maintains content, but also details about how the site itself is organized. That is, it structures how content is related.

The principle way that it does this is through the menu subsystem. This system provides APIs for generating, retrieving, and modifying elements that describe the site structure. Put in common parlance, it handles the system's navigational menus.

Two menu systems?

One source of frustration for developers new to Drupal is the fact that the application's front controller is called the **menu router**. However, this system is not identical to the menu subsystem. Its responsibility is to actually map the URLs to callback functions. We will return to the menu router in later chapters.

Menus are hierarchical, that is, they have a tree-like structure. A menu item can have multiple children, each of which may have their own children, and so on. In this way, we can use the menu system to structure our site into sections and subsections.

Nodes

Perhaps the most important subsystem to know is the **node system**. In Drupal parlance, a node is a piece of text-based, publishable content. It can have numerous fields defined, but typically it has a title, a body, and various pieces of auxiliary data, such as timestamps, publishing state, and author identification.

Nodes are content

In computer science, the term "node" often has a special meaning. Drupal's own definition of node is distinct. It is not a point on a graph, but rather a piece of content. One might prefer to think of a Drupal node as a structured document.

The node system is mostly implemented in the **node module**. This sophisticated module provides dozens of hooks, though means that many other modules can and do interact with the node module via hook implementations.

Since nodes account for the content of the site, understanding the node system is an indispensable requirement for the Drupal developer. For that reason, we discuss aspects of the system throughout the book.

Files

In previous versions of Drupal, externally generated files (notably images) were not handled directly by Drupal itself. Instead, there were a plethora of modules available for working with files.

This has changed in Drupal 7, which now has a file-centered subsystem. This means working with images, documents, and so on is now substantially easier.

While Drupal has long had a sophisticated suite of tools for dealing with the filesystem (in the `files.inc` core library) there is now also a `file` module.

Chapter 11 discusses this new API.

Users

Drupal is not designed to be merely a CMS, but also a platform for social media. Central to any concept of social media is a robust user system that can support not only administrative users, but also site members. Drupal offers a powerful user subsystem that allows developers to work with just about all aspects of user lifecycle, from what fields show up on a user profile, to what permissions (at a fine-grained level) users have, to what particular encryption scheme is used to encrypt the user's password.

Drupal's user system even provides tools for making authentication and other aspects of user management pluggable. Modules provide, for instance, LDAP integration or authentication through many of the publicly available authentication services like OpenID.

We discuss the user system, particularly the permissions aspects, throughout this book.

Comments

Perhaps the most common social media tool is comments. Drupal provides a subsystem that provides comment functionality for nodes (and by extension, other data types).

While one could imagine that comments are merely a type of node (and, in fact, there are modules that do this), Drupal developers have chosen to implement comments as a separate type. The `comment` module contains the majority of the comment code. However, again, as with the node system, it provides numerous hooks, and thus many other modules interact with the comment system.

Fields and entities

In previous versions of Drupal, the node system was really the only system for creating structured pieces of textual content. (Comments are too focused to be generally useful for extension.) In order to extend node content beyond simple title and body fields, one needed to either write custom node types or use the **Content Construction Kit (CCK)** to build node types.

However, Drupal 7 introduces two substantial subsystems that change this:

- The **fields system** brings most of CCK's functionality into core
- The **entities system** makes it possible to define other structured data types that are *not nodes*

Already these new systems are making waves among Drupal developers, with the Drupal Commerce module leading the way in defining sophisticated entities that are not nodes.

These two subsystems are new, important, and also complex. So we will cover them in detail in *Chapter 6*.

Forms API

Another remarkable subsystem that is provided in Drupal's core is the Forms API (FAPI). This system provides a robust programmatic tool for defining, displaying, validating, and submitting forms. It takes much of the busy-work out of developing forms, and also adds a layer of security. FAPI is so integral to Drupal that we use it numerous times throughout the book.

Installation Profiles

More sophisticated Drupal use-cases may benefit from the ability to customize the installation process. Drupal provides an installation profile subsystem that can be leveraged to create a custom installer.

Using this, developers can set custom themes and modules, change installation parameters, and generally streamline the process of installing sophisticated Drupal sites.

Simple test

Programmatically testing code is a well-established practice in the software development industry. In Drupal 7, it is a capability of the core Drupal distribution. Using the Simple Test framework, developers can now use functional and unit tests to validate their code.

We employ testing throughout this book. In fact, we will write some of our first tests in *Chapter 2*.

Blocks

Along with the primary content, most web pages also have additional content displayed along the top, bottom, or sides of the page. Drupal's block subsystem handles the configuration and display of these units of content.

Most of this functionality is concentrated in the `block` module, and we will develop our first custom block in *Chapter 2*.

Other subsystems

In this section, we have provided some basic information on several high-profile subsystems. However, this list is not exhaustive. There are numerous others, and even some very important ones (like **Views**) that are not in core, but provided by third party modules.

Some of these other subsystems will be introduced and discussed throughout this book. However, Drupal is a sophisticated system, and no book of a manageable length can go into all of the details. For that reason, we provide references throughout the book pointing developers to the appropriate resources on the web and elsewhere.

Tools for developing Drupal code

Drupal is a sophisticated platform, and from the glimpse above we can see already that there are numerous systems and structures to keep track of. In this section, we try to provide tools that simplify or streamline the development process.

We assume that you have your own web server stack and your own PHP development tools. The authors of this book each use different editors, operating systems, and web server stacks, so we collectively understand that there are many good tools for developing PHP applications. And Drupal itself doesn't require anything special.

If you are just getting started, you may want to look at Acquia Drupal (`http://acquia.com`). They offer entire application stacks to get you started on Windows, Linux, or Mac OS X.

While running a PHP debugger is certainly not necessary, you may find running **Xdebug** or the **Zend Debugger** to be useful. (One of the authors of this book first learned how Drupal worked by stepping through an entire page load.)

Version control with Git and CVS

Managing source code is a major part of any software development lifecycle. In this regard, Drupal 7 coincides with a major transition period for the Drupal community.

In years past, Drupal's source code has been maintained in the venerable old CVS (Concurrent Versioning System) tool. However, Drupal has grown and the needs of the community have changed. Drupal is now moving to the Git distributed version control system.

As we begin working with Drupal code, it will help to be able to have the tools necessary to work with Git. From command-line programs to full-featured desktop applications, there is no shortage of tools for this.

The book's code and Git

The authors of this book have been working with Git for some time (one, in fact, is leading the CVS-to-Git conversion). We have done our best to make sure that all of the code contributions in this book are available from a Git repository.

You can access the code for this book, view it online in a web browser, submit patches, or even branch your own copy and build your own tool. All the code is located at GitHub:

`http://github.com/LearningDrupal7Development`

From there you will be able to access each chapter's code—and in some cases, multiple versions of the same code.

The API site and coding standards

A lot of background knowledge is required for writing good Drupal code. Of course, the aim of a book such as this is to provide that background knowledge. However, there are two reference resources that a burgeoning Drupal developer should have on-hand.

The first is the official online API documentation. Just about every function in Drupal is documented using in-line code documentation. The **Doxygen** program is then used to extract that documentation and format it. You can access the full API documentation online at `http://api.drupal.org`.

Along with using the Drupal APIs, we strive to comply with Drupal's coding conventions. Best practices in software development include keeping code clean, consistent, and readable. One aspect of this is removing nuances in code formatting by following a fixed standard.

This is particularly important on a platform like Drupal where thousands of developers all contribute to the code. Without coding standards, the code would become a cluttered mishmash of styles, and valuable development time would be spent merely deciphering code instead of working on it.

The Drupal site has a manual on best practices (`http://drupal.org/node/360052`) that includes a section on coding standards (`http://drupal.org/coding-standards`). All Drupal developers abide by these standards.

While we have attempted to follow all of the coding guidelines in this book, we don't always explicitly point out what these standards are. So new developers are encouraged to peruse the coding standards given on the previously mentioned web address.

Developer-oriented modules

There are a few Drupal-specific development and administrative modules that deserve a mention. These are tools that are installed on the server to help simplify Drupal development.

The developer module

The Developer module provides several sophisticated tools designed to help developers create and debug Drupal code. For this, please refer to the following page: `http://drupal.org/project/devel`

The following are a few of the features of this module:

- Functions used for dumping objects and arrays into formatted Drupal output
- Tools for analyzing database usage and performance
- A theme tool which indicates (graphically) which elements of a page were themed by which functions or templates
- A content generator for quickly populating your site with testing content

Drush (the Drupal shell)

Sometimes it is much easier to run some tasks with a single command in a console. Drush provides a command-line Drupal interface. It can be used to execute tasks with a few keystrokes at the console: `http://drupal.org/project/drush`

When developing, we often have to clear caches, run specific tasks, or deploy data to a remote server. Drush can help accomplish tasks like this.

Coder

The Coder module provides two big features:

- It can examine code for compliance against the Drupal coding standards
- It can automatically convert modules from one version of Drupal to another: `http://drupal.org/project/coder`

For those new to Drupal, it is nice to be able to have a module automatically evaluate whether or not new code follows the existing standards.

Summary

This chapter has been an overview of Drupal for developers. We saw what technologies Drupal uses. We looked at Drupal's architecture. We took a cursory glance at several prominent subsystems of Drupal's. We also got a feel of which developer-oriented tools are to be used while working with Drupal.

Starting in the next chapter, we will be working with code. In fact, each of the subsequent chapters will focus on practical aspects of working with Drupal. Coming up next is an introduction to the block system, where we will write our first module.

2
Creating Your First Module

The focus of this chapter is module creation. In the last chapter we surveyed Drupal's architecture advanced. We learned about the basic features and subsystems. We also saw some tools available for development. Now we are going to begin coding.

Here are some of the important topics that we will cover in this chapter:

- Starting a new module
- Creating `.info` files to provide Drupal with module information
- Creating `.module` files to store Drupal code
- Adding new blocks using the **Block Subsystem**
- Using common Drupal functions
- Formatting code according to the Drupal coding standards
- Writing an automated test for Drupal

By the end of this chapter, you should have the foundational knowledge necessary for building your own module from scratch.

Our goal: a module with a block

In this chapter we are going to build a simple module. The module will use the **Block Subsystem** to add a new custom block. The block that we add will simply display a list of all of the currently enabled modules on our Drupal installation.

 The block subsystem was introduced in the previous chapter alongside other important Drupal subsystems.

We are going to divide this task of building a new module into the three parts:

- Create a new module folder and module files
- Work with the Block Subsystem
- Write automated tests using the SimpleTest framework included in Drupal

We are going to proceed in that order for the sake of simplicity. One might object that, following agile development processes, we ought to begin by writing our tests. This approach is called **Test-driven Development (TDD)**, and is a justly popular methodology.

> Agile software development is a particular methodology designed to help teams of developers effectively and efficiently build software. While Drupal itself has not been developed using an agile process, it does facilitate many of the agile practices. To learn more about agile, visit `http://agilemanifesto.org/`.

However, our goal here is not to exemplify a particular methodology, but to discover how to write modules. It is easier to learn module development by first writing the module, and then learn how to write unit tests. It is easier for two reasons:

- SimpleTest (in spite of its name) is the least simple part of this chapter. It will have double the code-weight of our actual module.
- We will need to become acquainted with the APIs we are going to use in development before we attempt to write tests that assume knowledge of those APIs.

In regular module development, though, you may certainly choose to follow the TDD approach of writing tests first, and then writing the module.

Let's now move on to the first step of creating a new module.

Creating a new module

Creating Drupal modules is easy. How easy? Easy enough that over 5,000 modules have been developed, and many Drupal developers are even PHP novices! In fact, the code in this chapter is an illustration of how easy module coding can be. We are going to create our first module with only one directory and two small files.

Module names

It goes without saying that building a new module requires naming the module. However, there is one minor ambiguity that ought to be cleared up at the outset, a Drupal module has two names:

- **A human-readable name**: This name is designed to be read by humans, and should be one or a couple of words long. The words should be capitalized and separated by spaces. For example, one of the most popular Drupal modules has the human-readable name **Views**. A less-popular (but perhaps more creatively named) Drupal 6 module has the human-readable name **Eldorado Superfly**.

- **A machine-readable name**: This name is used internally by Drupal. It can be composed of lower-case and upper-case letters, digits, and the underscore character (using upper-case letters in machine names is frowned upon, though). No other characters are allowed. The machine names of the above two modules are `views` and `eldorado_superfly`, respectively.

By convention, the two names ought to be as similar as possible. Spaces should be replaced by underscores. Upper-case letters should generally be changed to lower-case.

Because of the convention of similar naming, the two names can usually be used interchangeably, and most of the time it is not necessary to specifically declare which of the two names we are referring to. In cases where the difference needs to be made (as in the next section), the authors will be careful to make it.

Where does our module go?

One of the less intuitive aspects of Drupal development is the filesystem layout. Where do we put a new module? The obvious answer would be to put it in the `/modules` directory alongside all of the core modules.

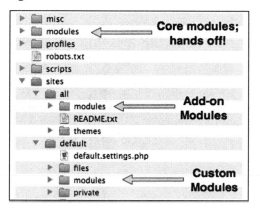

As obvious as this may seem, the /modules folder is not the right place for your modules. In fact, you should never change anything in that directory. It is reserved for core Drupal modules only, and will be overwritten during upgrades.

The second, far less obvious place to put modules is in /sites/all/modules. This is the location where all unmodified add-on modules ought to go, and tools like **Drush** (a Drupal command line tool) will download modules to this directory.

In some sense, it is okay to put modules here. They will not be automatically overwritten during core upgrades.

However, as of this writing, /sites/all/modules is not the recommended place to put custom modules unless you are running a multi-site configuration and the custom module needs to be accessible on all sites.

The current recommendation is to put custom modules in the /sites/default/ modules directory, which does not exist by default. This has a few advantages. One is that standard add-on modules are stored elsewhere, and this separation makes it easier for us to find our own code without sorting through clutter. There are other benefits (such as the loading order of module directories), but none will have a direct impact on us.

> Throughout this book, we will always be putting our custom modules in /sites/default/modules. This follows Drupal best practices, and also makes it easy to find our modules as opposed to all of the other add-on modules.

The one disadvantage of storing all custom modules in /sites/default/modules appears only under a specific set of circumstances. If you have Drupal configured to serve multiple sites off of one single instance, then the /sites/default folder is only used for the default site. What this means, in practice, is that modules stored there will not be loaded at all for other sites.

In such cases, it is generally advised to move your custom modules into /sites/all/modules/custom.

> **Other module directories**
>
> Drupal does look in a few other places for modules. However, those places are reserved for special purposes.

Creating the module directory

Now that we know that our modules should go in `/sites/default/modules`, we can create a new module there.

Modules can be organized in a variety of ways, but the best practice is to create a module directory in `/sites/default/modules`, and then place at least two files inside the directory: a `.info` (pronounced "dot-info") file and a `.module` ("dot-module") file.

The directory should be named with the machine-readable name of the module. Similarly, both the `.info` and `.module` files should use the machine-readable name.

We are going to name our first module with the machine-readable name `first`, since it is our first module. Thus, we will create a new directory, `/sites/default/modules/first`, and then create a `first.info` file and a `first.module` file:

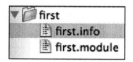

Those are the only files we will need for our module.

For permissions, make sure that your webserver can read both the `.info` and `.module` files. It should not be able to write to either file, though.

In some sense, the only file absolutely necessary for a module is the `.info` file located at a proper place in the system. However, since the `.info` file simply provides information about the module, no interesting module can be built with just this file.

Next, we will write the contents of the `.info` file.

Writing the .info file

The purpose of the `.info` file is to provide Drupal with information about a module—information such as the human-readable name, what other modules this module requires, and what code files this module provides.

A `.info` file is a plain text file in a format similar to the standard INI configuration file. A directive in the `.info` file is composed of a name, and equal sign, and a value:

```
name = value
```

By Drupal's coding conventions, there should always be one space on each side of the equals sign.

Some directives use an array-like syntax to declare that one name has multiple values. The array-like format looks like this:

```
name[] = value1
name[] = value2
```

Note that there is no blank space between the opening square bracket and the closing square bracket.

If a value spans more than one line, it should be enclosed in quotation marks.

Any line that begins with a ; (semi-colon) is treated as a comment, and is ignored by the Drupal INI parser.

 Drupal does not support INI-style section headers such as those found in the php.ini file.

To begin, let's take a look at a complete first.info file for our first module:

```
;$Id$

name = First
description = A first module.
package = Drupal 7 Development
core = 7.x
files[] = first.module

;dependencies[] = autoload
;php = 5.2
```

This ten-line file is about as complex as a module's .info file ever gets.

The first line is a standard. Every .info file should begin with ;Id. What is this? It is the placeholder for the version control system to store information about the file. When the file is checked into Drupal's CVS repository, the line will be automatically expanded to something like this:

```
;$Id: first.info,v 1.1 2009/03/18 20:27:12 mbutcher Exp $
```

This information indicates when the file was last checked into CVS, and who checked it in.

CVS is going away, and so is Id. While Drupal has been developed in CVS from the early days through Drupal 7, it is now being migrated to a Git repository. Git does not use Id, so it is likely that between the release of Drupal 7 and the release of Drupal 8, Id tags will be removed.

Throughout this book you will see all PHP and .info files beginning with the Id marker. Once Drupal uses Git, those tags may go away.

The next couple of lines of interest in first.info are these:

```
name = First
description = A first module.
package = Drupal 7 Development
```

The first two are required in every .info file. The name directive is used to declare what the module's human-readable name is. The description provides a one or two-sentence description of what this module provides or is used for. Among other places, this information is displayed on the module configuration section of the administration interface in **Modules**.

▼ CORE			
ENABLED	NAME	VERSION	DESCRIPTION
☐	Aggregator	7.x–dev	Aggregates syndicated content (RSS, RDF, and Atom feeds).
☑	Block	7.x–dev	Controls the visual building blocks a page is constructed with. Blocks are rendered into an area, or region, of a web page. Required by: Dashboard (enabled)
☐	Blog	7.x–dev	Enables multi-user blogs.

In the screenshot, the values of the name and description fields are displayed in their respective columns.

The third item, package, identifies which family (package) of modules this module is related to. Core modules, for example, all have the package Core. In the screenshot above, you can see the grouping package **Core** in the upper-left corner. Our module will be grouped under the package Drupal 7 Development to represent its relationship to this book. As you may notice, package names are written as human-readable values.

When choosing a human-readable module name, remember to adhere to the specifications mentioned earlier in this section.

The next directive is the `core` directive: `core = 7.x`. This simply declares which main-line version of Drupal is required by the module. All Drupal 7 modules will have the line `core = 7.x`.

Along with the core version, a `.info` file can also specify what version of PHP it requires. By default, Drupal 7 requires Drupal 5.1 or newer. However, if one were to use, say, **closures** (a feature introduced in PHP 5.3), then the following line would need to be added:

```
php = 5.3
```

Next, every `.info` file must declare which files in the module contain PHP functions, classes, or interfaces. This is done using the `files[]` directive. Our small initial module will only have one file, `first.module`. So we need only one `files[]` directive.

```
files[] = first.module
```

More complex files will often have several `files[]` directives, each declaring a separate PHP source code file.

> JavaScript, CSS, image files, and PHP files (like templates) that do not contain functions that the module needs to know about needn't be included in `files[]` directives. The point of the directive is simply to indicate to Drupal that these files should be examined by Drupal.

One directive that we will not use for this module, but which plays a very important role is the `dependencies[]` directive. This is used to list the other modules that must be installed and active for this module to function correctly. Drupal will not allow a module to be enabled unless its dependencies have been satisfied.

> Drupal does not contain a directive to indicate that another module is recommended or is optional. It is the task of the developer to appropriately document this fact and make it known. There is currently no recommended best practice to provide such information.

Now we have created our `first.info` file. As soon as Drupal reads this file, the module will appear on our **Modules** page.

Modules ⊕

Home » Administer

Download additional contributed modules to extend Drupal's functionality.

Regularly review available updates to maintain a secure and current site. Always run the update script each time a install modules and themes.

▸ CORE

▾ DRUPAL 7 DEVELOPMENT

ENABLED	NAME	VERSION	DESCRIPTION
☐	First		A first module.

In the screenshot, notice that the module appears in the **DRUPAL 7 DEVELOPMENT** package, and has the **NAME** and **DESCRIPTION** as assigned in the `.info` file.

With our `.info` file completed, we can now move on and code our `.module` file.

 Modules checked into Drupal's version control system will automatically have a `version` directive added to the `.info` file. This should typically not be altered.

Creating a module file

The `.module` file is a PHP file that conventionally contains all of the major hook implementations for a module. We discussed hooks at a high level in the first chapter. Now we will gain some practical knowledge of them.

A **hook implementation** is a function that follows a certain naming pattern in order to indicate to Drupal that it should be used as a callback for a particular event in the Drupal system. For Object-oriented programmers, it may be helpful to think of a hook as similar to the Observer design pattern.

When Drupal encounters an event for which there is a hook (and there are hundreds of such events), Drupal will look through all of the modules for matching hook implementations. It will then execute each hook implementation, one after another. Once all hook implementations have been executed, Drupal will continue its processing.

In the past, all Drupal hook implementations had to reside in the .module file. Drupal 7's requirements are more lenient, but in most moderately sized modules, it is still preferable to store most hook implementations in the .module file.

 Later in this book you will encounter cases where hook implementations belong in other files. In such cases, the reasons for organizing the module in such a way will be explained.

To begin, we will create a simple .module file that contains a single hook implementation – one that provides help information.

```php
<?php
// $Id$

/**
 * @file
 * A module exemplifying Drupal coding practices and APIs.
 *
 * This module provides a block that lists all of the
 * installed modules. It illustrates coding standards,
 * practices, and API use for Drupal 7.
 */

/**
 * Implements hook_help().
 */
function first_help($path, $arg) {
  if ($path == 'admin/help#first') {
    return t('A demonstration module.');
  }
}
```

Before we get to the code itself, we will talk about a few stylistic items.

To begin, notice that this file, like the .info file, contains an Id marker that CVS will replace when the file is checked in. All PHP files should have this marker following a double-slash-style comment: // Id.

Next, the preceding code illustrates a few of the important coding standards for Drupal.

Source code standards

Drupal has a thorough and strictly enforced set of coding standards. All core code adheres to these standards. Most add-on modules do, too. (Those that don't generally receive bug reports for not conforming.) Before you begin coding, it is a good idea to familiarize yourself with the standards as documented here: `http://drupal.org/ coding-standards` The Coder module mentioned in the last chapter can evaluate your code and alert you to any infringement upon the coding standards.

> Throughout this book we will adhere to the Drupal coding standards. In many cases, we will explain the standards as we go along. Still, the definitive source for standards is the URL listed above, not our code here.

We will not re-iterate the coding standards in this book. The details can be found online. However, several prominent standards deserve immediate mention. I will just mention them here, and we will see examples in action as we work through the code.

- **Indenting**: All PHP and JavaScript files use *two spaces to indent*. Tabs are never used for code formatting.

- **The** `<?php ?>` **processor instruction**: Files that are completely PHP should begin with `<?php`, but should omit the closing `?>`. This is done for several reasons, most notably to prevent the inclusion of whitespace from breaking HTTP headers.

- **Comments**: Drupal uses Doxygen-style (`/** */`) doc-blocks to comment functions, classes, interfaces, constants, files, and globals. All other comments should use the double-slash (`//`) comment. The pound sign (#) should not be used for commenting.

- **Spaces around operators**: Most operators should have a whitespace character on each side.

- **Spacing in control structures**: Control structures should have spaces after the name and before the curly brace. The bodies of all control structures should be surrounded by curly braces, and even that of `if` statements with one-line bodies.

- **Functions**: Functions should be named in lowercase letters using underscores to separate words. Later we will see how class method names differ from this.

- **Variables**: Variable names should be in all lowercase letters using underscores to separate words. Member variables in objects are named differently.

As we work through examples, we will see these and other standards in action.

Doxygen-style doc blocks

Drupal uses Doxygen to extract API documentation from source code. Experienced PHP coders may recognize this concept, as it is similar to PhpDocumentor comments (or Java's JavaDoc). However, Drupal does have its idiosyncrasies, and does not follow the same conventions as these systems.

We will only look at the documentation blocks as they apply to our preceding specific example. As we proceed through the book, we will see more advanced examples of correct documentation practices.

Let's take a closer look at the first dozen lines of our module:

```
<?php
// $Id$

/**
 * @file
 * A module exemplifying Drupal coding practices and APIs.
 *
 * This module provides a block that lists all of the
 * installed modules. It illustrates coding standards,
 * practices, and API use for Drupal 7.
 */
```

After the PHP processor instruction and the `$Id$` line, the part of the code is a large comment. The comment begins with a slash and two asterisks (`/**`) and ends with a single asterisk and a slash (`*/`). Every line between begins with an asterisk. This style of comment is called a **doc block** or documentation block.

A doc block is a comment that contains API information. It can be extracted automatically by external tools, which can then format the information for use by developers.

> **Doc blocks in action: api.drupal.org**
>
> Drupal's doc blocks are used to generate the definitive source of Drupal API documentation at `http://api.drupal.org`. This site is a fantastic searchable interface to each and every one of Drupal's functions, classes, interfaces, and constants. It also contains some useful how-to documentation.

All of Drupal is documented using doc blocks, and you should always use them to document your code.

The initial doc block in the code fragment above begins with the `@file` decorator. This indicates that the doc block describes the file as a whole, not a part of it. Every file should begin with a file-level doc block.

From there, the format of this doc block is simple: It begins with a single-sentence description of the file (which should always be on one line), followed by a blank line, followed by one or more paragraph descriptions of what this file does.

The Drupal coding standards stipulate that doc blocks should always be written using full, grammatically correct, punctuated sentences.

If we look a little further down in our module file, we can see our first function declaration:

```
/**
 * Implements hook_help().
 */
function first_help($path, $arg) {
  if ($path == 'admin/help#first') {
    return t('A demonstration module.');
  }
}
```

Before moving onto the function, let's take a look at the doc block here. It is a single sentence: `Implements hook_help()`. This single-sentence description follows a Drupal doc block coding standard, too. When a function is a hook implementation, it should state so in exactly the format used above: `Implements NAME OF HOOK`. Why the formula? So that developers can very quickly identify the general purpose of the function, and also so that automated tools can find hook implementations.

Note that we don't add any more of a description, nor do we document the parameters. This is okay when two things are true:

*   The function implements a hook
*   The function is simple

In such cases, the single-line description will do, since coders can simply refer to the API documentation for the hook to learn more.

Later we will see how non-hook functions and more complex hook implementations have an extended form of doc block comment. For now, though, we have addressed the basics of doc blocks. We will move on and look at the help function.

The help hook

Drupal defines a hook called `hook_help()`. The help hook is invoked (called) when a user browses the help system. Each module can have one implementation of `hook_help()`. Our module provides brief help text by implementing the help hook.

```
function first_help($path, $arg) {
  if ($path == 'admin/help#first') {
    return t('A demonstration module.');
  }
}
```

How does this function become a hook implementation? Strictly by virtue of its name: `first_help()`. The name follows the hook pattern. If the hook is named `hook_help()`, then to implement it, we replace the word `hook` with the name of the module. Thus, to implement `hook_help()`, we simply declare a function in our `first` module named `first_help()`.

Each hook has its own parameters, and all core Drupal hooks are documented at `http://api.drupal.org`.

A `hook_help()` implementation takes two arguments:

* `$path`: The help system URI path
* `$arg`: The arguments used when accessing this URL

In our case, we are only concerned with the first of these two. Basically, the help system works by matching URI paths to help text. Our module needs to declare what help text should be returned for specific URIs.

Specifically, the module-wide help text should be made available at the URI `admin/help#MODULE_NAME`, where `MODULE_NAME` is the machine-readable name of the module.

Our function works by checking the `$path`. If the `$path` is set to `admin/help#first`, the default help screen for a module, then it will return some simple help text.

If we were to enable our new module and then look at Drupal's help text page with our new module enabled, we would see this:

Notice that **Help** now shows up under **OPERATIONS**. If we were to click on the **Help** link, we would see our help text:

The key to make this system work is in the use of the $path checking, which displays the help information only when the context-sensitive help for this module is enabled via hook_help().

```
if ($path == 'admin/help#first') {
  return t('A demonstration module.');
}
```

Since this is our first module, we will dwell on the details a little more carefully than we will do in subsequent chapters.

First, the previous code conforms to Drupal's coding standards, which we briefly covered earlier. Whitespace separates the if and the opening parenthesis (, and there is also a space between the closing parenthesis) and the opening curly brace ({). There are also spaces on both sides of the equality operator ==. Code is indented with two spaces per level, and we never use tabs. In general, Drupal coders tend to use single quotes (') to surround strings because of the (admittedly slight) speed improvement gained by skipping interpolation.

Also important from the perspective of coding standards is the fact that we enclose the body of the if statement in curly braces even though the body is only one line long. And we split it over three lines, though we might have been able to fit it on one. Drupal standards require that we always do this.

Finally, in the example above we see one new Drupal function: t().

The t() function and translations

Every natural language string that may be displayed to a user should be wrapped in the t() function. Why? Because the t() function is responsible for translating strings from one language into other.

Drupal supports dozens of languages. This is one of the strongest features of Drupal's internationalization and localization effort. The method by which Drupal supports translation is largely through the t() function.

There are three features of this function that every developer should understand:

- What happens when t() is called
- How Drupal builds the translation table
- Additional features you get by using the t() function

First, let's look at what the t() function does when it is called. If no language support is enabled and no second argument is passed to t(), it simply returns the string unaltered. If more languages are enabled and the user's language is something other than English, Drupal will attempt to replace the English language string with a string in the appropriate language.

The second thing to look at is how Drupal builds the translation information. There are two aspects to this: The human aspect and the technical one. The translations themselves are done by dozens and dozens of volunteers who translate not only Drupal's core, but also many of the add-on modules. Their translations are then made into downloadable language bundles (.po files) that you can install on your site.

On the more technical side, this dedicated group of translators does not simply search the source code looking for calls to the t() function. Instead, an automated tool culls the code and identifies all of the translatable strings. This automated tool, though, can only extract string literals. In other words, it looks for calls like this:

```
t('This is my string');
```

It cannot do anything with lines like this, though:

```
$variable = 'This is a string';
t($variable);
```

Why won't the translation system work in the case above? Because when the automated translation system runs through the code, it does not execute the code. It simply reads it. For that reason, it would become cumbersome (and many times impossible) to determine what the correct value of a variable is.

The locale module can, under certain circumstances, identify other strings that were not correctly passed into the t() function and make them available to translators. This, however, should not be relied upon.

So the t() function should *always* be given a literal string for its first argument.

The third thing to note about the t() function is that it does more than translate strings. It offers a method of variable interpolation that is more secure than the usual method.

In many PHP applications, you will see code like this:

```
print "Welcome, $username.";
```

The code above will replace $username with the value of the $username variable. This code leaves open the possibility that the value of $username contains data that will break the HTML in the output – or worse, that it will open an avenue for a malicious user to inject JavaScript or other code into the output.

The t() function provides an alternate, and more secure, method for replacing placeholders in text with a value. The function takes an optional second argument, which is an associative array of items that can be substituted. Here's an example that replaces the the previous code:

```
$values = array('@user' => $username);
print t('Welcome, @user', $values);
```

In the previous case, we declare a placeholder named @user, the value of which is the value of the $username variable. When the t() function is executed, the mappings in $values are used to substitute placeholders with the correct data. But there is an additional benefit: these substitutions are done in a secure way.

If the placeholder begins with @, then before it inserts the value, Drupal sanitizes the value using its internal check_plain() function (which we will encounter many times in subsequent chapters).

If you are sure that the string doesn't contain any dangerous information, you can use a different symbol to begin your placeholder: the exclamation mark (!). When that is used, Drupal will simply insert the value as is. This can be very useful when you need to insert data that should not be translated:

```
$values = array('!url' => 'http://example.com');
print t('The website can be found at !url', $values);
```

In this case, the URL will be entered with no escaping. We can do this safely only because we already know the value of URL. It does not come from a distrusted user.

Finally, there is a third placeholder decorator: the percent sign (%) tells Drupal to escape the code and to mark it as emphasized.

```
$values = array('%color' => 'blue');
print t('My favorite color is %color.', $values);
```

Not only will this remove any dangerous characters from the value, but it will also insert markup to treat that text as emphasized text. By default, the preceding code would result in the printing of the string **My favorite color is blue**. The emphasis tags were added by a theme function (`theme_placeholder()`) called by the `t()` function.

There are more things that can be done with `t()`, `format_plural()`, translation contexts, and other translation system features. To learn more, you may want to start with the API documentation for `t()` at `http://api.drupal.org/api/function/t/7`.

We have taken a sizable detour to talk about the translation system, but with good reason. It is a tremendously powerful feature of Drupal, and should be used in all of your code. Not only does it make modules translatable, but it adds a layer of security. It can even be put to some interesting (if unorthodox) uses, as is exemplified by the String Overrides module at `http://drupal.org/project/stringoverrides`.

At this point, we have created a working module, though the only thing that it does is display help text. It's time to make this module a little more interesting. In the next section we will use the Block API to write code that generates a block listing all of the currently enabled modules.

Working with the Block API

In the first chapter we talked about blocks, and in your passing usage of Drupal, you have already no doubt encountered block configuration and management. In this section, we are going to learn how to create blocks in code. The Block API provides the tools for hooking custom code into the block subsystem.

 The Block API has changed substantially since Drupal 6. In Drupal 6, there was only one function used for all block operations. Now there is a family of related functions.

We are going to create a block that displays a bulleted list of all of the modules currently enabled on our site.

There are half a dozen hooks in the Block API, providing opportunities to do everything from declaring new blocks to altering the content and behavior of existing blocks. For our simple module, we are going to use two different hooks:

- `hook_block_info()`: This is used to tell Drupal about the new block or blocks that we will declare
- `hook_block_view()`: This tells Drupal what to do when a block is requested for viewing

One thing to keep in mind, in the context of the Block API as well as other APIs is that each module can only implement a given hook once. There can be only one `first_block_info()` function.

Since modules should be able to create multiple blocks, that means that the Block API must make it possible for one block implementation to manage multiple blocks. Thus, `first_block_info()` can declare any number of blocks, and `first_block_view()` can return any number of blocks.

> The entire Block API is documented in the official Drupal 7 API documentation, and even includes an example module: `http://api.drupal.org/api/drupal/developer--examples--block_example.module/7`.

To keep our example simple, we will be creating only one block. However, it is good to keep in mind that the API was designed in a way that would allow us to create as many blocks as we want.

Let's start with an implementation of `hook_block_info()`.

The block info hook

All of the functions in our module will go inside of the `first.module` file — the default location for hook implementations in Drupal. Before, we created `first_help()`, an implementation of `hook_help()`. Now, we are going to implement the `hook_block_info()` hook.

The purpose of this hook is to tell Drupal about all of the blocks that the module provides. Note that, as with any hook, you only need to implement it in cases where your module needs to provide this functionality. In other words, if the hook is not implemented, Drupal will simply assume that this module has no associated blocks.

Here's our 'block info' hook implementation declaring a single block:

```
/**
 * Implements hook_block_info().
 */
function first_block_info() {
  $blocks = array();

  $blocks['list_modules'] = array(
    'info' => t('A listing of all of the enabled modules.'),
    'cache' => DRUPAL_NO_CACHE,
  );

  return $blocks;
}
```

Once again, this function is preceded by a doc block. And since we are writing a trivial implementation of `hook_block_info()`, we needn't add anything other than the standard documentation.

An implementation of `hook_block_info()` takes no arguments and is expected to return an associative array.

Associative arrays: Drupal's data structure of choice

Arrays in PHP are very fast. They are well supported, and because they serve double duty as both indexed arrays and dictionary-style associative arrays, they are flexible. For those reasons Drupal makes heavy use of arrays—often in places where one would expect objects, linked lists, maps, or trees.

The returned array should contain one entry for every block that this module declares, and the entry should be of the form `$name => array($property => $value)`.

Thus, the important part of our function above is this piece:

```
$blocks['list_modules'] = array(
  'info' => t('A listing of all of the enabled modules.'),
  'cache' => DRUPAL_NO_CACHE,
);
```

This defines a block named `list_modules` that has two properties:

- `info`: This provides a one-sentence description of what this block does. The text is used on the block administration screens.
- `cache`: This tells Drupal how to cache the data from this block. Here in the code I have set this to `DRUPAL_NO_CACHE`, which will simply forgo caching altogether. There are several other settings providing global caching, per-user caching, and so on.

There are a handful of other possible properties that Drupal recognizes. You can read about these in the Drupal API documentation at `http://api.drupal.org/api/function/hook_block_info/7`.

We have now created a function that tells Drupal about a block named `list_modules`. With this information, Drupal will assume that when it requests that block for viewing, some function will provide the block's contents. The next function we implement will handle displaying the block.

The block view hook

In the section above we implemented the hook that tells Drupal about our module's new block. Now we need to implement a second hook—a hook responsible for building the contents of the block. This hook will be called whenever Drupal tries to display the block.

An implementation of `hook_block_view()` is expected to take one argument—the name of the block to retrieve—and return an array of data for the given name.

Our implementation will provide content for the block named `list_modules`. Here is the code:

```
/**
 * Implements hook_block_view().
 */
function first_block_view($block_name = '') {
  if ($block_name == 'list_modules') {
    $list = module_list();

    $theme_args = array('items' => $list, 'type' => 'ol');
    $content = theme('item_list', $theme_args);

    $block = array(
      'subject' => t('Enabled Modules'),
      'content' => $content,
```

```
      );

   return $block;
   }
}
```

By now, the doc block should be familiar. The Drupal coding style should also look familiar. Again, we have implemented `hook_block_view()` simply by following the naming convention.

The argument that our `first_block_view()` function takes, is the name of the block. As you look through Drupal documentation you may see this argument called `$which_block` or `$delta`—terms intended to identify the fact that the value passed in is the identifier for which block should be returned.

 The term `$delta` is used for historical reasons. It is not a particularly apt description for the role of the variable, and more recently it has been replaced by more descriptive terms.

The only block name that our function should handle is the one we declared in `first_block_info()`. If the `$block_name` is `list_modules`, we need to return content.

Let's take a close look at what happens when a request comes in for the `list_modules` block. This is the content of the `if` statement above:

```
$list = module_list();

$theme_args = array('items' => $list, 'type' => 'ol');
$content = theme('item_list', $theme_args);

$block = array(
  'subject' => t('Enabled Modules'),
  'content' => $content,
);

return $block;
```

On the first line, we call the Drupal function `module_list()`. This function simply returns an array of module names. (In fact, it is actually an associative array of module names to module names. This duplicate mapping is done to speed up lookups.)

Now we have a raw array of data. The next thing we need to do is format that for display. In Drupal formatting is almost always done by the theming layer. Here, we want to pass off the data to the theme layer and have it turn our module list into an HTML ordered list.

The next few chapters will take a detailed look at the theming system. For now, though, we will simply grant the fact that when we use the theme function in the way we have done above, it returns formatted HTML.

The main function for working with the theming system is theme(). In Drupal 7, theme() takes one or two arguments:

- The name of the theme operation
- An associative array of variables to pass onto the theme operation

Previous versions of Drupal took any number of arguments, depending on the theme operation being performed. That is no longer the case in Drupal 7. The details of this are covered in the later chapters.

To format an array of strings into an HTML list, we use the item_list theme, and we pass in an associative array containing two variables:

- the items we want listed
- the type of listing we want

From theme() we get a string of HTML.

Now all we need to do is assemble the data that our block view must return. An implementation of hook_block_view() is expected to return an array with two items in it:

- subject: The name or title of the block.
- content: The content of the block, as formatted text or HTML.

So in the first place we set a hard-coded, translatable string. In the second, we set content to the value built by theme().

One thing you may notice about the $block array in the code above is its formatting:

```
$block = array(
  'subject' => t('Enabled Modules'),
  'content' => $content,
);
```

This is how larger arrays should be formatted according to the Drupal coding standards. And that trailing comma is not a error. Drupal standards require that multi-line arrays terminate each line—including the last item—with a comma. This is perfectly legal in PHP syntax, and it eliminates simple coding syntax problems that occur when items are added to or removed from the array code.

Not in JavaScript!

Drupal programmers make the mistake of using a similar syntax in Drupal JavaScript. Object literal definitions (the JavaScript equivalent of associative arrays) do not allow the last item to terminate with a comma. Doing so causes bugs in IE and other browsers.

Now we have walked through our first module's code. For all practical purposes, we have written an entire module (though we still have some automated testing code to write). Let's see what this looks like in the browser.

The first module in action

Our module is written and ready to run. To test this out, we need to first enable the module, and then go to the block administration page.

The module can be enabled through the **Modules** menu. Once it is enabled, go to **Structure | Blocks**. You should be able to find a block described as **A listing of all of the enabled modules**. (This text came from our `first_block_info()` declaration.)

Once you have placed this module in one of the block regions, you should be able to see something like this:

Enabled Modules

1. block
2. color
3. comment
4. contextual
5. dashboard
6. dblog
7. field
8. field_sql_storage
9. field_ui
10. file
11. filter
12. first
13. help
14. image
15. list

The output from our module is a simple ordered list of modules. Like any other block, it can be positioned in any of the block regions on the site, and responds in all the ways that a block is expected to respond.

Now that we have a working module, we are going to write a couple of automated tests for it.

Writing automated tests

The final thing we are going to do in this chapter is write automated tests to verify that our module works as anticipated. Again, some development methodologies call for writing tests before writing code. Such a methodology is perfectly applicable with Drupal modules. However, we have delayed writing tests until we had a little Drupal coding under our belts. Now that we have worked up a complete module, we are ready to write some tests.

Drupal uses an automated testing tool called SimpleTest (or just **Testing**). It is largely derived from the Open Source SimpleTest testing framework, though with many modifications. SimpleTest comes with Drupal 7.

In Drupal 6, `SimpleTest` was an add-on module and required core patches. This is no longer the case in Drupal 7.

There are various types of test that can be constructed in code. Two popular ones are unit tests and functional tests.

A **unit test** is focused on testing discrete pieces of code. In object-oriented code, the focus of unit testing is often the exercising every method of an object (or class). In procedural code, unit tests focus on functions and even, occasionally, on global variables. The objective is simply to make sure that each piece (each unit) is doing its job as expected.

Most of the tests written for Drupal are not unit tests. Instead, they are **functional tests**. That is, the tests are designed to verify that when a given piece of code is inserted into Drupal, it functions as expected within the context of the application. This is a broader category of testing than unit tests. Larger chunks of code (like, say, Drupal as a whole) are expected to function correctly already before the functional test can accurately measure the correctness of the code being tested. And rather than calling the functions-to-be-tested directly, often times a functional test will execute the entire application under conditions which make it easy to check, whether the code being tested is working. For example, Drupal's functional tests often start Drupal, add a user, enable some modules, then retrieve URLs over an HTTP connection and finally test the output.

There are many excellent sources of information on testing strategies and their strengths and weaknesses. We will skip any discussion of this and dive right into the code. Just keep in mind as we go that our goal is to *verify that our block functions as expected*. Since unit tests are easier to construct, and since our module is extremely simple, we will construct a unit test for our module.

While the **Testing** module is included with Drupal 7, it is not enabled by default. Go to the **Modules** page and enable it. Once it is enabled, you should be able to go to the **Configuration** tab and, under the **Development** section, find the **Testing** configuration page. This is the point of entry into the testing user interface.

Creating a test

Tests should reside in their own file. Just as the module's main module code is in MODULENAME/MODULENAME.module, a test should be in MODULENAME/MODULENAME.test. The testing framework will automatically pick it up.

Starting out

As with other files in a module, the file containing the unit tests needs to be declared in the module's .info file. All we need to do is add it to the files array:

```
;$Id$

name = First
description = A first module.
core = 7.x
package = Drupal 7 Development
files[] = first.module
files[] = first.test
```

All we have done is added first.test beneath first.module. This simply tells Drupal to inspect the contents of this file during execution. When the testing framework is invoked, it will find the tests automatically by inspecting the contents of first.test.

Once your module is installed, Drupal caches the contents of the .info file. After adding a new item to the file, you should re-visit the **Modules** page to force Drupal to re-parse the .info file.

Now we are ready to add some code to first.test.

Writing a test case

There are a few areas of Drupal that make use of PHP's Object-oriented features. One is the database API that we will see later in the book. Another is the testing framework. It uses class inheritance to declare tests. This is primarily a vestige of the `SimpleTest` API upon which Drupal's testing is based.

Since this is a book on Drupal programming, not PHP, we will not spend time introducing PHP's Object-Oriented features. If you are not familiar with Object-oriented Programming (OOP) in PHP, you may want to learn the basics before moving on to this section. Since most tests follow a formulaic pattern, there is no need to master OOP before writing simple tests. However, some background knowledge will ease the transition. A good starting point is PHP.net's OOP manual available at the URL http://www.php.net/manual/en/language.oop5.php.

The basic pattern

Most test cases follow a simple pattern:

- Create a new class that extends `DrupalWebTestCase`
- Add a `getInfo()` function
- Do any necessary configuration in the `setUp()` method
- Write one or more test methods, beginning each method with the word `test`
- In each test method, use one or more assertions to test actual values

As we go through our own tests, we will walk through each of these steps

First, we will begin by adding a test class inside our `first.test` file. It should look something like this:

```php
<?php
/**
 * @file
 * Tests for the first module
 */

class FirstTestCase extends DrupalWebTestCase {
  // Methods will go here.
}
```

As usual, we begin the test file with a doc block. After that, we declare our new test case.

The examples you see in this chapter are derived largely from the `block.test` file that ships with Drupal core (`modules/block/block.test`). If you are anxious to dive into some detailed unit tests, that is one place to start.

We have just created a new `test case` class—that is, a class that handles testing a particular related group of features. In our case, we are going to test the block implementation we wrote in this chapter. You can, if you would like, create multiple test cases in the same `.test` file. For our simple case, there is no need to do this, though.

The test case extends a base class called `DrupalWebTestCase`. `DrupalWebTestCase` provides many utilities for running tests, as well as core testing logic that is not necessarily exposed to or used by individual test cases. For these two reasons, every Drupal test should extend either this class or another class that already extends `DrupalWebTestCase`.

Once we have the class declared, we can create our first method, `getInfo()`.

Naming conventions and Classes

Drupal functions are named in all lowercase, with words separated by underscore (_) Classes and methods are different. Classes should be named in uppercase "CamelCase" notation, with the first letter capitalized. Methods should be named in "camelCase" with the first letter in lowercase. Underscores should not be used in class or method names.

The getInfo() method

Already we have seen a few cases where Drupal uses nested associative arrays to pass information. Our `first_block_info()` function did just this. The `DrupalWebTestCase::getInfo()` method also returns an array of information. This time, the information is about the test.

The method looks like this (shown in the context of the entire class)

```php
<?php
/**
 * @file
 * Tests for the first module
 */

class FirstTestCase extends DrupalWebTestCase {
```

```
    public function getInfo() {
      return array(
        'name' => 'First module block functionality',
        'description' => 'Test blocks in the First module.',
        'group' => 'First',
      );
    }
  }
```

The `getInfo()` method returns an array with three items:

- `name`: The name of the test.
- `description`: A sentence describing what the tests do.
- `group`: The name of the group to which these tests belong.

All three of these are intended to be human-readable. The first two are used for purely informational purposes. The third, `group`, is also used to group similar tests together under the same heading.

When viewed from **Configuration | Testing**, the information above is displayed like this:

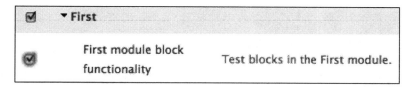

Clean the environment

If you have already run tests and your new test is not showing up, you may need to press the **Clean environment** button to reset the testing environment.

Above you can see how the value of `group` became a grouping field, and `name` and `description` were used to describe the test.

The `getInfo()` function might seem, at first blush, to be unimportant, but your test, absolutely must have it. Otherwise, the test case will not be made available for execution.

Setting up the test case

Often, a test case will require some setup and configuration, where shared values are initialized and subsystems made available.

Fortunately, Drupal handles most of the basics. The database layer, module system, and initial configuration are all done. However, test cases often have to handle some initialization themselves. In cases where you need to do this, there is an existing method that will be called before tests are executed. This is the setUp() method. While we don't need any set up for our module, I am going to show it anyway so that we can see a few important things.

```php
<?php
/**
 * @file
 * Tests for the first module
 */

class FirstTestCase extends DrupalWebTestCase {

  public function setUp() {
    parent::setUp('first');
  }

  public function getInfo() {
    return array(
      'name' => 'First module block functionality',
      'description' => 'Test blocks in the First module.',
      'group' => 'First',
    );
  }
}
```

Again, a setup method is not strictly necessary, but when you use one it must have at least the lines shown in the example above.

Of particular importance is this bit:

```php
parent::setUp('first');
```

This tells the setup method to call the setUp() method that exists on the DrupalWebTestCase class. Why would we do this?

`DrupalWebTestCase::setUp()` performs some necessary setup operations—things that need to be done before our tests will run successfully. For that reason, we need to make sure that when we override that method, we explicitly call it. We pass this function the name of the module we are testing (`first`), so that it knows to initialize that module for us. This means we do not need to worry about installing the module in our testing code.

When writing your own cases, you can add more lines of configuration code beneath the `parent::setUp()` call. Later in the book you will see more robust examples of setup methods.

For now, though, we are going to move on to the next type of method. We are going to write our first test.

Writing a test method

Most of the methods in a test case are test methods; that is, they run operations with the intent of verifying that they work. But, as you will notice, nowhere in our code do we explicitly call those test methods.

So how does `SimpleTest` know to call our methods? As with Drupal hooks, the answer is in the naming convention. Any method that starts with the word `test` is assumed to be a test case, and is automatically run by the testing framework.

Let's write two test methods, again shown in the context of the entire class.

```php
<?php
/**
 * @file
 * Tests for the first module
 */

class FirstTestCase extends DrupalWebTestCase {

  public function setUp() {
    parent::setUp();
  }

  public function getInfo() {
    return array(
      'name' => 'First module block functionality',
      'description' => 'Test blocks in the First module.',
      'group' => 'First',
```

```
    );
  }

  public function testBlockInfo() {
    $info = module_invoke('first', 'block_info');

    $this->assertEqual(1, count($info),
      t('Module defines a block.'));

    $this->assertTrue(isset($info['list_modules']),
      t('Module list exists.'));
  }

  public function testBlockView() {
    $data  = module_invoke('first', 'block_view',
      'list_modules');

    $this->assertTrue(is_array($data),
      t('Block returns renderable array.'));
    $this->assertEqual(t('Enabled Modules'), $data['subject'],
      t('Subject is set'));
  }

}
```

The code above has two test methods:

- `testBlockInfo()`
- `testBlockView()`

As the names imply, each method is responsible for testing one of the two block functions we wrote earlier.

We will begin by taking a close look at `testBlockInfo()`.

```
  public function testBlockInfo() {
    $info = module_invoke('first', 'block_info');

    $this->assertEqual(1, count($info),
      t('Module defines a block.'));

    $this->assertTrue(isset($info['list_modules']),
      t('Module list exists.'));
  }
```

This function does three things.

First, it runs a function called `module_invoke()`, storing its results in `$info`. The `module_invoke()` function calls a particular hook for a particular module.

 This function is the infrequently used counterpart of `module_invoke_all()`, which executes a hook in all of the modules in which that hook appears.

The `module_invoke()` method takes two parameters: The name of the module and the name of the hook to call. The call in this code, `module_invoke('first', 'block_info')` is semantically equivalent to calling `first_block_info()`. Our only advantage gained here is in ensuring that it can be called through the hook system.

Basically, then, we have simulated the circumstances under which our block info hook would have been executed by Drupal. The next thing to do is ensure that the information returned by our hook is as expected.

We do this by making a couple of statements — assertions, about what we expect. The testing framework then validates these exceptions. If the code functions as expected, the test passes. If not, the test fails.

Here are the two tests:

```
$this->assertEqual(1, count($info),
  t('Module defines a block.'));

$this->assertTrue(isset($info['list_modules']),
  t('Module list exists.'));
```

(Note that each of these two lines were split onto one line for formatting.)

Each assertion is typically of the form `$this->assertSOMETHING($conditions, $message)`, where `SOMETHING` is a type of assertion, `$conditions` are the conditions that must be satisfied for the test to pass, and `$message` is a message describing the test.

In our first test, the test asserts that `1` and `count($info)` should be equal. (The message is simply used by the testing interface to show what it was testing.)

You might notice that the function began `$this->assertEqual()` which is a member method, but one that we did not define. (`$this`, for those new to PHP's OOP, is a shorthand way of referring to the present object.) The parent class, `DrupalWebTestCase`, provides a dozen or so assertion methods that make writing tests easier. Many of these will come up in subsequent chapters, but in our tests we use two:

- `$this->assertEqual()`: Assert that the first (known) value equals the second (tested) value.
- `$this->assertTrue()`: Assert that the given value evaluates to TRUE.

While the first assertion validates that we defined one block in our block info hook implementation, the second assertion verifies that the name of this block is `list_modules`. Thus, by the time this test has run, we can be sure that our info hook is returning information about our single block.

The next test verifies that the `first_block_view()` function is returning the correct information.

```
public function testBlockView() {
  $data  = module_invoke('first', 'block_view',
    'list_modules');

  $this->assertTrue(is_array($data),
    t('Block returns renderable array.'));
  $this->assertEqual(t('Enabled Modules'), $data['subject'],
    t('Subject is set'));
}
```

Again, `module_invoke()` is used to execute a hook—this time the block view hook implementation. And again we perform two assertions. First, we check to make sure that an `array` is returned from `first_block_view()`. Second, we verify that the title is **Enabled Modules**, as we expect.

We could go on and add another assertion—something that makes sure that the `$data['content']` field has the expected data in it. But that information is a little volatile. We are not positive about which other modules will be enabled, and testing against that would be injecting an external dependency into our test, which is considered bad form.

At this point, we have defined one test case, `FirstTestCase`, which defines four methods. Two of those methods are tests, each containing two assertions. So when we run the test, we should see one test case, two tests, and two assertions for each test.

To run the test, go to **Configuration | Testing**. As long as your test case is implemented correctly (including the get Info() method), then it should show up in the list.

☑	▾ **First**	
☑	First module block functionality	Test blocks in the First module.

If we select our group of tests, and then press the **Run tests** button, our test case will be executed. Test cases often take a long time to run. Behind the scenes, Drupal actually builds a special installation of Drupal that will be used only for this round of tests. But after a minute or two, the test framework should print a report that looks something like this:

Test result ○

The test run finished in 10 sec.

ACTIONS

Filter All (1) ▾

(Run tests) Return to list

RESULTS

4 passes, 0 fails, and 0 exceptions

▾ FIRST MODULE BLOCK FUNCTIONALITY
Test blocks in the First module.
4 passes, 0 fails, and 0 exceptions

MESSAGE	GROUP	FILENAME	LINE	FUNCTION	STATUS
Module defines a block.	Other	first.test	24	FirstTestCase->testBlockInfo()	✓
Module list exists.	Other	first.test	25	FirstTestCase->testBlockInfo()	✓
Block returns renderable array.	Other	first.test	31	FirstTestCase->testBlockView()	✓
Subject is set	Other	first.test	32	FirstTestCase->testBlockView()	✓

The report above shows us that all four of our assertions were run (two for each test), and that all passed.

Should a test not pass, it will be displayed in red, with the status flag set to a red **X** instead of a green checkmark. A warning message may be displayed, too (depending on the error or failure).

Summary

We have now completed an end-to-end walk through the creation of a module. We began by creating the module directory, followed by the `.info` file. Next, we added a `.module` file and implemented three hooks, taking advantage of several core Drupal functions in the process. Finally, we wrote our first test for this module, learning about Drupal's OO testing framework as we went.

Along the way, we learned about basic coding guidelines, translation support, the mechanics of hooks, and using the block API.

In subsequent chapters, we will build on this knowledge to create more powerful modules, making use of the database layer, the menu system, nodes, and other tools. In the next few chapters, we will look at the theme system, a powerful and extensible mechanism for structuring and formatting output.

3
Drupal's Theme Layer

The most obvious part of Drupal's theming system is the **Appearance** page, which lists all of the themes installed on your website. When you choose a theme from the **Appearance** admin page, you are applying a specific graphic design to your website's data and functionality. However, the applied theme is in reality only a small part of the entire theming layer.

This book is mostly focused on building modules that encapsulate discrete chunks of functionality. However, since we're ultimately building a web application, everything outputted by your functionality will need to be marked up with HTML. Drupal calls the process of wrapping your data in HTML and CSS as **theming**.

For the next two chapters, we will discuss how your module should integrate with the theme layer. *Chapter 3* will talk about the architecture of the system, theme functions, templates, render elements, and the theme registry. *Chapter 4* will use these newly acquired concepts to integrate an example module with the theming layer.

Business logic versus presentation logic

So what would be the best way to get our data and functionality marked up? Do we simply wrap each piece of data in HTML and return the whole as a giant string? Like the following example:

```
return '<div class="wrapper">' . $data . '</div>';
```

Fortunately, we don't. Like all other well-designed applications, Drupal separates its business logic from its presentation logic. Traditionally, the primary motivations for this separation of concerns are as follows:

1. To make the code easier to maintain.
2. To make it possible to easily swap out one layer's implementation without having to re-write the other layers.

As we shall see, Drupal takes the "swap-ability" aspect to the extreme.

As we mentioned in the introduction of this chapter, the default theme selected on the **Appearance** page is the most obvious part of the theme layer. Also, you might think that the theme is responsible for applying the HTML and CSS for the website. However, there are thousands of contributed modules on drupal.org. Should the theme be responsible for marking up all of those modules' data? Obviously not.

Since a module is most intimately familiar with its own data and functionality, it's the module's responsibility to provide the *default* theme implementation. As long as the module uses the theme system properly, a theme will be able to override any HTML and CSS by hot-swapping its own implementation for the module's implementation.

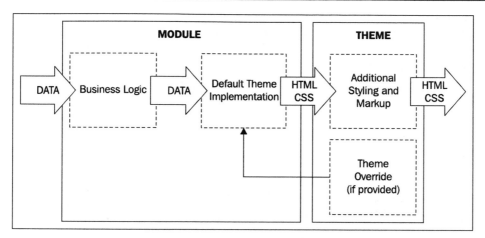

After the data has been retrieved and manipulated in the heart of your module (the business logic), it will need to provide the default theme implementation. Sometimes a particular theme will need to override your implementation in order for it to achieve a specific design goal; if the theme provides its own implementation, Drupal will use the theme implementation instead of the module's default implementation.

When building our first module in *Chapter 2*, we saw a brief example of this in action as follows:

```
$variables = array('items' => $list, 'type' => 'ol');
$content = theme('item_list', $variables);
```

By calling the theme() function, we are delegating the responsibility of determining and using the proper theme implementation. We're saying:

"Hey, theme()! I want to markup my data as an item_list. Can you do that for me? I don't need to know the details. kthxbye."

Our module just needs to decide which theme hook it wants to use to markup its data. Should the data be displayed in an unordered list, a table, or a wordle?

Hook crazy?

> In addition to API **hooks**, Drupal also has **theme hooks**. A theme hook is simply the *name* of a particular way to markup some data. For example, passing data to the item_list theme hook will result in different markup then passing data to the links theme hook. However, while normally every module's hook function will be called when Drupal invokes an API hook, only one theme hook implementation will be invoked when Drupal invokes a theme hook.

There are actually two different ways you can make an implementation (which we will discuss later), but for now we'll only talk about the simplest method for module developers—**theme functions**. When you call `theme()`, it will look for a default theme function named `theme_HOOKNAME` and for an optional theme override function called `THEMENAME_HOOKNAME`. If you dig into Drupal's internals, you'll find a `theme_item_list()` inside `includes.inc` or `theme.inc`. This is Drupal's default theme implementation for an `item_list`. If our active theme was **Bartik**, and if **Bartik** implemented a theme override called `bartik_item_list()`, then `theme()` would use the **Bartik** theme's implementation instead of the default one.

The preceding figure shows one piece of data as it passes through a module and a theme. However, in order for you to understand the full power of Drupal's theme layer, you also need to understand how the entire page is built.

However, since all of the active theme's modifications occur after any module modifications, from a module developer's perspective, all of this theme inheritance is transparent. Since modules don't need to know anything about the structure of the theme and its ancestry, we'll simply talk about "the theme" in this book. Just be aware that the actual theme may be more complex.

Base themes and sub-themes

If you've previously read anything about Drupal theming, you've probably heard about **base themes** and **sub-themes**. Any theme can declare a parent theme in its `.info` file using the base theme key and it will inherit all the hook implementations from its parent theme (and its parent's parent theme, and so on).

Data granularity

One of the things that makes Drupal theming so powerful is its granularity. Each piece of content is handled separately as it's passed through the theming system. Each bit of data is themed individually, then combined into ever-larger chunks. At each step in the aggregation process, it's themed again. The following illustration will make this clearer:

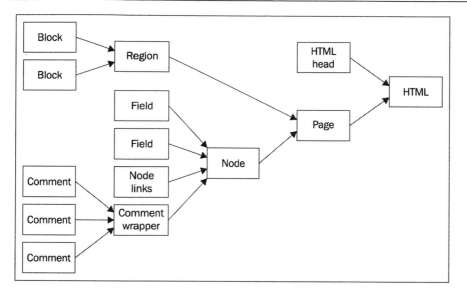

As you can see in the preceding illustration, for a typical blog post, each comment is pulled from the database and sent through the theme system to get HTML markup added to it. Then all the comments are aggregated together into a "comment wrapper" where additional markup and, usually, a "new comment" form is added. Then the single group of comments is passed to the node theming where it is combined with other pieces of the blog post's content. This process of theming bits of content, aggregation, and theming again is repeated until we've built the entire HTML page ready to be sent to a web browser.

There are two advantages to this granular system. First, since each module is responsible for theming its own data, it can either create a very specialized theme hook for its data or it can re-use an existing theme hook. Re-using a theme hook ensures a consistent set of markup for similar data structures while still allowing customized CSS classes (Most theme hooks allow custom classes to be passed as parameters.) For example, the list of links after a node (**read more**, **add new comment**, and so on) re-uses the `links` theme hook, and the links after each comment use the same `links` theme hook.

The second advantage is for the theme developer. Having a fine-grained theming system means that a theme, if it chooses to, can literally rewrite all of the markup for its own design purposes. As module developers we need to be keenly aware of the themer's desire to have granular theming overrides.

Theme engines

Some themes require alternate theme engines. Theme engines can provide alternate template syntax, naming standards, and helper functions. Several theme engines are available for download at `http://drupal.org/project/theme+engines`. However, we won't be discussing any theme engines except for Drupal's default theme engine, **PHPTemplate**. The PHPTemplate theme engine has been the default theme since Drupal 4.7, has been continuously improved with each version, and has proven its worth again and again. Over 99% of themes available for download on `drupal.org` use the default PHPTemplate theme engine. All of the examples in this book assume you are using PHPTemplate. So, enough said.

Two ways to theme

So now that we have a good understanding of higher level concepts, let's get down to the nitty-gritty of theme implementations. As mentioned earlier in the chapter, there are actually two different ways to implement a theme hook:

- **Theme functions**: pass data to a PHP function to wrap it in markup
- **Templates**: pass data to a template which is a PHP file mixed with markup and PHP print statements

Let's look at each of these in turn.

Theme functions

For a module developer, the easiest type of implementation to understand is a **theme function**. Theme functions just need to follow a few simple rules in order for them to work properly.

First, the name of the theme function follows the pattern:

```
theme_[theme hook name]
```

> Since the theme hook name is used directly in the theme function's name, theme hook names have the same constraints on naming as regular PHP function names; the only valid characters in theme hook names are alphanumeric characters and underscores. So if a module has created an `example_format` theme hook, it would implement it with theme function named `theme_example_format()`.

Second, the theme function will only have a single parameter, as follows:

```
function theme_THEME_HOOK_NAME($variables) {…}
```

The theme function variables are an associative array containing the pieces of data we wish to markup and any options we want to pass to the function. It may seem extremely odd not to use multiple parameters and PHP's ability to specify default values for each parameter. In fact, previous versions of Drupal did use multiple parameters. We'll see why Drupal now only uses one parameter in just a moment when we talk about preprocess functions.

For an example of a `$variables` array, let's look at how the DocBlock of the `theme_item_list()` function defines it:

- **Items**: An array of items to be displayed in the list. If an item is a string, then it is used as is. If an item is an array, then the "data" element of the array is used as the contents of the list item. If an item is an array with a "children" element, those children are displayed in a nested list. All other elements are treated as attributes of the list item element.
- **Title**: The title of the list.
- **Type**: The type of list to return (e.g. `ul`, `ol`).
- **Attributes**: The attributes applied to the list element.

The `items` and `title` keys hold the actual data, and the `type` and `attributes` keys are options that specify how to build the item list.

Third, the theme function should return a string that contains the rendered representation of the data. This is usually a string of HTML, but some theme hooks return other types of themed markup. For example, `theme_syslog_format` returns a simple string with pipe-separated data values for use in a `*NIX syslog` error log.

That's it! As you can see, theme functions have very simple requirements and in every other way are standard PHP functions.

The major difference between most functions and theme functions is that you should never call theme functions directly. It may be tempting to take your data and call `theme_item_list($vars)` directly, but you should instead call `theme("item_list", $vars)`. This method of calling theme functions indirectly ensures that themes are able to override any module's default theme function (or template). It also allows the `theme()` function to work additional magic, including allowing other modules to alter the theme function's variables before they are used.

Preprocess functions

Now we're starting to see the real flexibility of the theme system. Preprocess functions allow one module to alter the variables used by another module when it calls a theme hook. So if some code passes data to `theme()` for a particular theme hook, preprocess functions will be called to alter the data before the actual theme hook implementation is called. The following steps are carried out:

1. Code calls `theme('hook_name', $variables)`.
2. `theme()` calls preprocess functions for `hook_name`.
3. Preprocess functions modify variables.
4. `theme()` calls actual implementation for `hook_name` with modified variables.

All preprocess functions take the form of:

```
[module]_preprocess_[theme hook name](&$variables)
```

So if the `foo` module wants to alter the variables for the `item_list` theme hook, it could define the function as follows:

```
function foo_preprocess_item_list(&$variables) {
  // Add a class to the list wrapper.
  $variables['attributes']['class'][] = 'foo-list';
}
```

Notice that the `$variables` parameter is defined with an ampersand in front of it. That's PHP notation to pass the parameter *by reference*. Instead of getting a copy of the variables, the `foo_preprocess_item_list()` function will get access to the actual `$variables` which is later passed to the theme function implementation. So any modifications that the preprocess function makes to the `$variables` parameter will be preserved when those variables are passed to the theme function. That's the reason our example `foo_preprocess_item_list()` function doesn't return anything; its work is done directly on the original `$variables`.

This is extremely handy for module developers as it allows all sorts of integration with other modules. Since the variables parameter is a mix of data and options, modules can alter both the raw data and change the way data will be rendered. This can be as simple as one module needing a special class for use in its JavaScript code and adding that class to another module's themed content by appending to the `$variables['attributes']['class']` array, or can be more complex interactions like the `i18n` module translating the language used in blocks.

Imagine we've built a retro module that integrates GeoCities and we want to replace all links to a user's profile page with a link to the user's **GeoCities** homepage. We can do that relatively easily with a preprocess function.

First let's look at the following `theme_username` function's documentation:

```
/**
 * Format a username.
 *
 * @param $variables
 *   An associative array containing:
 *   - account: The user object to format.
 *   - name: The user's name, sanitized.
 *   - extra: Additional text to append to the user's name, sanitized.
 *   - link_path: The path or URL of the user's profile page, home
 *     page, or other desired page to link to for more information
 *     about the user.
 *   - link_options: An array of options to pass to the l() function's
 *     $options parameter if linking the user's name to the user's
 *     page.
 *   - attributes_array: An array of attributes to pass to the
 *     drupal_attributes() function if not linking to the user's page.
 */
```

Quite conveniently, `theme_username()` has a handy `$link_path` variable that we want to alter to achieve our old-school giggles. Assuming that we've used some other business logic with the user module's hooks to load our GeoCities URL into the user's account (the "hard" part), replacing the link to the user's profile page can be accomplished with the following simple preprocess function:

```
/**
 * Implements awesomeness with hook_preprocess_username().
 */
function retro_preprocess_username(&$variables) {
  $variables['link_path'] = $variables['account']->geocities_url;
}
```

That's it! We don't have to override the user module's theme implementation; we just modify its parameters.

Theme overrides

While module developers usually don't have to worry about whether a theme overrides a particular theme function or not, it's still important to understand how this mechanism works.

A Drupal theme is normally composed of CSS, images, JavaScripts, template files (discussed shortly), a `.info` file, and a `template.php` file. The `template.php` file is analogous to a module's `.module` file. It contains all of the PHP functions for the theme and is automatically loaded when the theme is initialized.

If a theme wants to override a particular theme function, it needs to copy the theme function from its original location and paste it into its `template.php` file. Then it needs to change the function's prefix from `theme` to its own name and finally, it needs to start making the desired changes to the function.

For example, if the **Bartik** theme wants to override the `theme_menu_local_tasks()` function in order to add some markup around the page's tabs, it would copy the entire function from `includes/menu.inc`, paste it into Bartik's `template.php`, and rename it to `bartik_menu_local_tasks()`.

Fortunately, when a theme overrides a default theme function, a module's preprocess functions continue to work as normal.

Themes also have the ability to create preprocess functions. If the **Bartik** theme decides to format a user's name in "last name, first name" format, it can implement a `bartik_preprocess_username()` function. Fortunately, a theme's preprocess functions do not override a module's preprocess functions. All preprocess functions are run; first any module's preprocess functions and then the theme's preprocess function.

Template files

While **theme functions** might be the easiest for module developers to understand, **template files** are the easiest for themers to grasp. When a theme hook is implemented with template files, they are used instead of theme functions. However, from a module developer's standpoint, there is actually a remarkable amount of similarity between template files and theme functions. First, let's take a closer look at template files.

Templates are files primarily containing HTML but with some PHP statements mixed in using the template's variables. Instead of declaring a `theme_hook_name()` function, a module would instead create a `hook-name.tpl.php` file. The following are the contents of a typical template file, `typical-hook.tpl.php`:

```
<div class="<?php print $classes; ?>"<?php print $attributes; ?>>

  <?php if ($title): ?>
    <h2<?php print $title_attributes; ?>>
      <?php print $title; ?>
    </h2>
  <?php endif;?>
```

```
<div class="submitted">
<?php print t('By !author @time ago', array(
  '@time' => $time,
  '!author' => $author,
  )); ?>
</div>

<div class="content"<?php print $content_attributes; ?>>
  <?php
    // We hide the links now so that we can render them later.
    hide($content['links']);
    print render($content);
  ?>
</div>

<?php print render($content['links']); ?>
</div>
```

The preceding example shows the full gamut of the things that you are likely see in a template file. They are as follows:

- Printing a variable containing a string
- Printing a translatable string using t()
- Conditional if/else/endif statement
- Delaying rendering on part of a render element with hide()
- Printing a render element

All of the PHP in a template should be limited to printing out variables. This limited amount of PHP makes it much easier for non-programmers to learn how to use template files compared to theme functions. However, for module developers, the template implementation is still very similar to the theme function implementation; the handful of differences are relatively minor.

As with theme function implementations, our module would still need to invoke the theme hook using theme().

```
$variables = array('typical' => $typical_object);
$output = theme('typical_hook', $variables);
```

The `theme()` function would discover that the `typical_hook` theme hook was implemented as a template and render the corresponding `typical-hook.tpl.php` file.

> As we mentioned earlier in the chapter, the only valid characters in theme hook names are alphanumeric characters and underscores. This is true of all theme hooks, regardless of whether they are implemented as a theme function or as a template file. However, when `theme()` looks for template implementations, it will automatically convert any underscores in the theme hook name into hyphens while searching for the template file. For example, calling `theme('user_picture', $variables)` will result in the template file named `user-picture.tpl.php` being rendered.

Also, just like theme functions, other modules can modify the variables using preprocess functions.

In template files the focus is on printing out variables in various places in the markup. So for template files, the preprocess function takes on a more important role. The only difference between a theme function's preprocess functions and a template file's are the number and type of preprocess functions.

The preprocess zoo

When you write a theme function, its natural to pass the raw data in as parameters and generate any display-related meta-data inside the function. With a template file, that's not really possible without putting complex PHP inside the template. However, as was stated earlier, all of the PHP in a template file should be limited to just the bare minimum required to print out a PHP variable. Any processing that we need to do on the raw data parameters to ease it into print-ready variables should be done in preprocess functions.

"template_" preprocess functions

When a module defines a theme hook by creating a template file, that module should also create a corresponding preprocess function to set up and process any variables that are needed by the template file, but are not passed as parameters to `theme()`. By convention, that preprocess function should be of the following form:

```
template_preprocess_[theme hook name](&$variables)
```

The `template_` prefix tells Drupal's theme system that this preprocess function is the primary preprocessor for the theme hook's variables and should be run *before* any other module's preprocess function.

Here's an example that should make this concept a bit clearer. This is an actual code snippet from Drupal's block preprocess function. In each page region, all of the blocks in the region get a variable whose value alternates between "odd" and "even". These values can be used to create zebra-striped styling, that is, alternate styling on every other block in a region.

```
function template_preprocess_block(&$variables) {
  // We store all block counters using drupal_static().
  $block_counter = &drupal_static(__FUNCTION__, array());

  // All blocks get an independent counter for each region.
  if (!isset($block_counter[$variables['block']->region])) {
    $block_counter[$variables['block']->region] = 1;
  }

  // Generate the zebra striping variable.
  $variables['block_zebra'] = ($block_counter[$variables['block']-
>region] % 2) ? 'odd' : 'even';

  // Increment the region's block count.
  $block_counter[$variables['block']->region]++;
}
```

The PHP logic in this function is directly related to the display of the block and not to the general business logic of this data. So, it doesn't make sense that the block module would calculate that meta data before calling theme(); the meta data clearly belongs to the display logic, which is why it's placed in the block module's preprocess function.

Multi-hook preprocess functions

In some rare circumstances, you may need to alter or provide some variables for all theme hooks. In fact, Drupal's theme system does provide some variables to all templates; the preprocess function that provides these variables is both a "template_" preprocess function and a **multi-hook preprocess function**. Multi-hook preprocess functions are simply functions that don't have a _HOOK suffix added to their name and are run for *every single template file*. Their name is of the following form:

```
[module]_preprocess(&$variables, $hook)
```

Obviously, there can be a big performance hit if a module needlessly implements a multi-hook preprocess function. If you're contemplating writing one, if at all possible, consider writing several preprocess functions that target the specific hooks you need instead, rather then hit all hooks.

Now, if you were paying close attention to the form of the name, you'll also notice that these functions actually receive two parameters, namely, the `$variables` array and a `$hook` parameter. `$hook`, as the name suggests, contains the name of the actual theme hook currently being run. So, while a `foo_preprocess(&$variables, $hook)` function is run for every template file, it will still be able to tell which template is currently being requested. In fact, `$hook` is the second parameter for *all* preprocess functions, but `$hook` is only useful for multi-hook preprocess functions.

For a good example of a multi-hook preprocess function, let's look at the function that the theme system uses to set up several variables common to all template files—the `template_preprocess()` function, which is as follows:

```
function template_preprocess(&$variables, $hook) {
  // Tell all templates where they are located.
  $variables['directory'] = path_to_theme();

  // Initialize html class attribute for the current hook.
  $variables['classes_array'] = array(drupal_html_class($hook));
}
```

As you can see, this preprocess function creates a `$directory` variable which can be used to tell where the template file is located on the web server. In the `$classes_array` variable, it also starts to set up the CSS classes used in the outer-most wrapping `div` of the template.

Process functions

Obviously, inside our template file, when we print out our dynamically created list of classes, we'll need the variable to be a string. `<?php print $classes_array; ?>` will, most unhelpfully print out "array". In earlier versions of Drupal, classes were dynamically created but were immediately concatenated into strings. So themes would see one long string with multiple classes in it, `menu-block-wrapper menu-block-1 menu-name-management`, for example. This made removing or altering classes difficult as themers had to master PHP's string-manipulation functions or even (gasp!) *regular expressions*.

In Drupal 7, this problem for themers has been solved using the new **process functions**. Process functions are an additional phase of variable processing functions that run after the initial preprocess functions. In all respects, process functions are exactly like preprocess functions; there are `template_` prefixed process functions, multi-hook process functions, module-provided process functions, and theme-provided process functions. The only difference is that process functions are run after all preprocess functions have been run.

Process functions are extremely useful when you have meta data that is likely to be manipulated by other modules or themes and you wish to delay the rendering of the meta data until just before the template file itself is rendered.

In the preceding code example, the `template_preprocess()` function creates a `$classes_array` variable that holds an array of classes to be used on the wrapping `div` in the template file. Modules and themes can easily add classes by simply adding an additional array element from inside their preprocess function, as follows:

```
$variables['classes_array'][] = 'extra-savoir-faire';
```

Themes can use much simpler array manipulation functions in order to remove or alter classes.

```
// Search for the bogus class and return its array key
// location. If not found, array_search returns FALSE.
// Remember that 0 is a valid key.
$key = array_search('bogus', $variables['classes_array']);
if ($key !== FALSE) {
  // Alter the class.
  $variables['classes_array'][$key] .= '-dude';
}
// Or remove the no-soup class.
$variables['classes_array'] = array_diff($variables['classes_array'],
array('no-soup'));
```

In addition to the `$classes_array` variable, the `template_preprocess()` function also creates `$attributes_array`, `$title_attributes_array`, and `$content_attributes_array` variables which are used for HTML attributes on the outermost wrapping `div`, the title's heading tag, and the content's wrapping `div`, respectively. You'll see each of these variables used in the `typical-hook.tpl.php` example, given earlier in the chapter.

After modules and themes are given an opportunity to alter these variables, the theme system uses the `template_process()` function to render those arrays into a simple string, as follows:

```
function template_process(&$variables, $hook) {
  // Flatten out classes.
  $variables['classes'] = implode(' ', $variables['classes_array']);

  // Flatten out attributes, title_attributes, and content_attributes.
  $variables['attributes'] = drupal_attributes(
$variables['attributes_array']);
  $variables['title_attributes'] = drupal_attributes(
$variables['title_attributes_array']);
  $variables['content_attributes'] = drupal_attributes(
$variables['content_attributes_array']);
}
```

A similar problem troubled module developers in Drupal 6. It was impossible to call `drupal_add_css()` or `drupal_add_js()` in a `MODULE_preprocess_page()` function because the lists of CSS files and JavaScript files were already generated *before* any of the preprocess functions were run. Again, process functions come to the rescue. Drupal 7 delays the generation of these lists until the `template_process_html()` function is run.

Order of preprocess execution

Now with all these different flavors of processing functions, it can get a bit confusing as to which function runs in what order. Fortunately, there are just three simple rules that are used to determine the order of processing. They are as follows:

- All preprocess functions run before all process functions
- `template_` prefixed functions run first. `[module]_` prefixed functions run next. `[theme]_` prefixed functions run last
- Multi-hook functions run before hook-specific functions

This results in the following order of execution for a particular theme hook:

1. `template_preprocess()`
2. `template_preprocesss_HOOK()`
3. `MODULE_preprocess()`
4. `MODULE_preprocess_HOOK()`
5. `THEME_preprocess()`
6. `THEME_preprocess_HOOK()`
7. `template_process()`
8. `template_processs_HOOK()`
9. `MODULE_process()`
10. `MODULE_process_HOOK()`
11. `THEME_process()`
12. `THEME_process_HOOK()`

Whew.

If the THEME is actually a list of inherited base and sub-themes, each `THEME_`-prefixed item above could be a list of each base theme's and sub-theme's functions, which would make the list even longer. See the "Base themes and sub-themes" tip near the beginning of this chapter if you haven't read it already.

By the way, does your brain hurt yet? You may want to take a break now; go out and get some air, or, at the very least, have a strong drink handy when you start reading the next section.

Render elements

Render elements are new to Drupal 7's theme layer. They've existed since Drupal 4.7 as part of the Form API, but they've now been injected into the heart of the theme system. A **Render element** is a complex data structure passed as a single parameter to theme(), as one of its variables. Render elements are fundamentally nested arrays that can include:

- The data to be rendered
- Other render elements which are considered "children" of the element
- An array of structures such as CSS and JavaScript files, that should be attached to the page when it is rendered
- A list of theme hooks that can be used to theme the data
- A list of callback functions to run on the element before and after it is themed

In template files, render elements are handled slightly differently then normal variables, using the syntax we saw earlier in our typical-hook.tpl.php example:

```php
<?php print render($element); ?>
```

In theme functions, render elements are included with its output using the drupal_render() function:

```php
$output .= drupal_render($element);
```

Let's look at a simple render element:

```php
$element = array(
  '#prefix' => '<div class="plain">',
  '#markup' => '<p>' . t('There is no spoon.') . '</p>',
  '#suffix' => '</div>',
);
```

In the preceding render element our main property is the #markup property which uses a string containing HTML markup as-is for the rendered element. The other properties do exactly what they hint at, prepending or appending HTML markup to the rendered element. If drupal_render($element) was called, it would simply return the three strings concatenated together.

Now, that was an extremely simple example, but when we start looking at more complex render elements, we'll see that each array key in a render element can be one of the following three things:

1. A render element **property**. These are prefixed by #.

2. A **child element**. All array keys not prefixed by # are considered to be a child elements.

3. A **variable** to be passed to a theme function. In the render element these variable's names are prefixed with # (just like properties are), but `theme()` will strip the # from the name before sending it on to the actual theme implementation.

Taking these slightly mush rules, we can examine the following render element:

```php
$element = array(
    '#prefix' => '<div class="less-simple">',
    '#suffix' => '!</div>',
    'kitten' => array(
        '#type' => 'link',
        '#title' => t('Kill me'),
        '#href' => 'admin/core/hack',
    ),
    'separator' => array(
        '#markup' => '<br />',
    ),
    'domo' => array(
        '#theme' => 'username',
        '#account' => $account,
    ),
);
```

First, we should identify the children since they are the simplest to spot. `kitten`, `separator`, and `domo` are the child elements of our render element. The `separator` child element is another example of a simple #markup render element.

Looking at the `domo` element, we see that its #theme property is set to username. `drupal_render()` will take that child element and pass it to `theme()` with a theme hook of `username`; meaning that `theme('username', $element['domo'])` will be called and `theme()` will strip the # characters from the front of all of the variables before passing the data to `theme_username()`.

Lastly, the `kitten` element's `#type` property is set to `link`. The `#type` property tells `drupal_render()` how to render that element. When we learn about `hook_element_info()`, we'll understand why, but for now `drupal_render()` will pass the `kitten` element to the `drupal_pre_render_link()` function which will render the element using `l()` and return its output.

Render properties

Render element properties are defined in two places. The first place where properties are defined is directly inside `drupal_render()` and its helper functions. The following is a complete list of properties used by `drupal_render()`:

- `#access`: A Boolean indicating if the current user has access to view the element.

- `#cache`: An array indicating whether the element should optionally be retrieved from cache or stored in cache after rendering. See `drupal_render()` for more information.

- `#markup`: A string containing markup (such as HTML). If this property is set, the `#type` property does not need to be set, as it will automatically be set to **markup**.

- `#type`: A string indicating which element is being rendered. The default properties for this type of element are extracted from the data specified with `hook_element_info()` and merged with the render element.

- `#defaults_loaded`: A Boolean indicating whether the element type's default properties have already been loaded. If this is `false` or not set, the default properties from `element_info()` are added before `drupal_render()` looks at any other render properties (except for `#access` and `#cache`).

- `#pre_render`: An array of callbacks to apply to the element before theming.

- `#theme`: A string specifying the theme hook to be used on the element.

- `#theme_wrappers`: An array of theme hooks to be used on the element after initial theming and/or after the child elements have been rendered. Theme functions that are to be used as wrappers need to be specially written to look for the `#children` property in the render element passed to it from theme.

- `#post_render`: An array of callbacks to apply to the element after theming.

- `#children`: The rendered element and its children. It is normally built up internally by `drupal_render()` as it renders the elements, but can also be set by a `#pre_render` callback.

- `#prefix`: A string containing markup to be prepended to the `#children` property.

- **#suffix**: A string containing markup to be appended to the #children property.

- **#weight**: A number used to sort child elements.

- **#sorted**: A Boolean indicating if the child elements have already been sorted. Since sorting a render array is expensive, if you know the data is already sorted (for example, the data was sorted when retrieved from the database), you should set this property to TRUE.

- **#states**: JavaScript state information.

- **#attached**: An array of CSS, JavaScript, libraries, or other associated attachments related to the element. See drupal_process_attached() for more information.

- **#printed**: A Boolean indicating if the element has already been rendered.

hook_element_info

The second place properties are defined is inside hook_element_info(). Each #type of render element needs to be defined in an implementation of hook_element_info(). system_element_info() defines most of Drupal core's render elements, which include several useful elements such as the markup element, the link element, and all the form elements. The following is a short snippet from system_element_info():

```
/**
 * Implements hook_element_info().
 */
function system_element_info() {
  // HTML markup.
  $types['markup'] = array(
    '#markup' => '',
    '#pre_render' => array('drupal_pre_render_markup'),
  );
  // A HTML link.
  $types['link'] = array(
    '#pre_render' => array('drupal_pre_render_link',
'drupal_pre_render_markup'),
  );
  // A hidden form element.
  $types['hidden'] = array(
    '#input' => TRUE,
    '#process' => array('ajax_process_form'),
    '#theme' => 'hidden',
  );

  return $types;
}
```

As you can see, the link type specifies that the render element should be passed to two #pre_render functions. And it is the drupal_pre_render_link() function that looks for the special render element properties in our example's link element, namely, #title, #href, and #options.

So to reiterate, hook_element_info() defines the default properties for its render element types, and it also specifies render callbacks that have their own internal API, defining render element properties.

Using this framework, modules can create their own complex render element by implementing hook_element_info(), using the properties specified by drupal_render(), and by creating any render callbacks and associated APIs.

hook_page_alter()

So what's the point? By creating these complex render elements, we delay rendering of the data and allow opportunities to alter that data before it is rendered into a string. Before render elements were used in Drupal's theme system, themers and module developers often had to completely re-render data after it had been rendered the default way. This was obviously inefficient. Now each of these render elements can be altered in preprocess functions or even directly in a template file with the show() and hide() functions.

Now that we've looked at the guts of the Render API, it becomes much easier to understand how the template-embedded hide() function works. If a template file calls hide($element['child']); it simply sets the #printed property to TRUE, so when print render($element); is later called, the child element is not printed. We can then later call print render($element['child']); and render() will set #printed to FALSE and pass $element to drupal_render().

Drupal's theme implementations use render elements in various places throughout its theme hooks. But the two primary places render elements get used are in the block and page theme hooks.

Any hook_block_view() implementation should return a renderable element, and any menu callback which supplies a page's main content should also return a render element.

Once the page's main content is retrieved, drupal_render_page() will decorate the $page element using hook_page_build(). During the block module's block_page_build(), all of the page's regions are added to the $page element as child elements; and each of the region's child elements contain child elements for each of the blocks in that region. drupal_render_page() will then allow modules to modify the giant $page render element using hook_page_alter().

Two powerful use cases for `hook_page_alter()` would be to allow the insertion of a block inside the page's main content, or doing the reverse, moving a "Field" into a certain spot in a page region. Of course, you'll have to read the Field API chapter (*Chapter 7, Creating New Fields*) **first!**

The power of theme()

It turns out that the `theme()` function has to do quite a bit of work once it's called. The following diagram should make its responsibilities and its order of operations clearer:

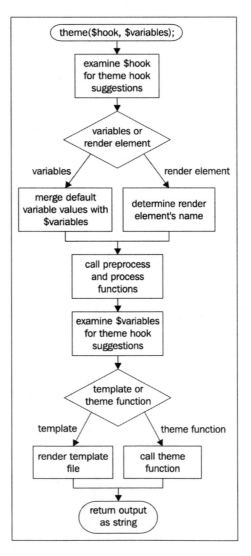

We've actually already discussed most of the work flow of theme(). There's only one aspect we haven't yet seen. So far, we've only called theme() with a simple string passed to its $hook parameter. However, we can actually pass more complex data to it and make use of the theme system's **theme hook suggestions**.

Theme hook suggestions

So re-using theme hooks in various places in our code is a good thing, of course. However, one problem you'll encounter is that theme functions lose context when a theme hook is re-used. For example, theme_links() has no idea if it's theming node links or comment links, which makes it difficult to style them differently. Fortunately, we can provide context to the theme system by providing a **theme hook pattern** as its first parameter:

```
[base hook]__[context]
```

The parts of the pattern are separated with a double underscore since some theme hooks (like user and user_profile) could be confusing if we were to use a single underscore to delineate the parts of the pattern. In fact, we can provide additional contexts if needed, as follows:

```
[base hook]__[context]__[even more context]__[don't get crazy]
```

So how does this work and how does it help? In Drupal 7, we theme the node's links by calling theme('links__node', $vars). So theme() will use a theme_links__node() function if one has been provided. However, if one doesn't exist, it will use theme_links(). This allows us to know the context based on the theme function we are implementing. A more complex example is when Drupal 7 themes the node's contextual links; it calls theme('links__contextual__node', $vars). So, theme() will search for a theme_links__contextual__node(), then for theme_links__contextual(), and lastly theme_links(), shortening the pattern by one unit of context each time.

The theme hook pattern is an easy-to-use method of providing context, but some contributed modules need to provide more complex lists of context than the simple string pattern can provide. For this reason, an *array* of possible hook suggestions can also be passed to theme(). For example, both Views and the Menu block module use this method. While theming trees of menus, Menu block provides the following array to theme:

```
$hook = array(
  'menu_tree__menu_block__' . $delta,
  'menu_tree__menu_block__' . $menu_name,
  'menu_tree__menu_block',
```

```
    'menu_tree__' . $menu_name,
    'menu_tree',
);
theme($hook, $tree);
```

This allows themers to provide either a `THEME_menu_tree__menu_block__1()` function to override the display of just the 1st configured menu block (with a delta ID of 1), or to override the display of all trees displaying the **management** menu with a `THEME_menu_tree__menu_block__management()`. Of course, if the theme provides none of those functions, `theme()` will continue to use the default implementation, `theme_menu_tree()`. To be clear about how this works, `theme()` takes the array of suggestions and checks them from left to right until it finds an actual implementation.

If you look at the preceding figure again, you'll notice that after the preprocess and process functions have been run, `theme()` examines the $variables for additional theme hook suggestions. Of course, only the calling code can specify hook suggestions in the first parameter to `theme()`. In order to allow other modules and themes to add its own suggestions, `theme()` will examine two variables `$theme_hook_suggestion` and `$theme_hook_suggestions`. `theme()` will first check the singular form of that variable name. If the `$theme_hook_suggestion` string doesn't match an actual implementation, `theme()` will check the `$theme_hook_suggestions` array from left to right to find an implementation. If `theme()` doesn't find any implementations from those two variables, it will continue to use the theme hook it had previously been using.

Since themes can completely override the value of `$theme_hook_suggestion`, it is recommended that modules stick to modifying the `$theme_hook_suggestions` array. This is how it is done:

```
// Add our suggestions to the front of the list, since our
// module is the most important one in the universe!
array_unshift($variables['theme_hook_suggestions'],
             'links__retro__geocities', 'links__retro');
```

Note that `$theme_hook_suggestions` and `$theme_hook_suggestion` do not take patterns. If you want `theme()` to look for `links__retro__geocities` and `links__retro`, you'll need to provide both of those strings in the `$theme_hook_suggestions` array.

One last note, all of the above examples assumed theme functions, but the same is true for theme hook suggestions of template files. If you provide a `node__blog__1` pattern to `theme()`, it will search for a `node--blog--1.tpl.php` file and then for a `node--blog.tpl.php` file.

Theme registry

So all of the wonderful things that theme() does, take a considerable amount of work. It's extremely inefficient for theme() to determine all of this information about theme hooks on the fly each time it's called. So to help its load and improve performance, Drupal uses a **theme registry**.

The theme registry holds a list of all the theme hooks known by the system, and for each theme hook, it also stores the following:

- Whether it's a theme function or a template
- The list of preprocess functions to run
- The list of process functions to run
- The path to the template file (which includes whether the original module template file is used or a theme version of it.)
- The theme function name (which indicates if it's the original module theme function or one overridden by a theme.)
- The list of variables that should be passed to theme() when this theme hook is called and a default value for each variable
- Whether, instead of a list of variables, the theme function expects a single render element as its parameter, and what that render element should be named

While this theme registry does improve performance for the website user, it does cause some inconvenience for module and theme developers. Since Drupal is caching data about theme hooks, if you are actively writing or altering a theme hook, you'll need to make sure that you rebuild the theme registry before testing your changes. Fortunately, this can easily by accomplished by clicking the **Clear all caches** button on the **Performance** page found in the **Configuration** admin (admin/config/development/performance). The devel module also has a handy **Rebuild the theme registry on every page load** option in its settings.

Variable default values

Earlier when we talked about theme functions and the single $variables parameter, you may have noticed one short-coming of that parameter. When you have a normal list of parameters in a function definition, you specify the default values for parameters that are optional. This allows code to only list a few parameters when calling the function and have the additional parameters just get sensible default values.

If a function were defined as follows:

```
function foo_spaghettify($code, $type = 'thin', $sticky = TRUE) { }
```

Then, code that called it could just call `foo_spaghettify($code)` and the `$type` and `$sticky` parameters would get the default values defined in the function definition. With a single `$variables` parameter we have an issue. If we tried the following:

```
function foo_spaghettify($variables = array('code' => array(),
                          'type' => 'thin', 'sticky' => TRUE) { }
```

And then called:

```
$variables = array('code' => $code);
$result = foo_spaghettify($variables);
```

Then, we would discover that `$variables['type']` and `$variables['sticky']` don't get the default value, and they are also undefined. The reason is simple; default parameter values only get used if the parameter is not specified when calling the function, but we *did* specify the `$variables` parameter, so its default is not used.

So how do we solve this problem in Drupal? We have modules that define the default variables in their `hook_theme` functions.

hook_theme

A module's `hook_theme` is primarily responsible for specifying a few things, as follows:

- The theme hooks that the module is responsible for
- The type of theme implementation (theme function or template)
- The theme hooks' default variable values
- If the hook expects a render element instead of variables

In addition to those main responsibilities, the `hook_theme` can optionally specify:

- Which file contains the theme function or preprocess functions (if it isn't in the main module file)
- A pattern to use during the auto-discovery search of a theme's overridden theme hook suggestions
- Some other esoteric things you can read about in its documentation:
  `http://api.drupal.org/api/function/hook_theme/7`

A module's `hook_theme` implementation just needs to return an array of theme hooks it is creating. For example:

```php
/**
 * Implements hook_theme().
 */
function retro_theme() {
  return array(
    // The array key is the name of the theme hook.
    'wonder' => array(
      // Use a template and give the template's name.
      'template' => 'wonder',

      // Specify the default variable names and their values.
      'variables' => array(
        'twin' => 'zen',
        'with_monkey' => FALSE,
        'activations' => array(),
      ),

      // Add a partial pattern to help hook theme suggestion
      // matches.
      'pattern' => 'wonder__',
    ),

    'austinite' => array(
      // Specify the name of the render element.
      'render element' => 'my_element',

      // We don't use this theme function often, so let's put
      // it in a separate file that is lazy loaded, if needed.
      'file' => 'retro.texas.inc',
    ),
  );
}
```

Let's examine this data. By default a theme hook will be assumed to be implemented as a theme function named `theme_hook_name()`. We can override the hook name using a `function` key/value inside our `austinite` array, but please don't confuse our poor themers; leave the default function name alone. If a theme hook instead wants to use template implementation, it needs to specify the name of the template file (without the `.tpl.php` extension) in the `template` key/value. Our `wonder` theme hook will use a `wonder.tpl.php` template.

We've also specified a pattern for that hook. After the theme registry retrieves the information from our `retro_theme()` function, it will try to auto-discover any template files whose names begin with the `pattern` that we specify. So the theme registry will search for any template beginning with `wonder__` and will add an entry for it in the theme registry. When `theme()` is passed theme hook suggestions, it doesn't search the file directory, it searches the theme registry instead, so this pattern is *essential* to making theme hook suggestions work.

Lastly in our `wonder` definition, we specified several variables with the `'variables'` key/value set, namely, `twin` (a string), `with_monkey` (a boolean), and `activations` (an array), and gave them each a default value.

Instead of a list of variables, the `theme_austinite()` function expects a single render element as its parameter, so we need to specify the name of the render element. We'll be able to access the render element of `theme_austinite()` from `$variables['my_element']`. In the preceding example, we used `my_element` to make it obvious that the value specified in `render element` is the key that needs to be used in `$variables` to access that element. However, by convention, Drupal core usually uses `element` or `elements` for that value.

To be clear, a theme hook should either use `'render element'` or `'variables'` in its dataset. Note that even if you use `'variables'`, one of those variables can still be a render element.

Finally, we used a `file` key to specify that we're storing our `theme_austinite()` function in a `retro.texas.inc` file. `theme()` will lazy load this file if it needs to use this theme hook on a particular page.

Full documentation can be found in the DocBlock for the `hook_theme()` API at the following site:

http://api.drupal.org/api/function/hook_theme/7

hook_theme_registry_alter

There are some extreme cases where a module may want to alter the registry entry for a particular theme hook. Fortunately, there's a hook for that.™ The `hook_theme_registry_alter()` hook can be implemented to alter the theme registry directly after it has been built with `hook_theme()` and the theme system's auto-discovery mechanisms. Let's suppose a `Spook` module wants to control whether Drupal's **status messages** are displayed to the user. If you look at `template_preprocess_page()`, you'll see that the `$show_messages` variable controls whether the status messages are displayed. Unfortunately, if we tried to simply implement a `spook_preprocess_page()` function, it would be run *after* `template_preprocess_page()` and, thus, too late. So, instead we need to implement the following code:

```
/**
 * Implements hook_theme_registry_alter().
 */
function spook_theme_registry_alter(&$theme_registry) {
  // Add our custom preprocess function to the beginning of
  // the preprocess function list.
  array_unshift($theme_registry['page']['preprocess functions'],
'spook_control_page_messages');
}

/**
 * Implements a custom preprocess function; one that is not
 * auto-discovered during the theme registry build.
 */
function spook_control_page_messages(&variables) {
  // Override #show_messages before template_preprocess_page()
  // accesses it.
  $variables['page']['#show_messages'] = spook_get_control();
}
```

The order of preprocess functions described in the earlier section is created during the theme's system registry build and is based on the naming conventions. However, `hook_theme_registry_alter()` allows us to alter that ordering to suit our own nefarious purposes.

What else?

For most modules you write, the contents of this chapter cover everything you need to learn about the theme system. Actually, this chapter might have been TMI. However, the theme system is chock full of yummy goodness not covered here, including accessibility classes, `hook_theme_enable`, and `hook_theme_disable` to name just a few. Drupal's online documentation includes a theme reference guide which can be a very handy tool for understanding some of the more obscure topics. It can be found at the following site:

```
http://drupal.org/theme-guide
```

Summary

You've learned a lot in this chapter. Since many of these theme concepts are inter-related, its challenging to learn them (and explain them!), so that the entire complex system makes sense. We touched on almost all parts of the theme system, including:

- Theme functions and template files
- Preprocess and process functions
- Default theme implementations and theme overrides
- `drupal_render()`, render elements and their properties
- `hook_element_info()`
- `hook_page_alter()`
- `theme()`, theme hooks and theme hook suggestions
- Theme registry, `hook_theme()`, and `hook_theme_registry_alter()`

I once created a graph that showed all the parts of theme system in one graphic, but it was more scary then useful. Or course, if you like horror, head over to:

`http://www.slideshare.net/JohnAlbin/default-theme-implementations`

In the next chapter, we'll take some of the most important topics in this chapter and use them to build a real world example.

4
Theming a Module

Now that you've learned the architecture of the theme layer, let's put that knowledge to practical use. In this chapter, we'll write some real code that both uses existing theme implementations and builds new theme implementations.

While the previous chapter was a whirlwind tour of the theme layer, this chapter will be a more thoughtful exploration of the system and how to best use it. We'll touch on the following ideas:

- The advantages of being lazy by reusing code
- Finding and reusing a theme hook
- Attaching CSS to render elements
- Creating stylesheets for RTL languages
- Building a theme hook

To help us learn these points, we're going to build a simple module in our examples. Drupal comes with the blog module, which creates multi-user blogs, one for each user and one aggregate blog. However, many websites only need a single blog. We're going to re-create some of the functionality of the blog module, and re-purpose it for a single blog that uses Drupal's default **article** content type. If you try out this chapter's code, you should disable Drupal 7's blog module first.

Reusing a default theme implementation

Now the first question you need to ask is "Should I reuse an existing theme hook or build my own?" Code reuse is one of the virtues of a lazy programmer. So the answer to that question is "Yes, be lazy!"

After all, if you choose an existing theme hook, you only have to build the data. You don't have to worry about building the implementation, registering it with `hook_theme`, building any helper pre-render functions, deciding on the best HTML to use, and building any supporting CSS and jQuery. What's not to like about skipping extra work?

However, laziness isn't the only reason you'll want to reuse existing theme hooks. Not only is it the easy way out, you'll also discover interesting integrations with other modules. As we learned in *Chapter 3, Drupal's Theme Layer*, modules can alter the way a theme implementation works by using preprocess/process functions. Those alterations aren't linked to only Drupal core's use of the theme hook; they are run even when *your* module uses the theme hook.

For example, when writing the `menu_block` module, I could have used my own theme hooks to theme the various parts of the menu trees that it displays. However, I decided to reuse core's menu tree-related theme hooks and just pump the data with lots of extra meta-data that core's usage lacked. I later discovered that another module was designed to modify core's menu trees and make them expand and collapse dynamically. That module did this by altering core's theme hooks. Since my `menu_block` module used the same hooks, the two modules were instantly interoperable. Neither module developer had to write any integration code. Score!

The hardest part to reusing existing theme hooks is simply finding the right one for you. You can browse all of Drupal core's default theme implementations at: `http://api.drupal.org/api/group/themeable/7`

Any hook implemented as a theme function is listed first. The template files are listed next, under the **Files** section.

In Drupal 7, there are 184 theme hooks that you could use in your own code. Many of those theme hooks are specific to a core module's usage, like theming an administration form, but it's still useful to go through the entire list to find hooks you could reuse. To make it even easier, we've included a list of the most commonly reused theme hooks:

Common theme hooks	
`file_link`	Returns HTML for a link to a file.
`html_tag`	Returns HTML for a generic HTML tag with attributes. This can often be too generic a theme hook to use, but is really useful for adding a tag to the `<head>` of a document or for theming a tag inside a render element.
`image`	Returns HTML for an image.
`image_style`	Returns HTML for an image using a specific image style.
`item_list`	Returns HTML for a list of items which can optionally be nested.

Common theme hooks

`links`	Returns HTML for a list of links (cannot be nested).
`more_link`	Returns HTML for a **more** link, often used on blocks.
`pager`	Returns HTML for a pager query element, a list of pages for result sets too long for one page.
`progress_bar`	Returns HTML for an indicator showing a task's progress.
`table`	Returns HTML for a table.
`username`	Returns HTML for a username.
`user_list`	Returns HTML for a list of users.
`user_picture`	Returns HTML for a picture configured for the user's account.

The theme hooks listed above are the most used hooks in Drupal core and also in Drupal `contrib` modules.

Drupal blocks revisited

So let's start building our `single_blog` module. We'll start with the `.info` file, of course. All of the lines in this `.info` file should be familiar to you:

```
;$Id$

name = Single blog
description = Enables a single blog for an individual or multiple
users.

core = 7.x
package = Drupal 7 Development

files[] = single_blog.module
```

One of the things that the blog module provides is a block listing recent blog entries. We're going to use the Block API that was introduced in *Chapter 2, Creating Your First Module*, as we build a couple basic hooks and an API function for our new module:

```
<?php
// $Id$

/**
 * @file
```

```
 * Enables a single-user blog.
 */

// After you learn Form API in Chapter 5, you'll be able to
// make these settings configurable.
define('SINGLE_BLOG_NODE_TYPE', 'article');
define('SINGLE_BLOG_LIST_COUNT', 3);

/**
 * Returns a list of blog entries.
 *
 * @param $number
 *    The number of blog entries to return.
 * @return
 *    A result set object containing the list of blog entries.
 */
function single_blog_list($number) {
  // Use the Database API to retrieve our data.
  // @see http://drupal.org/node/310069
  $query = db_select('node', 'n')
    ->fields('n', array('nid', 'title', 'created', 'uid'))
    ->condition('type', SINGLE_BLOG_NODE_TYPE)
    ->condition('status', 1)
    ->orderBy('created', 'DESC')
    ->range(0, $number)
    ->addTag('node_access')
    ->execute();

  return $query;
}

/**
 * Implements hook_block_info().
 */
function single_blog_block_info() {
  $blocks = array();

  // The array key defines the $delta parameter used in all
  // other block hooks.
  $blocks['recent'] = array(
    // The name of the block on the blocks administration page.
    'info' => t('Recent blog posts'),
  );

  return $blocks;
}
```

In *Chapter 5, Building an Admin Interface,* you'll learn how to build administration forms that could make our `single_blog` module configurable, but in this chapter we simply created a few PHP constants that define the node type to use for blog entries and the list count for block.

Next up, we provided a simple API for our module that allows any code to retrieve a list of blog nodes; we've called the function `single_blog_list()`. We're using Drupal's Database API to query for the data. You can learn more about it from Drupal's online documentation at `http://drupal.org/node/310069`. For now, you'll have to rely on DB API's *relatively* self-documenting method names. We selected the unique node ID, title, creation date and author (`uid` stands for user ID) fields of nodes that are of the `SINGLE_BLOG_NODE_TYPE` content type and that are published (`status` = 1). We only selected the `$number` latest nodes that have been created.

Why did we create a `single_blog_list()` function instead of just putting that database query code inside `hook_block_view()`? Some Drupal developers get so caught up in hooking into Drupal's APIs that they forget to write abstracted APIs for their own module's business logic. Don't make that same mistake. We *could* put the database query inside a Drupal hook, but that reduces the chance that other modules can integrate with your module in ways you could never anticipate. Remember, *be lazy.* If your module's API is good enough, some *other* developer will write the code to integrate your module with theirs.

Now that we have our API function written, let's use it to build the block using Drupal's Block API:

```
/**
 * Implements hook_block_info().
 */
function single_blog_block_info() {
  $blocks = array();

  // The array key defines the $delta parameter used in all
  // other block hooks.
  $blocks['recent'] = array(
    // The name of the block on the blocks administration page.
    'info' => t('Recent blog posts'),
  );

  return $blocks;
}

/**
 * Implements hook_block_view().
 *
```

```
 * First draft!
 *
 * @pararm $delta
 *    The name of the requested block.
 */
function single_blog_block_view($delta = '') {
  // Create an empty block.
  $block = array(
    'subject' => '',
    'content' => '',
  );

  // Check which block is being requested.
  if ($delta == 'recent') {
    // Set the block title.
    $block['subject'] = t('Recent blog posts');

    // Check if the user can access content.
    if (user_access('access content')) {
      // Retrieve the most recent nodes.
      $result = single_blog_list(SINGLE_BLOG_LIST_COUNT);

      // Create links for each blog entry.
      $items = array();
      foreach ($result as $node) {
        $items[] = array(
          'data' => l($node->title, 'node/' . $node->nid),
          'class' => array('node-' . $node->nid),
        );
      }

      if (!empty($items)) {
        // Theme the list of blog entries.
        $block['content'] = theme('item_list', array(
                            'items' => $items));
      }
    }
  }

  return $block;
}
```

Our `single_blog_block_info()` function is a simple `hook_block_info()` implementation as described in *Chapter 2*. We return an array of information that describes the blocks that our module provides. Each key in the array is the "delta" for that block. The delta, when combined with the name of the module, creates the unique block ID for a block which is stored in the `block.tpl.php` file's `$block_html_id`. For example, we've defined our "recent blog posts" block as having a delta of `recent`, so its full block ID is `single-blog-recent`. The block ID is used by Drupal to assign blocks to regions. The "info" returned by our `single_blog_block_info()` function defines the block "name" that you see on the block administration page.

The `single_blog_block_view()` function implements `hook_block_view()`. When Drupal wants to render a particular block, it calls the `hook_block_view()` implementation of the module responsible for the block, passing in the block's `$delta` as a parameter. Our function first checks the `$delta` given to it and then returns the requested block's data as an array containing the block title in the `subject` key and its contents in the `content` key. First, we're going to set the block title using the `t()` function. From *Chapter 2*, you should recall that `t()` translates English language strings into other languages. Then our function checks that the user viewing the page can access the website's content via `user_access('access content')`; this call checks if the current user has the `access content` permission. If the current user doesn't have the proper permission, you'll notice that our function returns an empty `content` key; this signals to Drupal that the requested block should not be rendered.

The last thing we're going to do before we *finally* start theming is to call our API function, `single_blog_list()`, in order to get the raw data from the database. Actually, `single_blog_list()` returns a result set object, but we haven't learned any special Database API functions to retrieve each row from the result set object. If we just iterate over this object using `foreach`, we'll get a series of objects that contain each row's data.

```
foreach ($result as $node) { }
```

Specifically, each time through the `foreach` loop, `$node` will be an object with properties for each database field we requested, `nid`, `title`, `created`, and `uid`. When the `$result` object has processed all the rows, the `foreach` loop will automatically end.

Theming a Drupal block

So, now that we know how to get all our data, we need to decide how we're going to theme it. We're actually going to build three versions of our `single_blog_block_view()`. This will allow us to try out several different methods of theming and to apply all the aspects of the theme layer we learned in *Chapter 3*.

Looking back at the previous table, *Common theme hooks*, will help us decide which existing theme hooks would be good candidates for our data. Initially, we're creating a list of links to our blog posts, so `theme_links()` would actually be a perfect match. However, in the next iteration of our `hook_block_view()` function we're going to create more then a simple list of links, so let's look again. The `item_list` hook will allow us to create a list that contains arbitrary data.

```
// Theme the list of blog entries.
$block['content'] = theme('item_list', array('items' => $items));
```

By looking at the documentation for `theme_item_list()` (available at `http://api.drupal.org/api/function/theme_item_list/7`) we can see that it expects as a parameter an `items` array. Each list item can be a simple string or the string can be placed in the `data` key of an array in which the other keys are treated as attributes for the list item:

```
$items[] = array(
    'data' => l($node->title, 'node/' . $node->nid),
    'class' => array('node-' . $node->nid),
);
```

On the surface, this construct looks similar to the Render API, but this is simply the convention used by this theme function; it doesn't use `drupal_render()` to convert the array to a string.

The internal path to a node is always "node/[node ID]". Fortunately, even if the author gives the blog post a URL alias, we don't have to figure out the alias as the `l()` function will automatically rewrite it to use the proper URL. So with the `l()` function, we're taking each node's title and node ID and constructing a simple link to the node and placing it in the list item's `data` element. `theme_item_list()` treats the `class` element as an attribute for the wrapping `<li>` element.

Okay. We've finished our first draft of our module. Looking at the following screenshot, you can see that our block displays as a simple unordered list of node titles. If this were a Drupal 6 theme implementation, we'd be done! However, in Drupal 7, all `hook_block_view()` and all page callbacks (the functions that return the main contents of a page) should return a renderable array instead of a string. So, while our code works (since Drupal 7 considers a plain string to be a degenerate renderable array), we'll need to fix that minor flaw in our second draft.

The following is a screenshot of version one of our module's block:

Render element and a theme hook suggestion

Ok, let's first fix the bug we left in our first version of `hook_block_view()` by converting that incorrect `theme()` call into a render array. This is actually quite easy, we simply need to edit our `single_blog_block_view()` and replace:

```
$block['content'] = theme('item_list', array('items' => $items));
```

with the following code:

```
$block['content'] = array(
  '#theme' => 'item_list__single_blog',
  '#items' => $items,
);
```

As you can see from the new code, we just need to convert all the array keys passed in the `$variables` parameter to `theme()` into # prefixed key names. `items` becomes `#items`, and so on. We're also going to take this opportunity to add a hook theme suggestion as described in *Chapter 3*. `theme()` will check for a `item_list__single_blog` implementation before using the default `item_list` theme hook.

Converting a theme call to a render element was rather painless, no? Let's add some more content to our block. Drupal core's blog module provides a page (and **menu callback**) that displays teasers of recent blog posts at the path **/blog**. Since menu callbacks aren't part of the theme system, we're going to leave that page unimplemented, but let's pretend that we *did* implement it. In that case, our block should provide a **more** link that goes to the blog page.

Adding additional content to a render element is easy. Since our $block['content'] is a single render element, we first need to move that existing render element as a child element, which we can do by moving it to $block['content']['list']. The list name is just an arbitrary label that we are giving to a child element; as long as it doesn't start with a #, it doesn't matter much what we call it. We'll add our new **more** link as a sibling to the list child:

```
// Theme the list of blog entries.
$block['content']['list'] = array(
  '#theme' => 'item_list__single_blog',
  '#items' => $items,
);
// Add a link to the full list of blog entries.
$block['content']['more'] = array(
  '#theme' => 'more_link',
  '#url' => 'blog',
  '#title' => t('Read the latest blog entries.'),
);
```

Glancing back at our common theme hooks list, you should have noticed the more_link theme hook which we used for our block's **more** link. Again we just need to examine the documentation for theme_more_link to determine how to structure the child element. See http://api.drupal.org/api/function/theme_more_link/7.

Creating a pre_render function

Now looking at our content, you'll probably notice that there is one piece of content that is still locked up in a string instead of being modifiable in a render element: the data element of each of the $items passed to our item_list render element. Converting the l() call to a render element is again straightforward; just change the following line:

```
'data' => l($node->title, 'node/' . $node->nid),
```

into these lines:

```
'data' => array(
  '#type' => 'link',
  '#title' => $node->title,
  '#href' => 'node/' . $node->nid,
),
```

`system_element_info()` defines the `link` element and we can see from its declaration and examining its `#pre_render` callbacks that render elements with a `#type` of `link` will be rendered into a link using `l()`.

Unfortunately, the `theme_item_list()` function does not expect a render element in its data key, so it will choke on these contents. Considering the push to make everything alterable with render arrays, this seems like an oversight. If you encounter a bug or inconsistency in Drupal (and you will!), you can contribute simply by making a note of it and creating an issue in Drupal's issue queue. In fact, I just created a new issue for this problem at `http://drupal.org/node/891112`.

In the meantime, we'll have to work around this problem rather then hacking Drupal core. Fortunately, a close inspection of the render element properties available to us (again, see *Chapter 3*) indicate that we can use a `#pre_render` callback to alter our render element before it is passed to the element's theme function. Let's add one to our `$block['content']['list']` child element:

```
$block['content']['list'] = array(
  '#theme' => 'item_list__single_blog',
  '#items' => $items,
  '#pre_render' => array('single_blog_item_list_child_render'),
);
```

Since `drupal_render()` will pass the entire child element to our `#pre_render` callback, we just need to make sure our callback modifies the `data` element of all our items.

```
/**
 * Render the child elements of theme_item_list() before its
 * data is themed.
 */
function single_blog_item_list_child_render($elements) {
  foreach (array_keys($elements['#items']) AS $key) {
    // Take the renderable array that we set in
    // single_blog_block_view() and render it into the string
    // that theme_item_list() expects.
```

```
    if (is_array($elements['#items'][$key]['data'])) {
      $elements['#items'][$key]['data'] =
          drupal_render($elements['#items'][$key]['data']);
    }
  }
  return $elements;
}
```

In our `single_blog_item_list_child_render()` function, we simply loop through all the `#items`, determine if they have an array in their `data` element and call `drupal_render()` on its contents.

Attaching CSS to render arrays

If you look at the screenshot of the first version, you can see that the default styling of our block is less then inspiring, so let's tweak that by giving our content some sensible default styling by adding a CSS stylesheet.

Since version 5, Drupal has had a `drupal_add_css()` function to add CSS stylesheets to pages. What's new in Drupal 7 is that, due to Drupal's block and page caching and the capabilities of `hook_page_alter()`, we now need to attach our stylesheet directly to the render element that we are creating. If we were to use `drupal_add_css()`, the stylesheet would not be cached with its block and it would also be considerably more difficult to alter the stylesheet if a `hook_page_alter()` implementation desired to (For example if it removed the block and wanted to remove the CSS too.)

So instead of calling `drupal_add_css()` from within our `single_blog_block_view()` function, we add it to the returned render array:

```
// Add a CSS file to style the block.
$block['content']['#attached']['css'][] = drupal_get_path('module',
                    'single_blog') . '/single-blog.css';
```

We use `drupal_get_path()` to find the path to our module relative to the website root. The `#attached` array can contain a list of CSS files and JS files to attach to our render element. For JavaScript files, just append them to the `js` array via `['#attached']['js'][]`.

And here are the contents of our **single-blog.css** stylesheet:

```
/* $Id$ */

.block-single-blog .content ul {
  padding-left: 0; /* LTR */
}
```

```
.block-single-blog .content ul li {
  margin-bottom: 10px;
  list-style-type: none;
}
```

RTL languages

One thing you'll need to be aware of when writing stylesheets is Drupal's support for **RTL languages**, those languages that are read **Right To Left**, for example Arabic or Hebrew. Users of RTL websites expect everything about that website to flow right-to-left instead of English's normal left-to-right. The convention used by websites that support both RTL and LTR languages is to flip the layout of the design horizontally depending on the directionality of the language.

A great live example of how right-to-left website layouts are flipped is Amnesty International's website; compare the Arabic language version at http://www.amnesty.org/ar with the English language version at http://www.amnesty.org/en. Notice how the sidebar changes sides depending on the language:

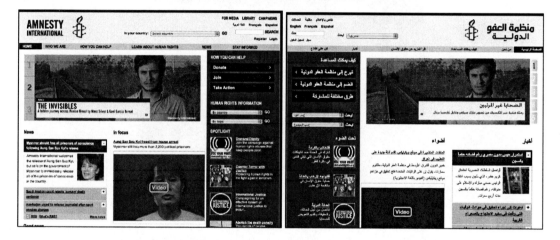

From a CSS standpoint, this means HTML elements whose left-side styling differs from their right-side styling need to have their styling altered when the current language is RTL. If a RTL language is being displayed, Drupal will, for each stylesheet, look for a supplemental RTL stylesheet to load. So, if Hebrew is the active language, Drupal will look for single-blog-rtl.css to load in addition to (and just after) the requested single-blog.css file. Since our -rtl stylesheet is loaded in addition to the standard stylesheet, we simply need to include the rules and properties needed to override the LTR version of our styles. To make it easier to keep track of those properties, Drupal modules should place a /* LTR */ comment next to each property that needs to be overridden.

Notice that the `.block-single-blog .content ul` rule in the `single-blog.css` stylesheet specifies a left padding. Since that's the only property that is directional, it's the only one we need to override in the `single-blog-rtl.css` file.

```
/* $Id$ */

.block-single-blog .content ul {
  padding-right: 0;
}
```

Note that if our original left padding was `10px`, we would have needed to override that in our RTL stylesheet by setting `padding-left` to `0` and then setting `padding-right` to `10px`. The following is a screenshot of version two of our module block:

If you look at the screenshot, you can see the new **More** link and how the display of our block has improved.

After all these modifications, the second draft of our `single_blog_block_view()` function is now complete and should look like this:

```
/**
 * Implements hook_block_view().
 *
 * Second draft!
 *
 * @pararm $delta
 *    The name of the requested block.
 */
function single_blog_block_view($delta = '') {
  // Create an empty block.
  $block = array(
    'subject' => '',
    'content' => '',
  );

  // Check which block is being requested.
  if ($delta == 'recent') {
    // Set the block title.
    $block['subject'] = t('Recent blog posts');

    // Check if the user can access content.
    if (user_access('access content')) {
      // Retrieve the most recent nodes.
      $result = single_blog_list(SINGLE_BLOG_LIST_COUNT);

      // Create links for each blog entry.
      $items = array();
      foreach ($result as $node) {
        $items[] = array(
          'data' => array(
            '#type' => 'link',
            '#title' => $node->title,
            '#href' => 'node/' . $node->nid,
          ),
          'class' => array('node-' . $node->nid),
        );
      }

      if (!empty($items)) {
        // Theme the list of blog entries.
```

```
          $block['content']['list'] = array(
            '#theme' => 'item_list__single_blog',
            '#items' => $items,
            '#pre_render' =>
                    array('single_blog_item_list_child_render'),
          );
          // Add a link to the full list of blog entries.
          $block['content']['more'] = array(
            '#theme' => 'more_link',
            '#url' => 'blog',
            '#title' => t('Read the latest blog entries.'),
          );
          // Add a CSS file to style the block.
          $block['content']['#attached']['css'][] =
     drupal_get_path('module', 'single_blog') . '/single-blog.css';
        }
      }
    }

    return $block;
}
```

Steps to build a default theme implementation

Okay, now it's time to exorcise our lazy-developer habit and practice building our own theme hook. From *Chapter 3*, you should recall that we'll need to do the following things:

1. Register the theme hook and define default variables.
2. Build the default implementation of our theme hook.
3. Re-build the theme registry.
4. Build a render element to use the theme hook.

Our current implementation of the **Recent blog posts** block simply shows a list of blog titles. But it would be nice to include the date of each post, as well as the author (if we have multiple people creating posts). So in this third and final version of our module, we're going to create a `single-blog-block-item.tpl.php` to render the contents of each item in our list of blog posts. By convention in Drupal, any CSS, JavaScript, or template files needed by a module should use dashes instead of underscores in their filenames.

Before we begin building the required `single_blog_block_item` theme hook, let's first add all the data we will need for the third version of our module. Looking back at how we generate the items for our list, we can see that all the data we want is in the `$node` variable.

```
// Create links for each blog entry.
$items = array();
foreach ($result as $node) {
  $items[] = array(
    'data' => array(
      '#type' => 'link',
      '#title' => $node->title,
      '#href' => 'node/' . $node->nid,
    ),
    'class' => array('node-' . $node->nid),
  );
}
```

So, instead of creating a simple render element using bits of the `$node` variable, let's just pass that entire variable to our new theme hook:

```
// Create links for each blog entry.
$items = array();
foreach ($result as $node) {
  $items[] = array(
    'data' => array(
      '#theme' => 'single_blog_block_item',
      '#node' => $node,
    ),
    'class' => array('node-' . $node->nid),
  );
}
```

hook_theme() implementations

We'll need to create a `single_blog_theme()` implementation of `hook_theme()` and register a `single_blog_block_item` theme hook.

```
/**
 * Implements hook_theme().
 */
function single_blog_theme($existing, $type, $theme, $path) {
  return array(
    'single_blog_block_item' => array(
```

```
        'variables' => array(
          'node' => NULL,
        ),
        'template' => 'single-blog-block-item',
      ),
    );
}
```

I'll explain the `variables` array in the very next section, but let's quickly go over the other key now.

Since this is a theme hook, and is to be implemented using a template instead of a theme function, we'll need to include the `template` key and specify the base name of the template file, `single-blog-block-item`. Drupal will automatically add the `.tpl.php` to the end of the base name when looking for the file, so we shouldn't include it.

Variables versus render element

In *Chapter 3*, we learned about the differences between using the `variables` key and using the `render element` key in your `hook_theme()`. One and only one of those keys must be present in each theme hook declaration. However it still can be somewhat confusing as to which to use when you are building your theme implementation.

There is only one situation in which you could use the `render element` key: if your data could be represented by a single render element or by a single renderable array containing nested render elements. If that is not the case, then you must specify the `variables` key and specify the variables you will be passed to `theme()` and their default values.

So does our data conform to the render element requirement above? Our `$node` variable is just a partial node object and not a render element, so we must use the `variables` key and specify the default values for all our variables.

As a side note, if we instead look at the way we've built the data element in the *second* version of our module (a `link` `#type` render element), we can see that we could go ahead and use `render element` as the key if our second version of the module had a `hook_theme()` implementation.

Since the node variable is an object, we set the default value to simply be the `NULL` value.

Preprocess functions

Our theme hook is now given a $node object, but template files expect variables containing strings or render elements. So we're going to need to transform the $node object's data into a series of variables. Technically, we could have performed this business logic directly inside our single_blog_block_view() function, but instead we're going to do this transformation in a preprocess function.

That's actually the purpose of the preprocess function: to transform raw data into variables needed for a theme hook's template or theme function. (Also, recall that preprocess functions should never query for raw data; the raw data should be passed as variables.)

Since we own this theme hook, we'll need to define our preprocess function with a template_ prefix.

```
/**
 * Preprocesses single blog block item variables.
 */
function template_preprocess_single_blog_block_item(&$variables) {
  $node = $variables['node'];
```

To make it easier to access all the object properties of our node variable, we're going to first create a $node local variable which we'll use inside the preprocess function:

```
// Create a renderable array for the title.
$variables['title'] = array(
  '#type'  => 'link',
  '#title' => $node->title,
  '#href'  => 'node/' . $node->nid,
);
```

Next we'll create the $title variable as a render element; it is identical to what we saw in the second version of our module:

```
// Format the creation date of the node.
$variables['created'] = $node->created;
$variables['date'] = format_date($node->created, 'custom',
                                  'F d, Y');
```

Date timestamps don't make very good render elements, so we'll just create two variables, one with the raw, unformatted date value and one with formatted date:

```
// Load the account object with the node's creator and store
// in a variable for themer convenience.
$variables['user'] = user_load($node->uid);
```

```
    // Theme the username.
    $variables['name'] = theme('username', array(
                        'account' => $variables['user']));
}
```

And finally, we'll pass the `$user` object of the author and theme the username.

All that's left is to order the variables the way we desire in our template file! However, since we've made the last change to our `.module` file, let's look at the finished product:

```php
<?php
// $Id$

/**
 * @file
 * Enables a single blog for an individual or multiple users.
 */

// After you learn Form API in Chapter 5, you'll be able to
// make these settings configurable.
define('SINGLE_BLOG_NODE_TYPE', 'article');
define('SINGLE_BLOG_LIST_COUNT', 5);
define('SINGLE_BLOG_DATE_FORMAT', 'F d, Y');

/**
 * Returns a list of blog entries.
 *
 * @param $number
 *    The number of blog entries to return.
 * @return
 *    A result set object containing the list of blog entries.
 */
function single_blog_list($number) {
  // Use the Database API to retrieve our data.
  // @see http://drupal.org/node/310069
  $query = db_select('node', 'n')
    ->fields('n', array('nid', 'title', 'created', 'uid'))
    ->condition('type', SINGLE_BLOG_NODE_TYPE)
    ->condition('status', 1)
    ->orderBy('created', 'DESC')
    ->range(0, $number)
    ->addTag('node_access')
    ->execute();
```

```
    return $query;
  }

/**
 * Implements hook_block_info().
 */
function single_blog_block_info() {
  $blocks = array();

  // The array key defines the $delta parameter used in all
  // other block hooks.
  $blocks['recent'] = array(
    // The name of the block on the blocks administration page.
    'info' => t('Recent blog posts'),
  );

  return $blocks;
}

/**
 * Implements hook_block_view().
 *
 * Third draft!
 *
 * @pararm $delta
 *    The name of the requested block.
 */
function single_blog_block_view($delta = '') {
  // Create an empty block.
  $block = array(
    'subject' => '',
    'content' => '',
  );

  // Check which block is being requested.
  if ($delta == 'recent') {
    // Set the block title.
    $block['subject'] = t('Recent blog posts');

    // Check if the user can access content.
    if (user_access('access content')) {
      // Retrieve the most recent nodes.
      $result = single_blog_list(SINGLE_BLOG_LIST_COUNT);
```

```
      // Create links for each blog entry.
      $items = array();
      foreach ($result as $node) {
        $items[] = array(
          'data' => array(
            '#theme' => 'single_blog_block_item',
            '#node' => $node,
          ),
          'class' => array('node-' . $node->nid),
        );
      }

      if (!empty($items)) {
        // Theme the list of blog entries.
        $block['content']['list'] = array(
          '#theme' => 'item_list__single_blog',
          '#items' => $items,
          '#pre_render' =>
                  array('single_blog_item_list_child_render'),
        );
        // Add a link to the full list of blog entries.
        $block['content']['more'] = array(
          '#theme' => 'more_link',
          '#url' => 'blog',
          '#title' => t('Read the latest blog entries.'),
        );
        // Add a CSS file to style the block.
        $block['content']['#attached']['css'][] =
      drupal_get_path('module', 'single_blog') . '/single-blog.css';
      }
    }
  }

  return $block;
}


/**
 * Render the child elements of theme_item_list() before its data is
themed.
 */
function single_blog_item_list_child_render($elements) {
  foreach (array_keys($elements['#items']) AS $key) {
    // Take the renderable array that we set in
```

```
    // single_blog_block_view() and render it into the string
    // that theme_item_list() expects.
    if (is_array($elements['#items'][$key]['data'])) {
      $elements['#items'][$key]['data'] =
            drupal_render($elements['#items'][$key]['data']);
    }
  }
  return $elements;
}

/**
 * Implements hook_theme().
 */
function single_blog_theme($existing, $type, $theme, $path) {
  return array(
    'single_blog_block_item' => array(
      'variables' => array(
        'node' => NULL,
      ),
      'template' => 'single-blog-block-item',
    ),
  );
}

/**
 * Preprocesses single blog block item variables.
 */
function template_preprocess_single_blog_block_item(&$variables) {
  $node = $variables['node'];

  // Create a renderable array for the title.
  $variables['title'] = array(
    '#type'  => 'link',
    '#title' => $node->title,
    '#href'  => 'node/' . $node->nid,
  );

  // Format the creation date of the node.
  $variables['created'] = $node->created;
  $variables['date'] = format_date($node->created, 'custom',
                                   SINGLE_BLOG_DATE_FORMAT);
```

```
// Load the account object with the node's creator and store
// in a variable for themer convenience.
$variables['user'] = user_load($node->uid);
// Theme the username.
$variables['name'] = theme('username', array(
                          'account' => $variables['user']));
}
```

Template files

In order to make template files as easy to understand by non-programmers, the template should be limited to the following PHP statements:

- `<?php print $variable; ?>`
- `<?php if ([condition]): ?>`
- `<?php elseif ([condition]): ?>`
- `<?php else: ?>`
- `<?php endif; ?>`
- `<?php print t('string'); ?>`
- `<?php hide($element['piece']); ?>`
- `<?php show($element['piece']); ?>`
- `<?php print render($element['piece']); ?>`
- `<?php print render($element); ?>`

The `print` and `if/elseif/else` PHP snippets should be self-explanatory. However, it's important to reiterate that, in order to make Drupal multi-lingual, we should never include a bare English word in our templates; instead we should use `t()` in a `<?php print t('string'); ?>` snippet.

Lastly, the `show()`, `hide()`, and `render()` functions are special themer-convenience functions that should only be used in template files; they should never be used in preprocess functions, theme functions or anywhere else. `render()` is basically the same thing as the `drupal_render()` function we've already learned about. The `hide()` function can be used on a render array's child element earlier in the template before the render array calls `render()`; this will prevent the child element from being included with the rest of the render array when it is rendered. For example (from Bartik's `node.tpl.php`):

```
<?php
  // We hide the links now so that we can render them later.
  hide($content['links']);
  print render($content);
```

```php
    // Only display the wrapper div if there are links.
    $links = render($content['links']);
    if ($links):
?>

<div class="link-wrapper">
  <?php print $links; ?>
</div>
```

As you can see, these convenience functions make it easier to tear apart, wrap, or remove pieces of render arrays.

So, let's create our `single-blog-block-item.tpl.php` template:

```php
<?php
// $Id$

/**
 * @file
 * HTML for an item in the single blog's block listing.
 *
 * Available variables:
 * - $classes: String of classes that can be used to
 *   style contextually through CSS. It can be manipulated
 *   through the variable $classes_array from preprocess functions.
 *   The default values can be one or more of the following:
 *   - single-blog-block-item: The current template type,
 *                             i.e., "theming hook".
 *   - $date: Formatted creation date. Preprocess functions can
 *            reformat it by calling format_date() with the desired
 *            parameters on the $created variable.
 *   - $title: A renderable array that that provides a title and
 *             link to the node.
 *   - $name: Themed username of node author output from
 *            theme_username().
 *
 * - $classes_array: Array of html class attribute values.
 *                   It is flattened into a string within the
 *                   variable $classes.
 *
 * Other variables:
 * The following variables are provided for contextual information.
 * - $node: Partial node object. Contains data that may not be safe.
 * - $created: Time the node was published formatted in Unix
 *             timestamp.
```

```
 * - $user: The user object of the node author.
 *
 * @see template_preprocess_single_blog_block_item()
 */
?>
<div class="<?php print $classes; ?>">

  <div class="date"><?php print $date; ?>:</div>

  <h4<?php print $title_attributes; ?>>
    <?php print render($title); ?></h4>

  <div class="name">
    <?php print t('by !username', array('!username' => $name)); ?>
  </div>

</div>
```

The first part of any template file should be a large docblock explaining all the variables available to themers, including convenience variables, not just the ones printed inside our template.

The only variable that we didn't explicitly create in our preprocess function was the `$classes` variable. This is a string that contains useful CSS classes that should be placed in the outer-most wrapping HTML element in our template file. The `$classes` variable is created by `template_processs()` and its corresponding `$classes_array` variable is created by `template_preprocess()`. If we want to add additional classes to the `$classes` string, we should append an array element to the `$classes_array` variable during our preprocess function and it will automatically be added to the `$classes` string before reaching the template file.

The string passed to the `t()` function, by `!username` includes the `!username` token to give context to translators when trying to translate "by"; see the `t()` API documentation for more information.

The last thing we should do, since we've updated the HTML markup returned by our block, is to also update the stylesheet:

```
/* $Id$ */

.block-single-blog .content ul {
  padding-left: 0; /* LTR */
}
```

```
.block-single-blog .content ul li {
  margin-bottom: 10px;
  list-style-type: none;
}

.block-single-blog .date {
  font-weight: bold;
}

.block-single-blog h4 {
  margin: 0;
}

.block-single-blog .name {
  font-style: italic;
}
```

Congratulations! We're done!

Take a look at our accomplishment shown in the following screenshot:

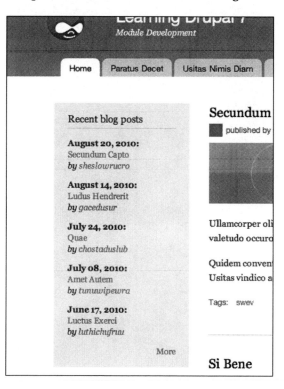

Summary

In this chapter we used our previous concepts and built an example theme implementation using real-world situations. In addition to the review of the theming concepts, you should have picked up on some of the strategies commonly used by Drupal developers and learned a little bit about contributing your experiences and knowledge back to the Drupal community.

In the next chapter, you'll learn about building admin interfaces for your module. So while the Single Blog module used slightly-funky constants that defined some hard-coded settings, the module in the next chapter will have a rich administrative interface to allow site admins to configure its settings.

5
Building an Admin Interface

In this chapter we will create a module with an administrative interface. This module will build upon many of the module creation concepts that were introduced in *Chapter 2*. Some of the concepts we will cover in this chapter are:

- Mapping Drupal functions to menu items using `hook_menu()`
- Creating basic forms with the Form API
- Managing Drupal settings using `variable_set()` and `variable_get()`
- Sending mail using `drupal_mail()` and `hook_mail()`
- Using Drupal 7's new token system

After this chapter is finished you should have a good handle on many concepts that are at the core of almost every module you will write in the future.

The User Warn module

In this chapter we will be creating the User Warn module. This module allows administrators to send users a warning via e-mail when that user violates a site's terms of service or otherwise behaves in a way that is inappropriate. The User Warn module will implement the following features:

- The module will expose configuration settings to site administrators, including default mail text
- This e-mail will include Drupal tokens, which allow the admin to replace and/or add site-specific variables to the e-mail
- Site administrators will be able to send a user mail via a new tab on their user profile page
- Warning e-mails will be sent using Drupal's default mail implementation

Starting our module

We will begin as we did in *Chapter 2*, by creating a new folder for our module called user_warn in the sites/default/modules directory in our Drupal installation. We can then create a user_warn.info file as shown in the following:

```
;$Id$
name = User Warn
description = Exposes an admin interface to send behavior warning
e-mails to users.
core = 7.x
package = Drupal 7 Development
files[] = user_warn.module
```

You should be pretty familiar with this now. We will also create our user_warn. module file and add an implementation of hook_help() to let site administrators know what our module does.

```php
<?php
// $Id$

/**
 * @file
 * User Warn module file
 *
 * This module allows site administrators to send a stock warning
 * e-mail to a specified user or users through the admin interface.
 * Administrators
 * can configure the default e-mail including token replacement.
 */

/**
 * Implement hook_help().
 */
function user_warn_help($path, $arg) {
  if ($path == 'admin/help#user_warn') {
    return t('User Warn allows site adminitrators to send a standard
e-mail to site users to notify them of improper behavior.');
  }
}
```

This is also nothing new so lets move on to the good stuff.

The Drupal menu system

Drupal's menu system is deceptively named. The name implies that it is responsible for the navigation of your site, and while this is true it does a great deal more. At its core, the menu system is responsible for mapping Drupal paths to the functions that generate the contents of the requested page. The menu system is also responsible for controlling access to Drupal pages, acting as one of the central gatekeepers of Drupal security.

Drupal module developers can map paths to Drupal functions by implementing `hook_menu()`, which adds paths to the menu system, assigns them access rules, and optionally creates navigational elements for them.

Defining a page callback with hook_menu

For our module we will need to implement two new pages—a configuration page for the User Warn module, and a tab in the user profile area where administrators can go to send the actual e-mails to a specific user. These will each require their own `hook_menu()` implementation as defined in the following example.

This example only scratches the surface of the options available in the menu system. For more details, developers should check out the API documentation at:

`http://api.drupal.org/api/function/hook_menu/7`

The example is as follows:

```
/**
 * Implement hook_menu().
 */
function user_warn_menu() {
  $items = array();

  $items['admin/config/people/user_warn'] = array(
    'title' => 'User Warn',
    'description' => 'Configuration for the User Warn module.',
    'page callback' => 'drupal_get_form',
    'page arguments' => array('user_warn_form'),
    'access arguments' => array('administer users'),
    'type' => MENU_NORMAL_ITEM,
  );
```

```
    $items['user/%/warn'] = array(
      'title' => 'Warn',
      'description' =>
            'Send e-mail to a user about improper site behavior.',
      'page callback' => 'drupal_get_form',
      'page arguments' => array('user_warn_confirm_form', 1),
      'access arguments' => array('administer users'),
      'type' => MENU_LOCAL_TASK,
    );

    return $items;
}
```

Like many Drupal hook implementations, `hook_menu()` returns a structured associative array with information about the menu items being defined. The first item in our example defines the module configuration page, and the second one defines the user tab where administrators can go to send the actual e-mail. Let's look at the first item in more detail.

Menu items are keyed off their path. This is an internal Drupal path with no leading or trailing slashes. This path not only defines the location of a page, but also its place in the menu hierarchy, with each part of the URL being a child of the last. In this example, `people` is a child of `config` which is itself a child of `admin`.

If a requested path does not exist, Drupal will work its way up the hierarchy until it encounters a page that does exist. You can see this in action by requesting `admin/config/people/xyzzy` which displays the page at `admin/config/people`.

If you are creating a menu item for site administration it must begin with `admin`. This places it into Drupal's administrative interface and applies the admin theme defined by the site settings.

 Module-specific settings should always be present under `admin/config`. Drupal 7 offers several categories which module developers should use to better organize their settings according to Drupal functional groups like People and Permissions or Content Authoring.

The value associated with this key is itself an associative array with several keys that define what action should be taken when this URL is requested. We can now look at those in detail. The first item defines your page title:

```
'title' => 'User Warn',
```

This is used in a variety of display contexts—as your page's heading, in the HTML `<title>` tag and as a subheading in the administration interface in combination with the description (if you are defining an administrative menu item).

```
'description' => 'Configuration for the User Warn module.',
```

The description is just that—a longer text description of the page that this menu item defines. This should provide the user with more detailed information about the actions they can take on this page. This description is also used as the title tag when you hover over a link.

> Menu item titles and descriptions are passed through `t()` internally by Drupal, so this is one case where we don't need to worry about doing that ourselves.

For an administration page, these two items define how your page is listed in Drupal's admin area as shown in the following:

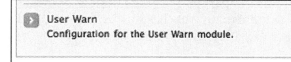

The next two items define what will happen when your page is requested:

```
'page callback' => 'drupal_get_form',
'page arguments' => array('user_warn_form'),
```

`'page callback'` defines the function that will get called (without the parentheses) and `'page arguments'` contains an array of arguments that get passed to this function.

Often you will create a custom function that processes, formats, and returns specific data. However, in our case we are calling the internal Drupal function `drupal_get_form()` that returns an array as defined by Drupal's Form API. As an argument we are passing the form ID of the form we want to display. We will dive into `drupal_get_form()` and the Form API in more detail later in the chapter.

The fifth item controls who can access your page.

```
'access arguments' => array('administer users'),
```

`'access arguments'` takes an array containing a permissions strings. Any user who has been assigned one of these permissions will be able to access this page. Anyone else will be given an **Access denied** page. Permissions are defined by modules using `hook_permission()`. You can see a full list of the currently defined permissions at `admin/people/permissions` as shown:

PERMISSION	ANONYMOUS USER	AUTHENTICATED USER	ADMINISTRATOR
User			
Administer permissions *Warning: Give to trusted roles only; this permission has security implications.*	☐	☐	☑
Administer users *Warning: Give to trusted roles only; this permission has security implications.*	☐	☐	☑
View user profiles	☐	☐	☑

You can see the `'administer users'` permission at the bottom of this list. In the preceding example, only the Administrator role has this permission, and as a result only those users assigned this role will be able to access our page.

Note that the titles of the permissions here do not necessarily match what you will need to enter in the access arguments array. Unfortunately, the only good way to find this information is by checking the `hook_perm()` implementation of the module in question.

Access rights, permissions, and security will be covered in greater detail in *Chapter 8, Drupal Permissions and Security*.

The final item defines what type of menu item we are creating:

```
'type' => MENU_NORMAL_ITEM,
```

The `'type'` is a bitmask of flags that describe what features we want our menu item to have (for instance, whether it is visible in the breadcrumb trail). Drupal defines over 20 constants for menu items that should cover any situation developers will find themselves in. The default type is `MENU_NORMAL_ITEM`, which indicates that this item will be visible in the menu tree as well as the breadcrumb trail.

This is all the information that is needed to register our path. Now when Drupal receives a request for this URL, it will return the results of `drupal_get_form(user_warn_form)`.

 Drupal caches the entire menu, so new/updated menu items will not be reflected immediately. To manually clear the cache, visit **Admin | Configuration | Development | Performance** and click on **Clear all caches**.

Using wildcards in menu paths

We have created a simple menu item, but sometimes simple won't do the job. In the User Warn module we want to have a menu item that is tied to each individual user's profile page. Profile pages in Drupal live at the path `user/<user_id>`, so how do we create a distinct menu item for each user? Fortunately the menu system allows us to use wildcards when we define our menu paths.

If you look at the second menu item defined in the preceding example, you will see that its definition differs a bit from our first example.

```
$items['user/%/warn'] = array(
    'title' => 'Warn',
    'description' => 'Send e-mail to a user about improper site
behavior.',
    'page callback' => 'drupal_get_form',
    'page arguments' => array('user_warn_confirm_form', 1),
    'access arguments' => array('administer users'),
    'type' => MENU_LOCAL_TASK,
);
```

The first difference is that the path is defined with % as one of the path entries. This indicates a wildcard; anything can be entered here and the menu item's hierarchy will be maintained. In Drupal, that will always be a user's ID. However, there is nothing stopping any user from entering a URL like `user/xyzzy/warn` or something else potentially more malicious. Your code should always be written in such a way as to handle these eventualities, for instance by verifying that the argument actually maps to a Drupal user. This would be a good improvement.

The other difference in this example is that we have added 1 as an additional argument to be passed to our page callback.

Each argument in a menu item's path can be accessed as an argument that is available to be passed to our page callback, starting with 0 for the root argument. So here the string user is item 0, and the user's ID is item 1. To use the user's ID as a page callback argument, we reference it by its number. The result in this case is that the user's ID will be passed as an additional argument to drupal_get_form().

We have one other difference in this second menu item:

```
'type' => MENU_LOCAL_TASK,
```

We have defined our type as MENU_LOCAL_TASK. This tells Drupal that our menu item describes actions that can be performed on the parent item. In this example, Warn is an action that can be performed on a user. These are usually rendered as an additional tab on the page in question, as you can see in the following example user profile screen:

Having defined the paths for our pages through hook_menu(), we now need to build our forms.

Form API

In standard web development, one of the most tedious and unrewarding tasks is defining HTML forms and handling their submissions. Lay out the form, create labels, write the submission function, figure out error handling, and the worst part is that from site to site much of this code is boilerplate—it's fundamentally the same, differing only in presentation. Drupal's Form API is a powerful tool allowing developers to create forms and handle form submissions quickly and easily. This is done by defining arrays of form elements and creating validation and submit callbacks for the form.

In past versions of Drupal, Form API was commonly referred to as FAPI. However, Drupal 7 now has three APIs which could fit this acronym—Form API, Field API (which you'll see in *Chapter 6* and *Chapter 7*) and File API (which you'll learn about in *Chapter 11*). We will avoid using the acronym FAPI completely, to prevent confusion, but you will still encounter it widely in online references.

Form API is also a crucial element in Drupal's security. It provides unique form tokens that are verified on form submission, preventing Cross-site Request Forgery attacks, and automatically validating required fields, field lengths, and a variety of other form element properties.

While Form API is one of the most useful and powerful tools in the module developer's toolbox, it can also be one of the most complicated. More detailed information beyond this simple example can be found at the following URLs:

- Form API Quickstart guide:

  `http://api.drupal.org/api/drupal/developer--topics--forms_api.html/7`

- Form API Full Reference:

  `http://api.drupal.org/api/drupal/developer--topics--forms_api_reference.html/7`

Using drupal_get_form()

In our first menu implementation seen earlier, we defined the page callback as `drupal_get_form()`. This Form API function returns a structured array that represents an HTML form. This gets rendered by Drupal and presented as an HTML form for the user. `drupal_get_form()` takes a form ID as a parameter. This form ID can be whatever you want, but it must be unique within Drupal. Typically it will be `<module_name>_<description>_form`.

The form ID is also the name of the callback function `drupal_get_form()` will call to build your form. The specified function should return a properly formatted array containing all the elements your form needs.

Since the form ID also serves as the form's callback function, it must be a valid PHP variable name. Spaces and hyphens are not allowed. All form IDs should be prefaced by the name of your module followed by an underscore, in order to prevent name collision.

Other parameters can be passed into `drupal_get_form()` in addition to the form ID. These extra parameters simply get passed through to the callback function for its own use. We will see how this works later in the chapter.

> In Drupal 6, `drupal_get_form()` returned a fully rendered HTML form. This has been changed in Drupal 7 in order to allow more flexibility in theming and easier form manipulation. `drupal_get_form()` now returns an unrendered form array which must be passed to `drupal_render()` for final output. In the preceding example the menu system handles the change transparently, but other code converted from Drupal 6 may need to be changed.

Building a form callback function

For the User Warn module we need a form that allows the site administrator to enter the following items:

- A subject line for our outgoing e-mail
- The text of our outgoing e-mail
- A checkbox indicating whether or not the administrator should be sent a Bcc on outgoing e-mails
- A submit button

Our menu definition specified `user_warn_form` as the `page arguments`, so we need to create that function and define our form within it.

> This function takes two parameters — `$form` and `$form_state`. We will not be using these parameters in the context of just displaying a form. But, for more information on their usage see the **Form API Quickstart Guide**.

```
/**
 * Form builder; Create and display the User Warn configuration
 * settings form.
 */
function user_warn_form($form, &$form_state) {
  // Text field for the e-mail subject.
  $form['user_warn_e-mail_subject'] = array(
    '#type' => 'textfield',
    '#title' => t('Warning e-mail subject'),
    '#description' => t('The subject of the e-mail which will be sent
to users.'),
```

```
        '#size' => 40,
        '#maxlength' => 120,
        '#required' => TRUE,
    );

    // Textarea for the body of the e-mail.
    $form['user_warn_e-mail_text'] = array(
        '#type' => 'textarea',
        '#rows' => 10,
        '#columns' => 40,
        '#title' => t('Warning e-mail text'),
        '#required' => TRUE,
        '#description' => t('The text of the e-mail which will be sent to
users.'),
    );

    // Checkbox to indicate if admin should be sent a Bcc on e-mails.
    $form['user_warn_bcc'] = array(
        '#type' => 'checkbox',
        '#title' => t('BCC admin on all e-mails'),
        '#description' => t("Indicates whether the admin user (as set in
site configuration) should be sent on all warning e-mails."),
    );

    // Submit button
    $form['submit'] = array(
        '#type' => 'submit',
        '#value' => t('Save settings'),
    );

    return $form;
}
```

The properties of a `form` element always begin with a # sign in order to
distinguish them from nested form fields. For more information visit the
Form API Quickstart Guide.

This is very similar to what we did earlier while implementing `hook_menu()`. We
create a specially formatted associative array and return it to the calling function.
In this case, each element in the array corresponds to an element in our form.

Lets look at the subject field first as an example.

```
    $form['user_warn_e-mail_subject'] = array(
```

Each element is keyed by a unique string, which will become the element's **name** attribute when the form is rendered. This element is then assigned an array of attributes.

 For a complete matrix of all the form elements defined by Drupal as well as the properties each one implements, visit:

```
http://api.drupal.org/api/drupal/developer--topics--
forms_api_reference.html/7
```

```
'#type' => 'textfield',
```

The first attribute is `'#type'` which defines what form element will be rendered. All the standard HTML form elements have types, as well as some Drupal-specific elements defined. In this case we are creating a basic textfield.

```
'#title' => t('Warning e-mail subject'),
'#description' => t(
          'The subject of the e-mail which will be sent to users.'),
```

The next two attributes, `'#title'` and `'#description'` define the element's label and an optional description.

Any attribute that a standard HTML element has are available as Form API properties or attributes as well. For instance, see the following two lines of code.

```
'#size' => 40,
'#maxlength' => 120,
```

As you would expect, these define the size and maxlength attributes of our text field. One of the nice things about Form API is that it will automatically validate many of the element's attributes when the form is submitted. In this case Drupal will throw an error if any text is submitted with a length greater than the element's maxlength. All this happens transparently with no extra code from the developer.

Form API also adds some convenience properties for validation purposes, like `'#required'`.

```
'#required' => TRUE,
```

When `'#required'` is set to TRUE, Drupal will throw an error if the form is submitted without a value in that element. Required fields are also marked with an asterisk in their labels. Again, this happens transparently without any extra code. Drupal will even highlight the field when an error applies to it! This on-the-fly error handling and form validation is one of the reasons Form API is such a boon to developers. It really reduces the amount of drudgery involved in creating and handling HTML forms.

The following is how this text field will appear when rendered by Drupal in the default admin theme:

Warning email subject *

The subject of the email which will be sent to users.

Moving on to the following elements, you can see this pattern repeat itself. For instance, the e-mail body field of type `'#textarea'` implements the `'#rows'` and `'#columns'` properties, just like the matching HTML attributes for a `textarea`. The checkbox element (indicating whether the admin should be sent a BCC on outgoing e-mails) and submit button are equally straightforward to operate.

When we visit the URL that we registered earlier (`admin/config/people/user_warn`), we get the form rendered as seen in the following screenshot:

Home » Administer » Configuration » People
User Warn ○

Warning email subject *

Administrative Warning

The subject of the email which will be sent to users.

Warning email text *

Hello [user:name],

We have been notified that you have posted comments on [site:name] that are
in violation of our terms of service. If this behavior continues your account will be suspended.

You can review our terms of service at [site:tos-url].

Sincerely,
[site:name]
[site:mail]

The text of the email which will be sent to users. Available variables are: [site:name], [site:slogan], [site:mail], [site:url], [site:url-brief],
[site:login-url], [site:tos-url], [user:uid], [user:name], [user:mail], [user:url], [user:edit-url], [user:last-login], [user:created]

Terms of Service URL

URL to this site's Terms of Service.

☐ BCC admin on all emails

Indicates whether the admin user (as set in site configuration) should be BCC'd on all warning emails.

[Save configuration]

Drupal also offers several custom form elements in addition to the standard HTML fields. You can see an example of one of these in the `drupal_get_form()` callback for our second menu item:

```
/**
 * Form builder; display the e-mail confirmation form.
 */
function user_warn_confirm_form($form, &$form_state, $uid) {
  $form['account'] = array(
    '#type' => 'value',
    '#value' => user_load($uid),
  );

  return confirm_form(
    $form,
    t('Are you sure you want to send a warning e-mail to this
    user?'),
    'user/' . $uid,
    t('This action can not be undone.'),
    t('Send e-mail'),
    t('Cancel')
  );
}
```

We will revisit this function in more detail later in the chapter, but for now we will focus on the highlighted area. As you'll remember from earlier in this chapter, we used a wildcard in the menu item path to grab the user's ID and pass it into the page callback. As you can see now, this is being passed as the third parameter into our callback function (after the required `$form` and `$form_state` parameters). We can now use this ID to retrieve data about the user for future use.

Also, you can see that we are defining a new form element of type `'value'`. The value element is similar to the HTML hidden fields with two distinct advantages. First, value elements can contain any data you want as opposed to just strings. Arrays, objects, or any other complex data structure can be stored and passed in a value element.

The second advantage is that value elements are not printed back to the browser in the HTML source. This can improve the security of your data by preventing users from viewing and/or modifying it on a local instance.

In this code sample we are assigning the value element `'account'` with the value of a Drupal user object. This object will be passed on when the form is submitted, and the receiving function will be able to use it as needed. Value elements are extremely useful and developers should always consider using them in places where they would otherwise use hidden fields.

Drupal also offers a Form API element of type `'hidden'`, should developers prefer to use it.

Form API makes form building incredibly simple, but right now this form has two problems. First, the module should provide some reasonable default settings for system administrators. Second, when you submit the form, none of the submitted data is actually handled in any way. Let's take a brief detour from form handling and look at how Drupal manages persistent system data.

Managing persistent data

Drupal provides a mechanism by which data, which needs to persist semi-permanently (like system settings), can be saved and retrieved. These items are somewhat confusingly referred to as 'variables' (we will refer to them specifically as **persistent variables** from here on to avoid confusion). Persistent variables are stored in a database table, keyed by a unique name provided by the module that implements them.

Persistent variables are saved using `variable_set()`, and retrieved using `variable_get()`. These variables can be any type of data that a developer needs, be it a simple string, an associative array, or a PHP object. The Drupal API for setting/getting them takes care of all the serialization/unserialization that is necessary behind the scenes.

`variable_get()` can also provide a default value, which is useful for situations where you need a variable which has not already been set, for instance, after a module is installed for the first time. We can use this to our advantage in our configuration form as shown in the following snippet:

```
$form['user_warn_e-mail_subject'] = array(
  '#type' => 'textfield',
  '#default_value' => variable_get('user_warn_e-mail_subject',
                                   'Administrative Warning'),
  '#title' => t('Warning e-mail subject'),
  '#size' => 40,
  '#maxlength' => 120,
  '#required' => TRUE,
  '#description' => t(
      'The subject of the e-mail which will be sent to users.'),
);
```

This is the same Form API element we created above, but with a new line added. This line adds the `'#default_value'` property of the form element. This property tells the form what data the element should contain when the form is first loaded.

We are assigning this property the results of a call to `variable_get()` using two parameters. The first parameter is the unique key associated with this data. It is common practice to give a persistent variable the same name as the form element it is associated with, and we have done so here.

 Like menu items, persistent variables are cached by Drupal, so you will often need to clear your caches after modifying them.

The second parameter specifies the data that should be returned if this variable has never been explicitly set. In this example we have set that to be the string `'Administrative Warning'`. If this variable had been explicitly set sometime previously, then that data will be returned by `variable_get()` instead. Otherwise, the default value will be returned.

Now the first time the form loads, whatever data is in the persistent variable `'user_warn_e-mail_subject'` will be set as the value of the e-mail subject form element. We can also do this to our other form elements as desired. In the end our function will be as follows. Note that we have also added a constant containing the default text of our e-mail. Removing this large block of text from our array definition makes our code more readable and maintainable down the road.

Drupal constants are typically defined at the top of a `.module` file, but for the sake of clarity this example includes the constant definition with the function:

```
define('USER_WARN_MAIL_TEXT',
'Hello,

We have been notified that you have posted comments on our site that
are in violation of our terms of service.  If this behavior continues
your account will be suspended.

Sincerely,
The administrative staff');

function user_warn_form($form, &$form_state) {
  $form = array();

  // Text field for the e-mail subject.
  $form['user_warn_e-mail_subject'] = array(
     '#type' => 'textfield',
```

```
          '#default_value' => variable_get('user_warn_e-mail_subject',
                                      'Administrative Warning'),
        '#title' => t('Warning e-mail subject'),
        '#size' => 40,
        '#maxlength' => 120,
        '#required' => TRUE,
        '#description' => t(
                'The subject of the e-mail which will be sent to users.'),
      );

      // Textarea for the body of the e-mail.
      $form['user_warn_e-mail_text'] = array(
        '#type' => 'textarea',
        '#rows' => 10,
        '#columns' => 40,
        '#default_value' => variable_get('user_warn_e-mail_text',
                                      USER_WARN_MAIL_TEXT),
        '#title' => t('Warning e-mail text'),
        '#required' => TRUE,
        '#description' => t(
                'The text of the e-mail which will be sent to users. '),
      );

      // Checkbox to indicate whether admin should be sent a Bcc
      // on e-mails.
      $form['user_warn_bcc'] = array(
        '#type' => 'checkbox',
        '#default_value' => variable_get('user_warn_bcc', FALSE),
        '#title' => t('BCC admin on all e-mails'),
        '#description' => t('Indicates whether the admin user (as set in
site configuration) should be BCC\'d on all warning e-mails.'),
      );

      // Submit button
      $form['submit'] = array(
        '#type' => 'submit',
        '#value' => t('Save settings'),
      );

      return $form;
    }
```

Persistent variables are an excellent way to store module settings and other user-configurable information. However, having given our configuration settings reasonable defaults, we are still left with the issue of how to save changes to these defaults.

Form submission process

When an HTML form built with Form API is submitted, Drupal looks for two specifically named functions—a validate function and a submit function. These functions are named by taking the form ID and appending either `_validate()` or `_submit()` depending on which function you are writing.

The validate function does additional validation beyond what Drupal provides. For instance if you wanted to check to see if a zip code is valid. Even if validation fails on one element, all validation functions are still called, so Drupal can return multiple errors in a single form. However, if any validation function fails, execution never proceeds to the submit function.

> Validate functions are optional. If you don't need any additional validation, then you don't have to write one. In this case, Drupal will just do its default validation. For more information on how to write validate functions, see the Form API documentation at the links referenced earlier in the chapter.

Once the form passes validation, the submit function is called. This is where the real work is done—saving settings, sending e-mail, and creating content among other things. The form submit function is one of the main workhorses of Drupal modules.

As a module writer you will spend an inordinate amount of time writing submit functions and support code for submit functions. This is good, because it means you are spending time on the code that is unique to your project, and not recreating the wheel every time you want to turn a field red because a required field is missing.

So let's apply this to the User Warn configuration form. The form ID for our configuration form is `user_warn_form`, so our submit function will be named `user_warn_form_submit()`.

Form submit functions take two arguments. `$form` is the original Form API array for the submitted form, and `$form_state` is an associative array containing information specific to this submission. In particular, `$form_state['values']` contains all the submitted form values keyed on their name properties. In general, `$form_state['values']` is the only thing you will need to worry about in validate and submit functions.

```
/**
 * Save configuration settings for User Warn module.
 */
function user_warn_form_submit($form, &$form_state) {
```

```
    variable_set('user_warn_e-mail_subject',
                $form_state['values']['user_warn_e-mail_subject']);
    variable_set('user_warn_e-mail_text',
                $form_state['values']['user_warn_e-mail_text']);
    variable_set('user_warn_bcc',
                $form_state['values']['user_warn_bcc']);

    drupal_set_message(t('The settings have been saved'));
}
```

After all that, our submit function is pretty simple. We are saving our submitted data using `variable_set()`, then setting a simple message indicating that the values have been saved successfully. Our needs for validation are handled by Drupal's built-in form validation, so we don't even need a validate function for this data.

> The function `drupal_set_message()` sets a simple message that is displayed in a specific area at the top of a Drupal page. For more details see `http://api.drupal.org/api/function/drupal_set_message/7`.

After a form is submitted, it will reload the form submission page. Since we have saved new data in our persistent variables through the submit function, and since the form is pre-loaded with default data based on the data in those variables, we should now be able to submit new data for these items and see them reflected after the form has been submitted.

> If you want Drupal to redirect to a different page after form submission, you can set `$form_state['redirect']` to the desired path in your submit function. If this isn't working, check whether you have specified for `$form_state` to be passed by reference by adding an ampersand to it in your function signature.

Form API provides us with a great deal of power with a pretty small amount of work, but Drupal offers some shortcuts which make common forms even easier.

A shortcut for system settings

The need to save configuration settings into persistent variables through a standard form is pretty common. Thankfully, once again Drupal has provided us with some magic to simplify this task. That magic is the `system_settings_form()` function. When you pass a standard Form API form array through this function and return the results, you get several benefits. Take a look at the following modified version of `user_warn_form()`:

```
/**
 * Form builder; Build the User Warn settings form.
 */
function user_warn_form($form, &$form_state) {

  // Text field for the e-mail subject.
  $form['user_warn_e-mail_subject'] = array(
    '#type' => 'textfield',
    '#default_value' => 'Administrative Warning',
    '#title' => t('Warning e-mail subject'),
    '#size' => 40,
    '#maxlength' => 120,
    '#required' => TRUE,
    '#description' => t(
        'The subject of the e-mail which will be sent to users.'),
  );

  // Textarea for the body of the e-mail.
  $form['user_warn_e-mail_text'] = array(
    '#type' => 'textarea',
    '#rows' => 10,
    '#columns' => 40,
    '#default_value' => USER_WARN_MAIL_TEXT,
    '#title' => t('Warning e-mail text'),
    '#required' => TRUE,
    '#description' => t(
        'The text of the e-mail which will be sent to users.'),
  );

  // Checkbox to indicate whether admin should be sent a Bcc
  // on e-mails.
  $form['user_warn_bcc'] = array(
    '#type' => 'checkbox',
    '#default_value' => FALSE,
    '#title' => t('BCC admin on all e-mails'),
```

```
       '#description' => t('Indicates whether the admin user (as set in
   site configuration) should be BCC\'d on all warning e-mails.'),
     );

   return system_settings_form($form);
}
```

The first thing you'll notice is that we no longer have a submit button element. That is because `system_settings_form()` adds one in for us automatically. It gets the label `'Save settings'`.

Additionally, `system_settings_form()` uses its own custom submit handler `system_settings_form_submit()`, which automatically saves all form elements into persistent variables of the same name. You don't have to write a submit function at all, Drupal takes care of everything behind the scenes.

It might seem silly to use an API function for something as simple as adding a submit button and automating the handling of persistent variables. However, the less code you have to write the less bugs you introduce. With just around 30 lines of code, we now have a fully functional form with extensive validation, customizable default settings, and the ability for users to change the default settings as they wish.

Having set up our module's configuration form, we now need to add a function that enables administrators to actually send this e-mail to users.

A shortcut for confirmation forms

Earlier in the chapter, we added a 'Warn' tab to user profile pages. System administrators should be able to click this tab to send the warning e-mail to users. However, it would be nice if we could add a confirmation step here, to prevent e-mails from being sent inadvertently.

This is another situation where Drupal offers a convenient shortcut function. Let's revisit the callback function we looked at earlier while discussing `'value'` form elements.

```
/**
 * Form builder; display the e-mail confirmation form.
 */
function user_warn_confirm_form($form, &$form_state, $uid)
{
  $form['account'] = array(
    '#type' => 'value',
    '#value' => user_load($uid),
  );
```

```
    return confirm_form(
      $form,
      t(
        'Are you sure you want to send a warning e-mail to this user?'),
      'user/' . $uid,
      t('This action can not be undone.'),
      t('Send e-mail'),
      t('Cancel')
    );
  }
```

The `confirm_form()` function allows developers to easily create confirmation forms associated with specific actions. It takes seven arguments, which seems intimidating but they are actually pretty intuitive.

The first argument contains additional form elements that we want merged into the resulting confirmation form. As we saw earlier, we have created a value element containing a user account object. We need this to be passed on to the form's submit function, so we set it to be added with all the other elements that `confirm_form()` creates on its own.

The second argument specifies the question you want to ask when the user is presented with the confirmation option. This is pretty straightforward and we have an appropriate message there.

The third argument indicates what URL the user should be sent to if the user cancels the form. Usually this will be an internal Drupal path without leading or trailing slashes. Typically site administrators will get to this page from a user profile page, so it is appropriate that when this form is canceled the administrators are returned to this profile page.

The final three arguments specify various captions used in the form. They are the additional description text to be displayed above the confirm button, the text of confirm button, and the text of the cancel link. All of these messages are optional, and Drupal will use sensible defaults if you don't change them here explicitly.

The code above displays the following:

Forms generated by `confirm_form()` only call their submit functions if the form is actually confirmed, so developers don't need to check for this themselves. If the form is canceled, then the user is simply redirected to the URL specified in the function call.

We have now gotten a pretty thorough introduction to Drupal's Form API. We can create forms from scratch, write, validate, and submit handlers, and use some of Drupal's internal functions to create common form types. We're two-thirds of the way into this chapter and we still haven't touched on the module's central purpose—sending an e-mail to a user!

Sending mail with drupal_mail() and hook_mail()

Drupal implements a custom e-mail templating system. Initially it may appear that this system is overly complicated, but it allows an enormous amount of flexibility for module developers.

Sending e-mail in Drupal is a multi-step process:

1. `drupal_mail()` is called, specifying what mail is being sent and what options are unique to this specific message (the recipient's e-mail address, the language the mail should be sent in, and so on).

2. Drupal then builds an e-mail message with standard headers combined with the information submitted to `drupal_mail()`.

3. The `hook_mail()` implementation specified in `drupal_mail()` is called. This is where the subject and body of the mail are added.

4. The fully composed mail array is then passed to `hook_mail_alter()`, allowing other modules to modify it (for instance, to add a common signature to all outgoing e-mails.).

5. The mail is passed to `drupal_send_mail()` for delivery.

That is a pretty long process just for sending a simple e-mail! However, in most cases developers will only have to worry about two of the above steps—calling `drupal_mail()` and implementing `hook_mail()`.

> **PHP mail configuration**
>
> In order for Drupal to send an e-mail, your server must be configured so that PHP's `mail()` function will work. Typically this involves installing and configuring a local mail server. Most shared hosting providers are already properly configured to do this, but if you are on a VPS or other custom-built server you may have to handle it yourself. This process varies wildly depending on your operating system and a variety of other factors. Searching for **php mail setup** on Google will most likely start you in the right direction.

Calling drupal_mail()

The following is the function that gets called when our confirmation form is submitted (indicating that we should in fact send an e-mail warning to the user in question).

```
/**
 * Send a warning e-mail to the specified user.
 */
function user_warn_confirm_form_submit($form, &$form_state) {
  $account = $form_state['values']['account'];

  drupal_mail(
    'user_warn',
    'warn',
    $account->mail,
    user_preferred_language($account),
    $form_state['values'],
    variable_get('site_mail', NULL),
    TRUE
  );
}
```

As you can see, `drupal_mail()` requires that we pass it quite a bit of information. Let's look at each of these arguments in detail:

- The first argument indicates what module should invoke `hook_mail()` to send this message. We are setting this to `'user_warn'` since we are doing our own `hook_mail()` implementation. However, you can send a mail implemented by another module if you need to. We will look at the `user_warn_mail()` implementation in a bit.

- The second argument, `warn`, is a key which is passed to `hook_mail()`. Any `hook_mail()` implementation can define several e-mails, uniquely identified by a text key. (Drupal's user module implements eighteen (!) for things like account confirmation and forgotten passwords). We specify which specific mail we want to send with this parameter.

- The third argument contains the recipient's address. We pull this out of the user object for the user whose profile we visited, as passed by the confirmation form above.

- The fourth argument specifies what language the mail should be sent in. This is important because individual users can specify a language preference that is different from the site's default language. We should honor this choice if possible when sending our e-mail to this user. The `user_preferred_language()` function makes this task easy by taking a user object and returning the user's language choice.

- The fifth argument is an associative array of parameters to be passed to `hook_mail()`. Any custom information needed to build the e-mail should be put here. In our case, any custom information we need to build the e-mail is already in the data submitted from the confirmation form, so we will just use `$form_state['values']` here.

- The sixth argument contains the e-mail address from whom this mail should be sent. When you first installed Drupal you had to specify an administrative e-mail address. This address is already being used as the source for other system e-mails (like account verification) so it makes sense to use it as our sender e-mail as well. The e-mail is stored as a persistent variable with the key `'site_mail'`, so we can easily grab it using `variable_get()` as discussed earlier in the chapter.

- Finally, the last variable indicates whether or not the mail should actually be sent. It will come as no surprise to learn that a mail message in Drupal is built in a specially structured associative array. At the end of the mail building process, this array is typically passed to the function `drupal_mail_send()` which handles the actual delivery of the mail. However, by setting this parameter to `FALSE`, `drupal_mail()` will bypass the delivery step, allowing you to take the structured array it returns and handle delivery yourself.

Implementing hook_mail()

In the last section, when we called `drupal_mail()`, we indicated that it should invoke `hook_mail()` in the `user_warn` module. This means that Drupal will be looking for a function named `user_warn_mail()`. This function is as follows:

```
/**
 * Implement hook_mail().
 */
function user_warn_mail($key, &$message, $params) {
  switch ($key) {
    case 'warn':
      $account = $params['account'];
      $subject = variable_get('user_warn_e-mail_subject',
                              'Administrative Warning');
      $body = variable_get('user_warn_e-mail_text',
                           'You\'ve been warned!');

      if (variable_get('user_warn_bcc', FALSE)) {
        $admin_mail = variable_get('site_mail', NULL);
        $message['headers']['bcc'] = $admin_mail;
      }

      $message['to'] = $account->mail;
      $message['subject'] = $subject;
      $message['body'][] = $body;
      break;
  }
}
```

As you can see the preceding function receives three arguments:

- The key we passed in parameter two of our call to `drupal_mail()`, indicating what message should be sent.

- The structured array that Drupal creates to represent an e-mail message. At this point this array has already been populated with the mail's default header information.

- The data we passed from `drupal_mail()` in the `$params` argument (in this case, a user's account object.)

As discussed earlier, it is possible for `hook_mail()` to handle multiple different e-mails as indicated by the key passed in from `drupal_mail()`. Even though we are only sending one e-mail with a key of `'warn'`, we still put it into a switch/case structure to make it easier to manage more mails later on if needed.

Now we can get on with the real purpose of our hook implementation—adding details to the `$message` array that are unique to our mail. Typically this is the subject, body, and any additional headers that we might need.

Our e-mail's subject and text have been set via the module's configuration page, so we retrieve them via `variable_get()` and set them to the `$message['subject']` and `$message['body]` properties here.

> Note that we do not pass the subject and body strings through `t()` as we have done in other contexts. These strings are supplied by the site administrator through the User Warn module's configuration form, and as such are not translatable. Only hardcoded system strings need to be passed through `t()`.

The other thing we need to do is to Bcc the site admin if that configuration setting has been set.

```
if (variable_get('user_warn_bcc', FALSE)) {
  $admin_mail = variable_get('site_mail', NULL);
  $message['headers']['bcc'] = $admin_mail;
}
```

As with the other configuration settings, we retrieve it using `variable_get()`. If it is TRUE, then we need to set the site admin to be Bcc'd. Unlike the e-mail recipient, Cc and Bcc are set by adding headers to the `$message` array. The headers are themselves an associative array held under the `'headers'` key, and we need to add a new header with the key `'Bcc'`. We assign this to the site admin's e-mail in the same manner as we did in `drupal_mail()` while setting the mail's sender.

This is all we need to do! `$message` is passed by reference, so we don't even need to return it. Drupal will just proceed on from here. After other modules get a chance to alter the mail through `hook_mail_alter()`, the `$message` array will be passed to `drupal_mail_system()` where the final mail message will be formatted and delivered (if you specified this option when you called `drupal_mail()`).

> **Debugging mail problems**
>
> There are a variety of reasons why an e-mail might not be delivered. If the the recipient's address does not exist or there is another problem on the receiving end, the mail will be bounced back to the e-mail address specified in the sixth argument of `drupal_mail()` (the site administrator in this example.). In the case of a misconfigured local system, you may be able to find more information in PHP's error logs. The Reroute Mail module can be helpful if you are having problems sending mail on your development server:
> `http://drupal.org/project/reroute_e-mail`

This is all good, and we actually have a fully functional module now. However, there is one more issue we should look at addressing.

The token system

It would be nice if we could include some personalized information in the mail text without having to hardcode it in the module configuration form. For instance, we should be able to include the login of the user being warned, or the name of the site admin. This leads us into our final topic, using Drupal's token system.

What are tokens?

A token is a small piece of text that can be placed into a piece of text via the use of a placeholder. When the text is passed through the function `token_replace()`, then the tokens are replaced with the appropriate information. Tokens allow users to include data that could change in text blocks, without having to go back and change it everywhere they're referenced.

> In previous versions of Drupal, tokens were implemented using the contributed module named, not surprisingly, Token. This functionality proved to be so popular and widely used that it was included in core for Drupal 7.

A sample token is `[site:name]`. When text containing this token is passed through `token_replace()`, it is replaced with your site's name as defined in **Home | Administer | Configuration | Site information**. If you change your site's name, then in the future all text containing this token will reflect this change. Drupal exposes a variety of tokens containing information on users, nodes, site-wide configuration, and more.

Tokens can also be 'chained' — a token can refer to another token which can refer to yet another one. As an example, the token [node:author] contains the name of a node's author, and the token [user:e-mail] contains the e-mail address of a given user. To retrieve the e-mail address of a node's author, you can chain the two together with the token [node:author:e-mail].

> Module developers can also expose their own tokens for other module developers to take advantage of. For more information on how to expose tokens in your module, see the following sites:
>
> http://api.drupal.org/api/function/hook_token_info/7
> http://api.drupal.org/api/function/hook_tokens/7

Drupal's token system is extremely flexible and prevents site builders and developers from having to replace information in site text every time it changes. So let's see how we can use tokens in our module.

> **How do we know what tokens are available?**
>
> Drupal 7 does not include a user interface for browsing available tokens, however the contributed Token module implements a very nice JavaScript tree-like browser for them. You can download and install it from the following site:
>
> http://drupal.org/project/token
>
> Additionally module developers can use the function token_info() to get a structured array containing all the tokens in the system. This can be parsed and/or displayed as desired.

Implementing tokens in your text

The obvious place where User Warn could use tokens is in the text of the outgoing e-mails. Let's expand the very simple default text we included above, and also put it into a constant, for easier module readability and maintainability. This will require updating some of the previous code, but in the future we will only need to change this information in one place.

```
define('USER_WARN_MAIL_TEXT',
'Hello [user:name],

We have been notified that you have posted comments on [site:name]
that are in violation of our terms of service.  If this behavior
continues your account will be suspended.

Sincerely,
[site:name]');
```

This text contains three tokens:

- `[site:name]`: the site's name as described earlier
- `[site:mail]`: the administrative e-mail address (this is the same e-mail address returned by `variable_get('site-mail')`
- `[user:name]`: the login name of a specified user

In order to make this work, we have to implement `token_replace()` in our `hook_mail()` implementation as highlighted below:

```
/**
 * Implement hook_mail().
 */
function user_warn_mail($key, &$message, $params) {
  switch ($key) {
    case 'warn':
      $account = $params['account'];
      $subject = variable_get('user_warn_e-mail_
subject','Administrative Warning');
      $body = variable_get('user_warn_e-mail_text',
                           USER_WARN_MAIL_TEXT);

      if (variable_get('user_warn_bcc', FALSE)) {
        $admin_mail = variable_get('site_mail', NULL);
        $message['headers']['bcc'] = $admin_mail;
      }

      $message['to'] = $account->mail;
      $message['subject'] = $subject;
      $message['body'][] = token_replace($body,
                             array('user' => $account));
      break;
  }

}
```

As you can see, we're now setting the e-mail body to the return value from `token_replace()`. This function is pretty simple, it only takes two arguments:

- The text with tokens in place.
- An array of keyed objects to be used in the token replacement process. In this case, the user object for the recipient of this e-mail as passed in the `$params` argument from `drupal_mail()`. If you need other replacements (like for a node) you would add additional objects into this array.

That's it! The text returned from `token_replace()` will now look something like this:

```
Hello eshqi,

We have been notified that you have posted comments on The Coolest
Site In The World that are in violation of our terms of service.  If
this behavior continues your account will be suspended.

Sincerely,
The Coolest Site In The World
```

This e-mail is much better and personalized for both the sender and the recipient.

Summary

In reality the User Warn module is probably of limited utility, but it does help to introduce many of the core concepts that Drupal developers will use on a day-to-day basis. You are now able to create pages at a specific URL using `hook_menu()`, and implement forms on those pages using the Form API. The values submitted from this form can be saved using functions like `system_settings_form()`, `confirm_form()`, or your own custom submit handler. You can also send the results of a form submission as a custom email using dynamic tokens for text replacement.

In *Chapter 7, Creating New Fields*, we will begin examining Drupal 7's new Field API, the core implementation of what was formerly the CCK module.

6
Working with Content

Drupal 7 introduces major changes to the way Drupal handles content. In earlier versions, nearly all content was considered a "node". By making content a standard object with a common API, any module could add data to and manipulate that object to create complex data models and workflows.

That worked extremely well, with the exception that Drupal had several other types of objects, such as users or comments, that were not really "content" per se but could still have benefited from the same rich API. For Drupal 7, therefore, most of those separate object types were merged into a single super-system known as "entities". Nodes, users, comments, and several other types of data objects are now particular instances of the generic Entity data object concept. That allows all types of data to have the same, or at least very similar, API and workflow, avoiding duplicate code and reducing the number of moving parts developers need to keep track of. Most importantly, it allows us to attach Fields, discrete structured pieces of information, to any type of entity rather than just to nodes.

In this chapter, we'll look at how to define new entity types. There are a lot of moving parts, and while the entity system automates much of the process for us it does not automate everything. Along the way we'll touch on several new pieces of Drupal and reiterate what we've covered in previous chapters about page callbacks and form handling.

Why create your own entities

It's generally not necessary to create a new entity type. Nodes are still extremely flexible, and more often than not can handle whatever use case we need. However, there are cases where it is necessary to create separate entities rather than separate node types, like for instance:

- We may need entities that have entirely different permission handling or workflow than nodes, such as products in an e-commerce system.

- We may be accessing entities that are not stored in Drupal's local database, such as a legacy data store.
- We may need to have internal variants, like node types, but nodes don't support "sub-type types".

For simplicity we'll not do anything too exotic for now. Instead, we'll look at a relatively simple use case and mirror node handling fairly closely.

The goal

For our example, we'll create a new entity called "artwork". This entity will represent a work of art held by a museum and managed through Drupal. Like nodes, artworks will have sub-types like "painting" and "sculpture". We will want to allow users to create, edit, and delete artworks, as well as configure what fields are available on each artwork type.

In practice most real museums would have their collection stored in a dedicated collection management system and we would need to just provide a wrapper that reads data from it in a Drupal-friendly way. For our purposes though we will assume a very small museum that wants to use Drupal itself as a simple collection management system, which implies full create, read, update, and delete capabilities.

Bundles

In earlier versions of Drupal only nodes had the ability to have sub-types. In Drupal 7, all entities have the ability to support sub-types. In Drupal parlance, these sub-types are called "bundles".

 A **bundle** is a sub-type of an entity that can be configured separately. Node types are an example of a bundle. Not all entity types have bundles. Users, for instance, do not have separate bundles.

For now, we'll hard-code two bundles, painting and sculpture. In a real use case we'd be likely to also include an administration system to create and manage bundles.

The Schema API

We will need a place to store our artwork data, so we need to create some new database tables. Rather than create them directly, though, we'll let Drupal do that for us using a part of the database layer called the Schema API.

> The Schema API allows database-agnostic definition and manipulation of the tables in Drupal's SQL database.

First, let's create a new module called "artwork". Start with the `artwork.info` and `artwork.module` files, as we've seen in previous chapters. However, we will also add another file, `artwork.install`. This file contains hooks that Drupal only ever uses when the module is being installed, removed, or updated so it only gets loaded at those times, saving considerable code on most page loads.

The most important hook in the `artwork.install` file is `hook_schema()`, which defines the database tables this module provides. We'll start with the following table definition, closely based on the node table:

```
function artwork_schema() {
  $schema['artwork'] = array(
    'description' => 'The base table for artworks.',
    'fields' => array(
      'aid' => array(
        'description' => 'The primary identifier for an artwork.',
        'type' => 'serial',
        'unsigned' => TRUE,
        'not null' => TRUE,
      ),
      'vid' => array(
        'description' =>
            'The current {artwork_revision}.vid version identifier.',
        'type' => 'int',
        'unsigned' => TRUE,
        'not null' => TRUE,
        'default' => 0,
      ),
      'type' => array(
        'description' => 'The {artwork_type} of this artwork.',
        'type' => 'varchar',
        'length' => 32,
        'not null' => TRUE,
        'default' => '',
      ),
      'title' => array(
        'description' => 'The title of this artwork.',
        'type' => 'varchar',
        'length' => 255,
        'not null' => TRUE,
```

```
        'default' => '',
      ),
      'created' => array(
        'description' =>
              'The Unix timestamp when the artwork was created.',
        'type' => 'int',
        'not null' => TRUE,
        'default' => 0,
      ),
      'changed' => array(
        'description' =>
      'The Unix timestamp when the artwork was most recently saved.',
        'type' => 'int',
        'not null' => TRUE,
        'default' => 0,
      ),

    ),
    'unique keys' => array(
      'aid_vid' => array('aid', 'vid'),
      'aid'     => array('aid')
      ),
    'primary key' => array('aid'),
  );

  return $schema;
}
```

That looks like a lot of code, but it's really just another big Drupal array. The keys of the $schema array are the names of tables to be created. Each table is then defined as another nested array that defines the fields, indices, and other data about the table. Most are self-explanatory.

> See http://drupal.org/node/146843 for more information on the Schema API.

Note that we're using an integer field called aid for our primary key. We also store the bundle that an artwork belongs to in a column called type (just like nodes), and we have a "version ID" field called vid. All entities can support versioning in a similar fashion to nodes, so let's build that in from the start.

To store old revisions, we'll need another table as well. We'll call that table artwork_revision:

```
$schema['artwork_revision'] = array(
  'description' =>
      'Stores information about each saved version of an {artwork}.',
```

```
    'fields' => array(
      'aid' => array(
        'description' => 'The {artwork} this version belongs to.',
        'type' => 'int',
        'unsigned' => TRUE,
        'not null' => TRUE,
        'default' => 0,
      ),
      'vid' => array(
        'description' => 'The primary identifier for this version.',
        'type' => 'serial',
        'unsigned' => TRUE,
        'not null' => TRUE,
      ),
      'title' => array(
        'description' => 'The title of this version.',
        'type' => 'varchar',
        'length' => 255,
        'not null' => TRUE,
        'default' => '',
      ),
      'created' => array(
        'description' =>
              'The Unix timestamp when the artwork was created.',
        'type' => 'int',
        'not null' => TRUE,
        'default' => 0,
      ),
    ),
    'indexes' => array(
      'aid' => array('aid'),
    ),
    'primary key' => array('vid'),
    'foreign keys' => array(
      'artwork' => array(
        'table' => 'artwork',
        'columns' => array(
          'aid' => 'aid',
        ),
      ),
    ),
  );
```

Note here as well that we're explicitly declaring the `aid` field of the revision table to be a foreign key to the `aid` field of the artwork table. Although Drupal does not leverage foreign key information itself, other modules may do so. By convention, tables in Drupal should be singular nouns.

With these two tables defined in `artwork_schema()`, Drupal will automatically create the corresponding tables for us in the database when the module is first enabled. If our module is uninstalled completely, it will also take care of removing them for us.

Declaring our entity

There are two parts to telling Drupal about our new entity. The first is another definition hook called `hook_entity_info()`. This hook tells Drupal about the entity or entities we're providing, and also provides the Field UI system with the information it needs to allow us to attach fields to entities—more on that later. The second part is a "controller class", which is a PHP class that will be responsible for loading and, in our case, creating, saving, and deleting our artwork.

Drupal includes a controller class called `DrupalDefaultEntityController` that handles the most common case, which we will be emulating. It is extremely basic, however, and only handles loading of objects. Fortunately it is very easy to subclass the default controller and add our own functionality so that is precisely what we will do.

 A **controller** is a loader object for an entity. All entity types must have a controller, but many can use the default. Different controllers may require additional keys on an entity definition.

The entity declaration

First let's tell Drupal about our entity type using `hook_entity_info()`:

```
/**
 * Implements hook_entity_info().
 */
function artwork_entity_info() {
  $return['artwork'] = array(
    'label' => t('Artwork'),
    'controller class' => 'ArtworkController',
    'base table' => 'artwork',
    'revision table' => 'artwork_revision',
    'uri callback' => 'artwork_uri',
```

```
      'fieldable' => TRUE,
      'entity keys' => array(
        'id' => 'aid',
        'revision' => 'vid',
        'bundle' => 'type',
        'label' => 'title',
      ),
      'bundle keys' => array(
        'bundle' => 'type',
      ),
      'static cache' => TRUE,
      'bundles' => array(),
      'view modes' => array(
        'full' => array(
          'label' => t('Full content'),
          'custom settings' => FALSE,
        ),
        'teaser' => array(
          'label' => t('Teaser'),
          'custom settings' => FALSE,
        ),
      ),
  );

  foreach (artwork_types() as $type => $info) {
    $return['artwork']['bundles'][$type] = array(
      'label' => $info->name,
      'admin' => array(
        'path' => 'admin/structure/artworks/manage/%artwork_type',
        'real path' => 'admin/structure/artworks/manage/' .
                       str_replace('_', '-', $type),
        'bundle argument' => 4,
        'access arguments' => array('administer artworks'),
      ),
    );
  }

  return $return;
}
```

Once again, our primary means of communicating with Drupal is through large structured arrays that define all the information we need. In this case, our $return array has a single entry, artwork. The string artwork, as the top-most key, will serve as the "machine name" of this entity, which is how it will be referred to in code. The label key specifies what name should be shown to the user. The base table, revision table, and object keys entries tell the entity system about how our artwork is going to be stored, and are used by the default controller:

- The main table where artworks are stored is called artwork, which has a primary key field (the "id" field) of aid.

- Revisions will be stored in a table called artwork_revision, and the revision's unique ID is called vid.

- Since we're supporting multiple bundles, we also tell the system what field will indicate to which bundle a given artwork belongs. In this case, we use the type field.

- The human-readable name of a given artwork is stored in the title field.

The view modes key defines the different ways that our entity can be viewed. In this case we are defining a "full" version and a "teaser" version, just as nodes use, but we could define whatever view modes we wanted. Other modules are free to inject additional view modes via hook_entity_info_alter() as well. As usual, the key of the view modes array is the machine name of the view mode and the label property is the human-friendly name. The custom settings flag indicates whether or not the Field UI should allow field formatters to be configured separately for that view mode by default. It is easily changed via the UI.

We also define a uri_callback function, namely artwork_uri(). That allows us to abstract out the definition of the path within Drupal where this artwork will be accessed. Instead of hard coding a path, such as artwork/$aid, we call a callback function to generate it for us. That is most important when listing entities of different types, as we can simply call a single function, entity_uri($type, $entity), and get back the correct information to pass to the url() or l() functions. Our simple callback looks like this:

```
function artwork_uri($artwork) {
  return array(
    'path' => 'artwork/' . $artwork->aid,
  );
}
```

The return value from the callback is an array with two keys: `path`, which is the Drupal path where the entity lives, and `options`, which defines other parameters to the `url()` and `l()` functions for things such as page anchors or GET query values. It is safe to omit the `options` key if it's not needed. Although our implementation is trivial, alternative implementations could, for instance, put all entities of a given type on a single page and have an anchor for each one.

> When creating a link to an entity, always use `entity_uri($type, $entity)` to generate the parameters to pass to either the `url()` or `l()` functions.

Note that these array keys assume we are using the default controller for our entity. A "controller" is an object that handles the loading of the entity object for us. The controller is defined as a PHP class, and can be written to load our entity from anywhere, not just the local database. In our case, we are defining a custom controller called `ArtworkController` that will extend from `DrupalDefaultEntityController`, so it uses the same keys. `DrupalDefaultEntityController` is a generic controller for entities that are stored in the local database and behave, more or less, like nodes. If we were pulling data from an entirely different system we would implement our own controller from scratch that implements the `DrupalEntityControllerInterface` interface, and we might then need different keys defined in the entity hook.

Two other important keys are the cacheable and fieldable flags:

- `static cache` indicates that the controller should keep a copy of an entity in memory after it's been requested so that if we try to load it a second time in the same page request we can just use that cached copy.
- `fieldable` indicates to the Field API that we can attach fields to this entity, in the same fashion as nodes. That's very important, as it is one of the main reasons to define a new entity type in the first place.

The second part of the hook is a little more involved. It is primarily there to support the Field API, which will be covered in the next chapter. Since we have multiple bundles, we need to tell the Field API what bundles we have and at what paths to put the extra field management interfaces for our entity. To do that, we define, for each of our bundles, a label that is shown to the user and the menu information that the Field API will need to add itself into the menu. The keys here, under `admin`, are fairly self explanatory. `path` defines the path that should be used in `hook_menu()` for the Field UI's pages, while `real path` is the exact path that should be used when generating links within the admin interface.

Because our path contains a menu placeholder, we also need to specify which index it is in the bundle argument. Remember that menu arguments are 0-based, so index 4 is the fifth part of the path, which here is `%artwork_type`. We also can control the permissions a user needs in order to access the field settings pages for this entity with the `access callback` and `access arguments` keys, which work the exact same way as in a normal menu item. If no access callback is specified then the `user_access` callback, which checks against user permissions, is the default.

Of course, since we've defined a new menu placeholder we need a callback for it. There is also the `artwork_types()` function, which doesn't exist yet. Let's create those now. They're really quite simple, but are a standard part of any entity.

```
function artwork_types() {
  $types = &drupal_static(__FUNCTION__);

  if (empty($types)) {
    $types['painting'] = (object)array(
      'type' => 'painting',
      'name' => t('Painting'),
      'description' => t('A picture made with paint.')
    );
    $types['sculpture'] = (object)array(
      'type' => 'sculpture',
      'name' => t('Sculpture'),
      'description' => t('A carving made out of stone or wood.')
    );
  }
  return $types;
}


function artwork_type_load($type) {
  $types = artwork_types();
  $type = str_replace('-', '_', $type);
  return isset($types[$type]) ? $types[$type] : FALSE;
}
```

The `artwork_types()` function returns a list of artwork type objects. Each artwork type object is simply a `stdClass` PHP object that contains whatever pertinent information there is about each bundle. There are two important attributes to the artwork type object:

- It must be an object
- There must be a property of that object that matches the `bundle keys` definition in `hook_entity_info()`

In our case, we defined the bundle to use the `type` property so our artwork types have a property called `type` that contains the machine name of the bundle. A property called `name` for the human-friendly name of the bundle is a standard convention but not strictly required, as is a human-readable `description` property.

The `artwork_type_load()` function is necessary for the menu placeholder to work, but is also a very nice convenience function to have available as well. Generally it is good practice to provide clean, flexible APIs to any system we develop, even if we don't expect to use them. Odds are that we'll either find a use for them later or someone else will think of a use we never expected.

Note that we are replacing dashes in a type name with underscores. That's because, by convention, all Drupal paths use dashes in place of underscores but bundle names need to use underscores, not dashes. When we use a type name in a URL we will always use a dash, and so here we first fold the dash back to an underscore to make sure we find the correct artwork type.

There is one other important detail here, and that is the `drupal_static()` function. That function acts as a central collector for static PHP variables, that is, those that are not technically global but should persist between calls to a function. They are quite commonly used as a lightweight cache to avoid re-processing or refetching the same data within the same page request, but that can in some cases lead to weird side effects when the data being cached changes mid-request, such as when writing unit tests.

The `drupal_static()` function acts as a central collector for such static variables. By putting all such static variables in one place and giving the variable a name that matches our function (that's what the `__FUNCTION__` PHP constant means), we allow systems that need to forcibly reset static caches without having a separate `$reset` parameter for every part of the system.

> Use the `drupal_static()` function to cheaply cache data structures for one page request. Don't cache data that is too large and too cheap to regenerate, though, as it does use up memory.

The entity controller

In the entity info hook we declared that we were going to use our own controller class. That means we need to provide one. However, a controller class may not always be small, and if it's only rarely used we don't want to parse that code on all pages. Fortunately PHP provides a way to load class definitions on demand, and Drupal makes it very easy to expose classes to PHP's autoloader.

> As a general rule, large, rarely used classes should be placed into a separate file while smaller or very frequently used classes should be left in the .module file to avoid the overhead of finding the class when needed. Additionally, classes that are typically used together can be placed into a single file so that we'll need to load only a single file.

Let's create a new file in our module called `artwork.controller.inc`. Next, add that file to the `files[]` array in the `artwork.info` file. In `artwork.controller.inc`, let's start with just the following code:

```
class ArtworkController extends DrupalDefaultEntityController {
}
```

Now when our module is enabled, Drupal will scan all files in the `files[]` array in `artwork.info`, find the `ArtworkController` class, and cache its location. Later on, when some code tries to create a new instance of `ArtworkController` it will lazy-load the `artwork.controller.inc` file, making the class available to be used.

Naturally the `ArtworkController` class needs to actually do something. We will add additional methods to it as we go. There is already a `load()` method, inherited from `DrupalDefaultEntityController`, as well as several others.

Most Drupal code prefers to work procedurally, however, even if the engine under the hood is object-oriented. Therefore, like the node module we will provide a set of utility API functions for us and other module developers to use.

```
function artwork_load($aid = NULL, $vid = NULL, $reset = FALSE) {
  $aids = (isset($aid) ? array($aid) : array());
  $conditions = (isset($vid) ? array('vid' => $vid) : array());
  $artwork = artwork_load_multiple($aids, $conditions, $reset);
  return $artwork ? reset($artwork) : FALSE;
}

function artwork_load_multiple($aids = array(), $conditions = array(),
$reset = FALSE) {
  return entity_load('artwork', $aids, $conditions, $reset);
}
```

Note that we're actually passing all of the loading logic back to the `entity_load()` function, which in turn will create a new instance of the `ArtworkController` as needed and call the `load()` method on it. The `load()` method assumes that all operations are multi-load. In fact, the entity system assumes multi-object operations wherever possible. That makes loading multiple objects at the same time much cheaper as we can load them all at once, while loading a single object is the exact same operation. "One" is a special case of "many". We can now load one or a dozen artwork objects with equal ease.

 Most entity operations in Drupal assume multiple objects.

Now that we have defined our entity and can load it, what can we do with it? Right now not much, since we have no way to create or edit entities. We still need to define the rest of the entity life cycle and expose a UI for it.

Entity management

In practice, different entity types will frequently need a different workflow for creating, editing, and deleting entities. Some may not even be editable through the UI. To keep things simple for now, though, we'll stick with the familiar node workflow and replicate that, more or less.

Because there are several parts, we'll tackle them one at a time:

1. Create an administrative workflow for managing artwork types.
2. Create pages to add and edit artworks.
3. Create a page to view artworks.
4. Create a form for deleting artworks.

Managing artwork types

We'll start with a stub of an admin section for managing artwork types. Although we will not allow users to create new artwork types we still need to have at least a very minimal administrative section on which the Field system can hang its interface. We'll start with a fairly simple `artwork_menu()` hook:

```
function artwork_menu() {
  $items['admin/structure/artworks'] = array(
    'title' => 'Manage artworks',
    'description' => 'Manage artworks.',
    'page callback' => 'artwork_overview_types',
    'access arguments' => array('administer artworks'),
  );
  $items['admin/structure/artworks/manage/%artwork_type'] = array(
    'title' => 'View artwork type',
    'title callback' => 'artwork_type_page_title',
    'title arguments' => array(4),
    'page callback' => 'artwork_information',
    'page arguments' => array(4),
```

```
      'access arguments' => array('administer artworks'),
    );
    $items['admin/structure/artworks/manage/%artwork_type/view'] =
array(
      'title' => 'View',
      'type' => MENU_DEFAULT_LOCAL_TASK,
    );

    return $items;
  }
```

Once again, while Drupal's big arrays look like a lot of code it is all fairly straightforward. The first item sets up our artwork type landing page at `admin/structure/artworks` (which deliberately parallels the `admin/structure/content` path for managing nodes). The second sets up a callback for viewing and editing each artwork type (bundle), although we won't do anything with it except show some static information. The third menu item creates a menu tab (or in Drupal parlance, "local task") called `View`, that is the default and will pass-through to the parent artwork-type-manage page.

The tab definition is important. Recall from the last section that our `artwork_entity_info()` function told the Field UI system that it should add its own administrative pages at `admin/structure/artworks/manage/%artwork_type`. When the Field UI module is enabled, therefore, it will add additional pages as tabs next to our **View** tab. If we don't declare our page as a tab, it will get lost when someone views the Field UI pages.

There are a few new functions we need here to support these pages, all of them very short.

```
function artwork_overview_types() {
  foreach (artwork_types() as $type => $info) {
    $type_url_str = str_replace('_', '-', $type);
    $label = t('View @type', array('@type' => $info->name));
    $items[] = l($label, 'admin/structure/artworks/manage/' .
              $type_url_str);
  }

  return theme('item_list', array('items' => $items));
}
```

This callback simply gives us an unordered list of all of the artwork types we have available. Each one is presented as a link to the **manage** page for that type. Note that we are converting the artwork type to use dashes instead of underscores in the path. That is a Drupal standard that we will use as well.

```
function artwork_type_page_title($type) {
  return t('Manage @type', array('@type' => $type->name));
}
```

We want the title of each page to be a string based on the type that is passed in, so we need to specify a title callback. The title callback couldn't be simpler:

```
function artwork_information($artwork_type) {
  return $artwork_type->name . ': ' . $artwork_type->description;
}
```

The summary page for each artwork type is trivial as well, at least in our case. A more complex entity type would have various configuration options here in a form, much the way nodes do. In our case, however, we will just show the title and description of the artwork type.

Believe it or not, that's it. Because we're not allowing any other user configuration of artwork types ourselves, setting up that minimal skeleton is all we need to do. However, if the Field UI module is enabled we should see **Manage fields** and **Manage display** tabs when viewing each of those artwork types.

Go to the **Painting** page, then select **Manage** fields. Add a new single-line text field called **Artist**, just as you would for a node. Now go to **Sculpture** and add the now existing **Artist** field to that artwork type.

That's the biggest advantage of making a new data object an entity. All of the power of Fields we get for free that way. Take note that even fields that normally attach to node types are available to us. We can now build up the entire data model of our artworks without writing any additional code, using all of the Field types available to us either in core or in contributed modules.

Adding artworks

Now that we have our artwork types hooked up, we need to be able to create them. Again modeling on the way nodes work let's add the following new entries to our menu hook:

```
function artwork_menu() {
  $items['artwork/add'] = array(
    'title' => 'Add new artwork',
    'page callback' => 'artwork_add_page',
```

```
      'access arguments' => array('create artworks'),
      'weight' => 1,
      'menu_name' => 'management',
      'file' => 'artwork.pages.inc',
  );
  foreach (artwork_types() as $type) {
      $type_url_str = str_replace('_', '-', $type->type);
      $items['artwork/add/' . $type_url_str] = array(
        'title' => $type->name,
        'title callback' => 'check_plain',
        'page callback' => 'artwork_add',
        'page arguments' => array(2),
        'access arguments' => array('create artwork'),
        'description' => $type->description,
      );
  }
  // ...
    return $items;
  }
```

The first menu item creates an index page of artwork types for us to be able to create artwork types. We then loop over all available artwork types and create a menu item for each, converting underscores in each artwork type into dashes. Each menu item's title is the name of the artwork type, but to be safe we run it through the check_plain() function. check_plain() will take whatever is specified in the title and escape any and all HTML in it, making it safe to use as the page title. That's always necessary when displaying a user-generated string as a page title to avoid both security risks and potentially broken pages.

The listing page is fairly simple, but does show a nice feature of the menu system. The following is an example:

```
function artwork_add_page() {
  $item = menu_get_item();
  $links = system_admin_menu_block($item);

  foreach ($links as $link) {
    $items[] = l($link['title'], $link['href'],
                 $item['localized_options'])
              . ': ' . filter_xss_admin($link['description']);
  }

  return theme('item_list', array('items' => $items));
}
```

This page will simply generate a bulleted list of menu items that are immediate children of the current page being viewed. `menu_get_item()` returns the current menu item while `system_admin_menu_block()`, despite its name, is a useful general purpose function for getting the children of an arbitrary menu item.

There are two other points to note here:

- First, the link takes the `localized_options` key of the menu item as its own options array. That way we allow the menu system to handle what attributes the link should have, any interaction with the translation system, and so on.
- Second, we run the description through `filter_xss_admin()`. The function will simply strip out HTML tags that are unsafe. The `filter_xss()` function lets us define an arbitrary list of allowed tags, while `filter_xss_admin()` is simply a wrapper that includes a fairly permissive set of allowed tags.

Adding new artwork

Now we need to provide a form to add our new artworks. We defined a menu callback named `artwork_add` earlier, so let's define that callback.

```
function artwork_add($type) {
  global $user;

  $types = artwork_types();
  $type = isset($type) ? str_replace('-', '_', $type) : NULL;
  if (empty($types[$type])) {
    return MENU_NOT_FOUND;
  }

  $artwork = entity_get_controller('artwork')->create($type);

  drupal_set_title(t('Create @name', array('@name' =>
                    $types[$type]->name)), PASS_THROUGH);
  return drupal_get_form($type . '_artwork_form', $artwork);
}
```

As before, we clean up the artwork type (bundle) name and then if there is no such artwork type we return a **404 not found** error page. Next we create a new, empty artwork object, set a page title, and then display a form.

There are a couple of moving parts here. First is the create method of the controller. The `entity_get_controller()` function creates a new instance of the controller class for artwork entities, which is the `ArtworkController` class we defined earlier. The create method is not part of the normal controller interface but is a really nice addition. It's quite simple:

```
public function create($type = '') {
  return (object) array(
    'aid' => '',
    'type' => $type,
    'title' => '',
  );
}
```

It's easier to define large data structures in PHP as arrays, so we'll do that and cast it back to an object to return it. We can now create a new artwork object from anywhere.

Next is the `PASS_THROUGH` constant we're passing as the second parameter to `drupal_set_title()`. Normally `drupal_set_title` will strip out HTML from the title to avoid security issues. Passing `PASS_THROUGH` as the second parameter tells the function to allow HTML in the string we're giving it because we've already checked to make sure it's safe.

> Use the `PASS_THROUGH` flag with `drupal_set_title()` to allow HTML in the page title. Remember that means it's up to us to sanity check and filter the title to avoid cross-site-scripting attacks.

Finally there's the form. We're giving the form a dynamic name so that `form_alter` implementations may uniquely target a specific artwork type. How then do we match that form name with the form builder function that defines it? Drupal provides another optional hook for us called `hook_forms()` that lets us dynamically define forms and how they should behave.

```
function artwork_forms() {
  $forms = array();
  if ($types = artwork_types()) {
    foreach (array_keys($types) as $type) {
      $forms[$type . '_artwork_form']['callback'] = 'artwork_form';
    }
  }
  return $forms;
}
```

This hook defines a new form on the fly for every artwork type we have, and declares that all of them should use the same callback function, `artwork_form()`. Now all we need is the `artwork_form()` function and all artwork forms will have the same processing.

```
function artwork_form($form, &$form_state, $artwork) {
  // Set the id to identify this as an artwork edit form.
  $form['#id'] = 'artwork-form';

  // Save the artwork for later, in case we need it.
  $form['#artwork'] = $artwork;
  $form_state['artwork'] = $artwork;

  // Common fields. We don't have many.
  $form['title'] = array(
    '#type' => 'textfield',
    '#title' => t('Title'),
    '#default_value' => $artwork->title,
    '#weight' => -5,
    '#required' => TRUE,
  );

  $form['revision'] = array(
    '#access' => user_access('administer artworks'),
    '#type' => 'checkbox',
    '#title' => t('Create new revision'),
    '#default_value' => 0,
  );

  // Add the buttons.
  $form['buttons'] = array();
  $form['buttons']['#weight'] = 100;
  $form['buttons']['submit'] = array(
    '#type' => 'submit',
    '#value' => t('Save'),
    '#weight' => 5,
    '#submit' => array('artwork_form_submit'),
  );
  if (!empty($artwork->aid)) {
    $form['buttons']['delete'] = array(
      '#access' => user_access('delete artworks'),
      '#type' => 'submit',
      '#value' => t('Delete'),
      '#weight' => 15,
```

```
        '#submit' => array('artwork_form_delete_submit'),
    );
}

$form['#validate'][] = 'artwork_form_validate';

field_attach_form('artwork', $artwork, $form, $form_state);

return $form;
}
```

Once again, a fair number of lines but all fairly simple. First we set a fake property on the form so that `form_alter` implementations may detect all artwork forms of any type and stick the artwork object itself into the form in case we need it later in **validate** or **submit** routines. We then add a `form` field for the title and a checkbox to indicate whether we should save a new revision or overwrite the existing revision. We then add not one but two buttons, one that is always available for the **save** operation and another for deleting an artwork if we're editing an existing artwork. More on that later.

The last line is very important. The `field_attach_form()` call is what passes our form off to the Field system so that any fields we've added to this artwork type can be added to the form. Think of it as a Field-specific `form_alter` operation. The form properties that the Field system adds are quite complex, but we don't have to worry about them. They just work.

Validation callback

Similar to the form, the validation callback passes most of its logic off to the Field system.

```
function artwork_form_validate($form, &$form_state) {
    $artwork = $form_state['artwork'];

    // Field validation.
    field_attach_form_validate('artwork', $artwork, $form, $form_state);
}
```

If we had any validation of our own we would include it here, but in this case any validation we'd do (checking for required fields) the Form API already does for us. All we need do is tell the Field system to do its own validation.

Submit callback

The submit callback is a little more interesting but not by much:

```
function artwork_form_submit($form, &$form_state) {
  global $user;

  $artwork = &$form_state['artwork'];

  // Set the artwork's uid if it's being created at this time.
  if (empty($artwork->uid)) {
    $artwork->uid = $user->uid;
  }

  $artwork->title = $form_state['values']['title'];
  $artwork->revision = $form_state['values']['revision'];

  // Notify field widgets.
  field_attach_submit('artwork', $artwork, $form, $form_state);

  // Save the artwork.
  artwork_save($artwork);

  // Notify the user.
  drupal_set_message(t('Artwork saved.'));

  $form_state['redirect'] = 'artwork/' . $artwork->aid;
}
```

First we pull the old artwork object out of the `$form_state` variable. Next we set its user, if it's a new artwork, and populate it with the few values we have from the form. We've already confirmed that those values are valid in the validation hook. `field_attach_submit()`, much like its sibling functions, lets the Field system respond to the fact that a form was just submitted and do whatever it wants to do. Then we simply save the artwork.

It is important to note here that the submit callback is doing extremely little. It's just glue code between the form and the `artwork_save()` function, really. That's a good thing. It means that artwork operations, such as saving, are not dependent on the form system.

 Never do serious processing in a form submit callback. The actual work of saving an entity and its data should happen in the entity's save routines. The form submit callback is just glue code.

Saving your artwork

What does `artwork_save()` look like, though? Like `artwork_load()` it's really just a thin wrapper:

```
function artwork_save($artwork) {
  return entity_get_controller('artwork')->save($artwork);
}
```

Once again, we let the controller class do the hard work. The `save()` method itself is actually broken into two parts, one for normal saving and one for revisions.

```
public function save($artwork) {
  $transaction = db_transaction();

  try {
    global $user;

    // Determine if we will be inserting a new artwork.
    $artwork->is_new = empty($artwork->aid);

    // Set the timestamp fields.
    if (empty($artwork->created)) {
      $artwork->created = REQUEST_TIME;
    }
    $artwork->changed = REQUEST_TIME;

    $artwork->revision_timestamp = REQUEST_TIME;
    $update_artwork = TRUE;

    // Give modules the opportunity to prepare field data for
    // saving.
    field_attach_presave('artwork', $artwork);

    if (!$artwork->is_new && !empty($artwork->revision) &&
        $artwork->vid) {
      $artwork->old_vid = $artwork->vid;
      unset($artwork->vid);
    }

    // If this is a new artwork...
    if ($artwork->is_new) {
      // Save the new artwork.
      drupal_write_record('artwork', $artwork);
```

```
      // Save the initial revision.
      $this->saveRevision($artwork, $user->uid);

      $op = 'insert';
    }
    else {
      // Save the updated artwork.
      drupal_write_record('artwork', $artwork, 'aid');

      if (!empty($artwork->revision)) {
        $this->saveRevision($artwork, $user->uid);
      }
      else {
        $this->saveRevision($artwork, $user->uid, TRUE);
        $update_artwork = FALSE;
      }

      $op = 'update';
    }

    // If the revision ID is new or updated, save it to the artwork.
    if ($update_artwork) {
      db_update('artwork')
        ->fields(array('vid' => $artwork->vid))
        ->condition('aid', $artwork->aid)
        ->execute();
    }

    // Save fields.
    $function = 'field_attach_' . $op;
    $function('artwork', $artwork);

    module_invoke_all('entity_' . $op, $artwork, 'artwork');

    // Clear internal properties.
    unset($artwork->is_new);

    // Ignore slave server temporarily to give time for the saved
    // order to be propagated to the slave.
    db_ignore_slave();

    return $artwork;
  }
```

```
    catch (Exception $e) {
      $transaction->rollback();
      watchdog_exception('artwork', $e, NULL, WATCHDOG_ERROR);
      return FALSE;
    }
  }
```

Most of the save routine is self-explanatory, and much of it is specific to the properties we've declared on our entity. A few parts bear further discussion, however.

We're wrapping the entire process in a PHP try-catch block. That's because the save process could be arbitrarily complex, involving a number of queries, any of which could, potentially, break. We therefore start a database transaction with the db_transaction() function. Transactions allow multiple database queries to either all succeed or all fail together. Any queries that run, from anywhere, between the db_transaction() call and when the $transaction variable goes out of scope at the end of the function will be part of that transaction.

If any queries, anywhere, fail, the database will throw an Exception. (There are other reasons an Exception could be thrown, too, but that is the most common.) In that case, we roll back the entire transaction with the rollback() method. Any queries that had already run get undone, and the entire save process effectively does not happen. That keeps us from ending up with a half-saved artwork, which requires manually editing the database to clean up. We also log the exception using a special utility function that decodes useful information from the exception for us.

Note that transactions are not available if using MySQL's MyISAM database tables. In that case code will still function but any attempt to roll back a transaction will be ignored and the database will still be left in a potentially unstable state. For that reason, when running on MySQL Drupal defaults to InnoDB tables, which support transactions.

Once we're done saving the artwork, we also call db_ignore_slave(). If we're running a high-traffic site then we may have both a master database and one or more slave databases configured, something Drupal supports natively. However, there may be a latency before our artwork gets propagated from the master server to the slave server. We therefore tell Drupal that, for the current user only, it should skip the slave server for a few minutes so that the user that submitted the artwork will see it immediately, even if there is a brief delay for other users.

> Master/slave database configurations are an advanced topic that we won't cover in detail. However, Drupal transparently falls back to single-database behavior if no slave is defined so it's always good to plan ahead for supporting a master/slave configuration.

Once again there are multiple points where we call the Fields system to let it do its part with our entity, which again should be self-explanatory. We also call `module_invoke_all()` in order to allow other modules to interact with any entity when they are created or updated.

Handling revisions

The only other complex part of the process involves revision handling, which can be a bit hard to wrap our head around. Looking at the `saveRevision()` method may help:

```
function saveRevision($artwork, $uid, $update = FALSE) {
  // Hold on to the artwork's original creator_uid but swap
  // in the revision's creator_uid for the momentary write.
  $temp_uid = $artwork->uid;
  $artwork->uid = $uid;

  if ($update) {
    drupal_write_record('artwork_revision', $artwork, 'vid');
  }
  else {
    drupal_write_record('artwork_revision', $artwork);
  }

  // Reset the order's creator_uid to the original value.
  $artwork->uid = $temp_uid;
}
```

After we've saved the artwork to the artwork table, we also save it to the artwork_revision table. If we're creating a new revision, we'll save a new record to the table and `drupal_write_record()` will populate the `vid` property for us with the new version ID. Then, back in `save()`, we update the record in the artwork table to point to the new revision record. If we just overwrote the old revision record then that step is not necessary.

That's it! We can now create new artwork objects straight from the UI with a simple form, including whatever Fields we've decided to attach to our artworks. Not only that, but since we put the saving logic in the controller rather than in the form submit callback we can easily create new artworks programmatically; we need only create a new artwork object with the properties we want and call `artwork_save()`.

Viewing artworks

The last line of our form submit handler redirected the user to the `artwork/$aid` page, presumably to view the artwork we just created. That would be great if there was a page there to display the artwork. Let's add that now.

First we need an appropriate menu item:

```
function artwork_menu() {
  $items['artwork/%artwork'] = array(
    'title callback' => 'artwork_page_title',
    'title arguments' => array(1),
    'page callback' => 'artwork_page_view',
    'page arguments' => array(1),
    'access arguments' => array('view artworks'),
    'type' => MENU_CALLBACK,
  );
  $items['artwork/%artwork/view'] = array(
    'title' => 'View',
    'type' => MENU_DEFAULT_LOCAL_TASK,
    'weight' => -10,
  );
  // ...
}
```

We are planning ahead for adding more tabs ("local tasks") later, but we definitely want the **View** tab to be the default. The menu item defines a `title callback` and `page callback`, both of which are reasonably straightforward.

```
function artwork_page_title($artwork) {
  return $artwork->title;
}
function artwork_page_view($artwork, $view_mode = 'full') {
  // Remove previously built content, if exists.
  $artwork->content = array();

  if ($view_mode == 'teaser') {
    $artwork->content['title'] = array(
      '#markup' => filter_xss($artwork->title),
      '#weight' => -5,
    );
  }

  // Build fields content.
  field_attach_prepare_view('artwork',
```

```
                          array($artwork->aid => $artwork),
                          $view_mode);
      entity_prepare_view('artwork', array($artwork->aid => $artwork));
      $artwork->content += field_attach_view('artwork', $artwork,
                                      $view_mode);


      return $artwork->content;
    }
```

The `title` `callback` needs no explanation. The `artwork_page_view()` function again doesn't do much beyond shepherd data off to the Field API. In particular, note that it does take a `$view_mode` parameter, which should be one of the view modes we defined back in the `artwork_entity_info()`. Even if we don't want to leverage it ourselves the Field system will require it.

If we're in "teaser" mode, we want to inject the title of the artwork into the viewable result. If not, we have no data to display other than the attached fields as the title is already being displayed as the page title. The field code is a fairly boilerplate three lines of code that produce a renderable array, which we simply return.

That wasn't so hard, was it?

Editing an artwork

Now that we have artworks we can see, we want to be able to go back and edit them. Fortunately most of the work we already did as part of the creation process. In fact, we're going to reuse the same form and same `save()` method of the controller. All we really need to add is the page callback to use it.

```
    function artwork_menu() {
      $items['artwork/%artwork/edit'] = array(
        'title' => 'Edit',
        'page callback' => 'artwork_page_edit',
        'page arguments' => array(1),
        'access arguments' => array('update artworks'),
        'weight' => 0,
        'type' => MENU_LOCAL_TASK,
        'context' => MENU_CONTEXT_PAGE | MENU_CONTEXT_INLINE,
      );

      // ...
    }
    function artwork_page_edit($artwork) {
      $types = artwork_types();
```

```
    drupal_set_title(t('<em>Edit @type</em> @title', array('@type' =>
    $types[$artwork->type]->name, '@title' => $artwork->title)),
    PASS_THROUGH);

    return drupal_get_form($artwork->type . '_artwork_form', $artwork);
}
```

The edit page callback is simple enough that we could almost get away with not having it at all and just calling the form directly from the menu system. However, since the form name is dynamic based on the artwork type we have to have a small function here. Note too that we're setting a dynamic title and again allowing HTML through.

That's it! The form we built earlier handles both new and existing artworks just the same, so editing an artwork, including saving new revisions, is done.

Deleting an artwork

The final missing piece is the ability to delete an artwork. Naturally we don't want to let users do so on a whim, so we'll give them a confirmation form.

Recall earlier that in our artwork edit form we had a **Delete** button with its own submit handler. First we need to define that submit handler:

```
function artwork_form_delete_submit($form, &$form_state) {
  $destination = array();
  if (isset($_GET['destination'])) {
    $destination = drupal_get_destination();
    unset($_GET['destination']);
  }
  $artwork = $form['#artwork'];
  $form_state['redirect'] = array('artwork/' . $artwork->aid . '/
delete', array('query' => $destination));
}
```

All this submit handler does is redirect the user to `artwork/$aid/delete`. The rest of the code there is simply to handle Drupal's page redirect system, which we can largely copy and paste. At that path we'll put a confirmation form so that users have to confirm they really mean to delete an artwork:

```
function artwork_menu() {
  $items['artwork/%artwork/delete'] = array(
    'title' => 'Delete',
    'page callback' => 'drupal_get_form',
    'page arguments' => array('artwork_delete_confirm', 1),
```

```
      'access arguments' => array('delete artworks'),
      'weight' => 1,
      'type' => MENU_LOCAL_TASK,
      'context' => MENU_CONTEXT_INLINE,
    );

    // ...
}
```

This menu item calls `drupal_get_form` directly, specifically loading the `artwork_delete_confirm` form created by the function of the same name:

```
function artwork_delete_confirm($form, &$form_state, $artwork) {
  $form['#artwork'] = $artwork;
  // Always provide entity id in the same form key as in the entity
edit form.
  $form['aid'] = array('#type' => 'value', '#value' => $artwork->aid);
  return confirm_form($form,
    t('Are you sure you want to delete %title?', array('%title' =>
$artwork->title)),
    'artwork/' . $artwork->aid,
    t('This action cannot be undone.'),
    t('Delete'),
    t('Cancel')
  );
}
```

Rather than build a complete form, we will simply pass data on to a utility function of the Form API called `confirm_form()`. `confirm_form()` takes a number of parameters: a form array, a question to ask, a path to redirect to if the user changes his mind, a label for the **Yes I mean it** button, and a label for the **No, I changed my mind** link.

The only form information we need is the artwork to be deleted. Neither will be displayed but we need to pass them along to the submit callback. The rest of the parameters are simply text to display to the user.

If the user submits the confirmation form, then we know he really means it. The submit callback handles deleting the artwork:

```
function artwork_delete_confirm_submit($form, &$form_state) {
  if ($form_state['values']['confirm']) {
    $artwork = artwork_load($form_state['values']['aid']);
    artwork_delete($form_state['values']['aid']);
```

```
        watchdog('artwork', '@type: deleted %title.', array('@type' =>
    $artwork->type, '%title' => $artwork->title));

        $types = artwork_types();
        drupal_set_message(t('@type %title has been deleted.', array(
                            '@type' => $types[$artwork->type]->name,
                            '%title' => $artwork->title)));
    }

    $form_state['redirect'] = '<front>';
}
```

Just to be certain, we first confirm that the `$form_state['values']['confirm']` property is set to TRUE. If so, the first thing we need to do is load the artwork. That's not really necessary for the deletion operation but we need the artwork object for displaying messages to the user and recording log messages. Then all we do is call `artwork_delete()`.

It should be no surprise that `artwork_delete()` is another simple wrapper:

```
function artwork_delete($aid) {
  return artwork_delete_multiple(array($aid));
}
function artwork_delete_multiple($aids) {
  return entity_get_controller('artwork')->delete($aids);
}
```

Like loading, deletion is a multi-value operation. We can delete an arbitrary number of artworks in one operation, and one is just a special case of many. The heavy lifting is again handed off to the controller:

```
public function delete($aids) {
  if (!empty($aids)) {
    $artworks = $this->load($aids, array());
    $transaction = db_transaction();

    try {
      db_delete('artwork')
        ->condition('aid', $aids, 'IN')
        ->execute();

      db_delete('artwork_revision')
        ->condition('aid', $aids, 'IN')
        ->execute();
```

```
      foreach ($artworks as $artwork_id => $artwork) {
        field_attach_delete('artwork', $artwork);
      }

      db_ignore_slave();
    }
    catch (Exception $e) {
      $transaction->rollback();
      watchdog_exception('artwork', $e, NULL, WATCHDOG_ERROR);
      return FALSE;
    }

    module_invoke_all('entity_delete', $artwork, 'artwork');

    // Clear the page and block and artwork caches.
    cache_clear_all();
    $this->resetCache();
  }

  return TRUE;
}
```

Once again we use a transaction to ensure that the entire deletion process either
succeeds or fails. We first load the artwork objects that we are about to delete,
as other operations will require them. We then handle our own deletion logic:
Removing the appropriate records from the artwork and artwork_revision tables. We
then call `field_attach_delete()` to let the Field system remove any field data that
was associated with those artworks, and finally disable the slave server as before.

There's one other task to take care of; we need to flush the cache. By default Drupal
caches most page requests for performance. If we've deleted an artwork, however,
we need to remove that page from the cache. There may be many other pages
affected by that deletion, however, so we simply clear the entire page cache with
`cache_clear_all()`. It will get rebuilt as needed. We also clear the static cache
of loaded artwork objects that the controller maintains so that if later in this same
request someone tries to load the artwork we just deleted they get an error rather
than a ghost object.

And we're done!

Summary

This has been quite a chapter. Not only have we learned how to create our own entities in Drupal, we have expanded our knowledge of many of Drupal's key systems.

- We've seen how to define new entities and encapsulate their loading and saving routines into a controller class.

- We've seen how to integrate our entity with the Field API, providing site administrators with enormous flexibility and power to build custom data models.

- We've learned how to define new tables in Drupal's database in a database-agnostic fashion.

- We've learned about database transactions, a simple way to ensure that a complex database operation succeeds completely or fails completely to avoid data corruption.

- We've learned about how to avoid stale data issues when using master/slave replication.

- We've seen how to display confirmation forms to users to ensure they didn't click a button by accident.

- We've learned how to have dynamically named forms which are built using the same process.

- We've seen how to leverage Drupal's autoloading capability for classes to help keep code size down.

As noted at the start of the chapter, in many cases a custom entity will not need the full life cycle of creation, editing, and deletion. Some may not even interact with Drupal's local database at all, relying on a `load()` method that calls out to a ReST service or SOAP server. We may need to define a complex set of permission controls for our custom entity, or in some cases there may not even be a way for users to view an entity directly.

By looking at a complete example, however, we have got a feel for most of the pieces we could implement if we needed to. Since our artwork example closely parallels the node entity type, although in a simplified form, it helps to provide a context for how the all-important node system works in Drupal.

7
Creating New Fields

In the last chapter we saw how to define new entities. The main advantage of defining our content as an entity, of course, was to make it accessible to the **Field API**. In this chapter, we will look at how fields work and how to define new fields to attach to either our own entities or to those already defined, such as nodes.

Along the way we'll cover:

- What Field API is and what it does
- How to use magic callbacks
- Using fields to store data
- Using widgets to hook fields into the **Form API**
- Using formatters to control the display of fields

When we're done, you should have an understanding of how all the key pieces of Drupal's main data handling system fit together and how to leverage them best.

Our goal: a "dimensions" field

In the last chapter, we created a new type of entity called **Artwork**. As a fieldable entity, we can attach any field we want to it. Sometimes though, we'll still need to create our own field types. That may happen if we want to treat a given piece of information atomically rather than building it up out of smaller parts. There are many reasons why that could be the case. They are as follows:

1. We want to conceptually treat that piece of data as a single chunk with its own meaning rather than as a series of chunks that together we know has meaning.
2. We have complex data but want to have multiple instances of that data on a single entity.

3. We want to present a unified custom interface to users while editing that data, especially if it is multi-value.

4. We want to display the data to the user in a custom format.

All of these are reasons why we may want to write our own field code.

In our case, we are dealing with artworks. Artworks have dimensions, either height and width, or height, width, and depth. Although we certainly could just add three numeric fields to our artwork bundles and call it a day, that is not very attractive either for the content editor or for site viewers. It gets even uglier if we want to allow multi-value fields; say if a given artwork is a collection of small statues or a series of similar paintings.

We will therefore define a new type of field to store dimensions, either height and width, or height, width, and depth. Although in our case we are talking about works of art, the field itself would apply just as well to cars, buildings, animals, or any other content that represents an object that takes up space. A good field type is generic enough to fit many different situations.

How Field API works

As hinted above, there are several different complementary parts to defining a field:

- **Field type**: this is strictly speaking, just the content definition. It defines the name of the field and what its inner data structure is, but not how to save it or how to display it.

- **Field**: this is a particular configuration of a field type.

- **Field instance**: this is the combination of a particular field with a bundle or subclass of an entity type

- **Widget**: this is a form element that exposes the field to a content editor. It could use simple text fields or be something as complex as an interactive Flash-based tool.

- **Formatter**: this is a piece of code that formats a field for display on screen. Typically it just wraps Drupal's theme system to do so.

Note that nowhere in any of the parts mentioned do we define how or where the data gets stored. That is handled by a field storage engine, which can be configured separately per field. By default all fields use a common storage engine that saves fields to Drupal's database. That's good enough for our needs, so we won't go into field storage engines in depth.

Although an advanced topic, **pluggable field storage** is one of the major new features of the Field API and is another option for handling remote data sources in Drupal.

Creating our new field type

Field types are defined by modules, so let's start by creating a new module called `dimfield.module`. Its info file is as follows:

```
name = Dimensions field
description = A Field offering height, width, and depth
package = Drupal 7 Development
core = 7.x
files[] = dimfield.module
```

Declaring the field

Now in `dimfield.module`, we need to implement `hook_field_info()`, which is how we tell Drupal about our new field type.

```
function dimfield_field_info() {
  return array(
    'dimensions' => array(
      'label' => t('Dimensions'),
      'description' => t(
                'This field stores a height and width, and depth.'),
      'settings' => array('num_dimensions' => 2),
      'instance_settings' => array(
        'max_height' => 0,
        'max_width' => 0,
        'max_depth' => 0,
      ),
      'default_widget' => 'dimfield_combined',
      'default_formatter' => 'dimfield_default',
    ),
  );
}
```

Like most "info hooks", this function returns a large definition array, defining one or more fields. Also as we would expect, there is a corresponding `hook_field_info_alter()` hook. In our case, we just have the one called `dimensions`. Let's look at each property in turn:

- `label` and `description` specify the human-readable name and explanation of this field.

- `settings` defines an array of configuration options for the field and their default values. These settings are fixed and after we create an instance of a field cannot be changed, so use with caution. Generally you only want field settings if changing the setting would affect how data gets saved.

- `instance_settings` is the same as the settings array, except that it can be changed after a field has been created. That makes it generally preferred over field-level settings.

- `default_widget` and `default_formatter` specify what widget and formatter Drupal should use for a given field before the user specifies one. Like fields, widgets and formatters have unique string names. We'll talk about how to write those later in this chapter.

The above code tells Drupal that there is a new field type called dimensions defined by our `dimfield` module, and gives a little metadata about it. However, Drupal still needs to know how that field is put together. For that, we implement a couple of other hooks.

Defining the field structure

Actually, no, we don't. Although called hooks in the Drupal documentation, these functions are pseudo-hooks: magically named module callbacks that are called individually by Drupal rather than together with that hook as used by all modules. Since our module is named `dimfield`, the supporting code for all of the field types we define in the `dimfield` module will live together in the same magic callback. For that reason, it's generally a good idea to not define too many field types in a single module as the code may get unwieldy. We also use a different name for the module and for the field type to help keep track of when we need to use which.

> A magic module callback, or pseudo-hook, looks like a hook, but is called individually rather than alongside implementations from all other active modules.

The most important magic callback for a field type is the schema callback, its definition can be seen in the following example:

```
function dimfield_field_schema($field) {
  if ($field['type'] == 'dimensions') {
    $schema['columns']['height'] = array(
      'type' => 'int',
      'not null' => FALSE,
    );
    $schema['columns']['width'] = array(
      'type' => 'int',
      'not null' => FALSE,
    );

    $schema['indexes'] = array(
      'height' => array('height'),
      'width' => array('width'),
    );

    if ($field['settings']['num_dimensions'] == 3) {
        $schema['columns']['depth'] = array(
          'type' => 'int',
          'not null' => FALSE,
        );
        $schema['indexes']['depth'] = array('depth');
    }

    $schema['columns']['units'] = array(
      'type' => 'varchar',
      'length' => 10,
      'not null' => FALSE,
    );

    return $schema;
  }
}
```

As we would expect from a name like `hook_field_schema()`, its return value is a Drupal schema array. Although fields will not always be saved in an SQL database, they usually are, and it's a convenient syntax to reuse. Note that in this case, we define two database columns, for height and width, and possibly a third for depth if our field is configured to have three dimensions. (We will skip over supporting four or five dimensions for now as it is an edge case.) The difference in the data structure is the reason the number of dimensions are a field setting rather than a field instance setting.

Since measurements of length do not really make sense without a unit, we will also record what unit the dimensions are in, such as inches or meters. To keep things simple we will only save integers, although in practice we would want to support float values. Also note that the whole function is wrapped in an `if()` statement to check for the field type. If we were defining multiple field types in this module, they would define their schema using the same function and we'd have to differentiate between them based on the value of `$field['type']`.

Defining empty

The second magic callback we need is to determine if a given field has an empty value. While that may seem like a simple question, it is actually dependent on our particular application.

Consider this: Is a dimension field empty if it has no height but only has a width, or only if both values are empty? Drupal doesn't know which we mean, so we need to tell it.

```
function dimfield_field_is_empty($item, $field) {
  if ($field['type'] == 'dimensions') {
    if (empty($item['height']) && empty($item['width']) &&
       ($field['settings']['num_dimensions'] == 2 ||
        empty($item['depth'])))
    {
      return TRUE;
    }
  }
  return FALSE;
}
```

In the preceding snippet, we define `empty` to mean that all dimensions in use are an empty value, which PHP defines to include an empty string or `0`. Again note that we are checking against the specific field type since we could add another field type to this module later.

Field settings

Although not absolutely required, we also need a configuration form for the field settings. Most fields will be configured through Drupal's web interface, so we need a form to allow users to set the available options. That's another magic callback. Let's look at an example:

```
function dimfield_field_settings_form($field, $instance, $has_data) {
  if ($field['type'] == 'dimensions') {
    $settings = $field['settings'];
    $form['num_dimensions'] = array(
```

```
        '#type' => 'select',
        '#title' => t('How many dimensions'),
        '#options' => array(
          2 => t('Height and width'),
          3 => t('Height, width, and depth'),
        ),
        '#default_value' => $settings['num_dimensions'],
        '#required' => FALSE,
        '#description' => t(
            'Is this for a 2-dimensional or 3-dimensional object?'),
      );
    return $form;
    }
  }
```

We only have a single form element here, that is, a select box that lets the user select whether we're dealing with a 2-dimensional or 3-dimensional object. It is this value that will determine the structure of the field itself, as defined in the schema callback.

Field validation

Although there are a couple of other callbacks we could implement, there's only one that we will cover for now, as it is rather important, namely, validation.

```
function dimfield_field_validate($obj_type, $object, $field,
                                 $instance, $langcode, &$items,
                                 &$errors) {
  if ($field['type'] == 'dimensions')'' {
    $columns = array(
      'height' => 'max_height',
      'width' => 'max_width',
    );
    if ($field['settings']['num_dimensions'] == 3) {
      $columns['depth'] = 'max_depth';
    }
    foreach ($items as $delta => $item) {
      foreach ($columns as $column => $max_key) {
        if ($instance['settings'][$max_key] &&
            !empty($item[$column]) &&
            $item[$column] > $instance['settings'][$max_key]) {
          $errors[$field['field_name']][$delta][] = array(
            'error' => 'dimfield_' . $max_key,
            'message' => t(
                '%name: The %column may not be larger than %max.',
                    array('%column' => $column,
                        '%name' => $instance['label'],
```

```
                                        '%max' => $instance['settings'][$max_key],
                                        ''x)
                          ),
                  );
              }
          }
        }
      }
    }
```

Just as all fields can be validated individually, so can all form elements. However, recall that fields can be saved from anywhere in code. We may not be using a form at all. We therefore must validate the field data itself, before we save it to the database. In this case, we're checking to make sure that if the dimension has a value, and if a maximum was set for it, it is within that maximum limit. If it's not, then we set an error in the $errors array, which is passed in by reference. That error consists of, naturally, an array of possible errors. It is up to the calling code to decide how to handle that error condition. It could show a message on screen if the error happens from a user form, or could send an invalid message object back over an SOAP connection if the field (and the entity it's attached to) is being saved by code triggered by a remote server.

> For more extensive information on each of the parameters to the Field API callback functions, see the examples in the field.api. php file in the field module.

Another important point to note here is that field is passed an array of items, not an individual item. From a code perspective, fields in Drupal are always multi-value. Even if there is only one value, even if the field is configured to only allow one value, it is still multi-value as far as our code is concerned. "One" is simply a special case of "many". That actually greatly simplifies most of our logic, as we don't need to handle two different possible cases. We can simply iterate with a foreach() loop over our data, and we will handle one or a hundred values equally well.

> Remember that fields in Drupal are always a multi-value array in code. That array may have only one entry, but it can still be treated as an arbitrarily large number of values.

Again, notice that nowhere in the field type definition or supporting code do we actually save data. In fact, there's not a single SQL query. We are simply describing the data. Saving the data itself, and deciding where to save it, is the responsibility of the core system. That allows a great deal of flexibility, as our dimension field can now be used to store data in a local SQL database or a remote SOAP server without any code changes on our part.

Exposing fields to the Form API with widgets

Although fields can be stored anywhere (or at least anywhere for which we write a storage engine) and accessed in a variety of ways, by far the most common user workflow is to create and edit an entity containing fields using a form embedded in a web page. In Drupal, all forms shown to the user are controlled by the Form API, introduced in *Chapter 5*. The way the field system exposes itself to the Form API is through widgets.

Widgets are simply Form API fragments that can get built into a larger form by Drupal. They can be very simple or very complex, depending on how we want to present information to the user. In fact, some of the greatest powers of widgets comes from the fact that the form elements the widget exposes do not have to map to the storage of the field type itself at all. Imagine, for example, a field that stored geographic points. While we could simply offer the user a series of text fields to enter X and Y values, it would be much nicer if we could offer them an interactive map to click on. The coordinate data would then get mapped back into X and Y values before it's stored, without the field itself being any the wiser. With widgets, we can do exactly that.

Declaring a widget

As with field types, widgets start with an info hook:

```
function dimfield_field_widget_info() {
  return array(
    'dimfield_simple' => array(
      'label' => t('Separate text fields'),
      'description' => t(
               'Allow the user to enter each dimension separately.'),
      'field types' => array('dimensions'),
      'behaviors' => array(
        'multiple values' => FIELD_BEHAVIOR_DEFAULT,
        'default value' => FIELD_BEHAVIOR_DEFAULT,
      ),
    ),
    'dimfield_combined' => array(
      'label' => t('Combined text field'),
      'description' => t(
               'Allow the user to enter all dimensions together.'),
      'field types' => array('dimensions'),
      'settings' => array('size' => 10),
```

```
        'behaviors' => array(
          'multiple values' => FIELD_BEHAVIOR_DEFAULT,
          'default value' => FIELD_BEHAVIOR_DEFAULT,
        ),
      ),
    );
}
```

In the preceding snippet, we are defining two widgets rather than just one. The first is a simple widget, consisting of simple text fields, one for each dimension. In the second, we offer only a single text field into which the user will enter all two or three dimensions in H×W×D format.

Both widgets explicitly specify the field types that they will work on. Although we are defining these widgets in the same module as the field type, that doesn't necessarily imply a relationship between them. In fact, any module may define widgets that work with any field type. The widget just needs to know how that field type wants its data. The second widget also includes a settings array, which allows us to configure the widget per-instance.

Also note the behaviors property. By default, widgets will handle only a single field value and Drupal itself will offer a dynamic way to add additional values from within the form. However, we can also tell Drupal to let our widget handle multi-value fields in case, for example, we want to offer a clickable map for multi-value coordinates we discussed earlier.

Simple widget forms

Let's look at the simple widget first, and then come back and look at the more complex one. The only callback we must define for a widget is its form callback, which defines the form fields that make up the widget. Let's look at an example:

```
function dimfield_field_widget_form(&$form, &$form_state, $field,
                                    $instance, $langcode, $items,
                                    $delta, $element) {
  $base = $element;

  if ($instance['widget']['type'] == 'dimfield_simple') {
    $element['height'] = array(
      '#type' => 'textfield',
      '#title' => t('Height'),
      '#default_value' => isset($items[$delta]['height']) ?
                          $items[$delta]['height'] : NULL,
    ) + $base;
```

```
    $element['width'] = array(
      '#type' => 'textfield',
      '#title' => t('Width'),
      '#default_value' => isset($items[$delta]['width']) ?
                          $items[$delta]['width'] : NULL,
    ) + $base;

    if ($field['settings']['num_dimensions'] == 3) {
      $element['depth'] = array(
        '#type' => 'textfield',
        '#title' => t('Depth'),
        '#default_value' => isset($items[$delta]['depth']) ?
                            $items[$delta]['depth'] : NULL,
      ) + $base;
    }

    $element['units'] = array(
      '#type' => 'select',
      '#title' => t('Units'),
      '#default_value' => isset($items[$delta]['units']) ?
                          $items[$delta]['units'] : NULL,
      '#options' => dimfield_units(),
      );
  }

  return $element;
}
```

Once again, notice that we're checking for which widget we are using in this
callback, since both widgets will use the same callback. Our parameters include
the form that this widget will be added to and its `$form_state`. Although they are
passed by reference, we will not actually be modifying them directly (most of the
time). Instead, we will return an `$element` Form API fragment that Drupal will
insert into the form in the correct place. The `$element` that is passed in contains basic
information about the widget itself, which we will store in our own variable to pass
forward. The Form API will ignore properties it doesn't recognize, but that data will
be available to us later.

In this simple case, all we're doing is creating two or three form elements for the dimensions, one for each dimension, and a select box to set the units. The available units are provided by a simple utility function that we also write:

```
function dimfield_units($unit = NULL) {
  static $units;

  if (empty($units)) {
    $units = array(
      'inches' => t('Inches'),
      'feet' => t('Feet'),
      'meters' => t('Meters'),
    );
  }

  if ($unit) {
    return isset($units[$unit]) ? $units[$unit] : '';
  }

  return $units;
}
```

That little utility function lets us get a consistent list of units we support anywhere we need it, plus it provides an easy mapping from the "internal name" of a unit to a translated human-friendly name.

It is important to note that the form elements we're creating are named exactly the same as the columns of the dimensions field. Drupal needs the "processed form" value to have the exact same "form element" names as the field columns so that it can save them properly. What makes this a simple widget is that the form maps one-to-one to the field definition, so we don't need to do any extra processing. At this point, we are in essence done. Users will be able to select our widget, Drupal will handle the multi-value logic for us, and save the data to the field, all without further interaction from us.

Complex widgets

Let's now look at the more complex widget. In this case, we will show all dimensions together in a single text field so that the user need only fill in a single field.

First off, because our more complex widget has settings that we need to implement, we use the `widget_settings_form` callback, given as follows:

```
function dimfield_field_widget_settings_form($field, $instance) {
  $form = array();

  $widget = $instance['widget'];
  $settings = $widget['settings'];
```

```
    if ($widget['type'] == 'dimfield_combined') {
      $form['size'] = array(
        '#type' => 'textfield',
        '#title' => t('Size of textfield'),
        '#default_value' => $settings['size'],
        '#required' => TRUE,
        '#element_validate' =>
                    array('_element_validate_integer_positive'),
      );
    }


    return $form;
  }
```

As with all of our other callbacks, we check the widget type and then return a form fragment for the field we want. Note that the textfield is named the same as the setting property we defined in `dimfield_field_widget_info()`, which is how Drupal knows which setting is which. We also are leveraging the Form API's ability to provide element-specific validators. In this case, we are using a validation callback that Drupal provides. It will throw a validation error if the user specifies anything other than a positive integer. (A widget size of -7.4 would not make much sense, would it?)

Now, we can expand our `field_widget_form` callback to include our new widget.

```
function dimfield_field_widget_form(&$form, &$form_state, $field,
                                    $instance, $langcode, $items,
                                    $delta, $element) {
  $base = $element;

  if ($instance['widget']['type'] == 'dimfield_simple') {
    // ...
  }
  elseif ($instance['widget']['type'] == 'dimfield_combined') {
    $element['#element_validate'] = array(
                                '_dimfield_combined_validate');

    $default = NULL;
    if (isset($items[$delta])) {
      $item = $items[$delta];
      if (isset($item['height'], $item['width'])) {
        $default = $item['height'] . 'x' . $item['width'];
        if ($field['settings']['num_dimensions'] == 3) {
          $default .= 'x' . $item['depth'];
        }
```

```
      }
    }

    $element['dimfield_combined_wrapper']['#theme'] =
                              'dimfield_combined_wrapper';

    $element['dimfield_combined_wrapper']['height_width_depth'] =
      array('#type' => 'textfield',
            '#default_value' => $default,
            '#size' => $instance['widget']['settings']['size'],
            ) + $base;

    $element['dimfield_combined_wrapper']['units'] = array(
      '#type' => 'select',
      '#title' => t('Units'),
      '#default_value' => isset($items[$delta]['units']) ?
                          $items[$delta]['units'] : NULL,
      '#options' => dimfield_units(),
    );
  }

  return $element;
}
```

In the first block of code, we assemble our default value for the form element out of the values available in the field. Since our widget is only handling a single instance, we have to check for just this one delta to see if we have a value defined. If so, we concatenate the height, width, and potential depth together with an × between them.

Then we set up our two form elements. One is our combined height, width, and depth text field and the other is the units, as we've seen before. The most important part, however, is that very first line:

```
$element['#element_validate'] = array('_dimfield_combined_validate');
```

Just as we specified an existing validation callback for a text field a moment ago, this time we will specify a custom validation callback. However, we won't be using it just for validation. Rather, we will be using it to modify the submitted form values. Let's have a look at that function given here:

```
function _dimfield_combined_validate($element, &$form_state) {
  // This function is also called when submitting the field
  // configuration form. If so, skip validation as it
  // won't work anyway.
  if ($form_state['complete form']['#form_id'] ==
```

```
                                      'field_ui_field_edit_form') {
    return;
  }


  $values = $form_state['values'];
  $language = $values['language'];
  $field_name = $element['#field_name'];


  $num_dimensions = 2;
  if (array_search('depth', $element['#columns'])) {
    $num_dimensions = 3;
  }


  foreach ($values[$field_name][$language] as $delta => $item) {
    if (substr_count($item['dimfield_combined_wrapper']['height_width_
depth'], 'x') == $num_dimensions - 1) {
      if ($num_dimensions == 2) {
        list($height, $width) = explode('x', $item['dimfield_combined_
wrapper']['height_width_depth']);
        $new_values = array(
          'height' => trim($height),
          'width' => trim($width),
          'units' => $item['dimfield_combined_wrapper']['units'],
        );
      }
      elseif ($num_dimensions == 3) {
        list($height, $width, $depth) = explode('x',
        $item['dimfield_combined_wrapper']['height_width_depth']);
        $new_values = array(
          'height' => trim($height),
          'width' => trim($width),
          'depth' => trim($depth),
          'units' => $item['dimfield_combined_wrapper']['units'],
        );
      }


    form_set_value($element, $new_values, $form_state);
    }
    else {
      form_set_error($field_name, t('You must specify all dimensions,
separated by an \'x\'.'));
    }
  }
}
```

During the validation phase of the form submission, this function will be called with the element it is attached to (the `height_width_depth` element) and the `$form_state` variable, which is passed by reference so that we can modify it. The first thing we check is that we're not displaying this widget on the field configuration page. If so, we don't bother validating it because nothing will be saved anyway.

Then, we check to see how many dimensions we're dealing with since the logic will be slightly different. We then iterate over each submitted value and, assuming that it has the requisite × character in it, break up the submitted string into three integers. The `explode()` function in PHP will take a string and split it into an array using the first parameter as a delimiter, while the `list()` operator will assign that array to two or three separate variables for us. We then take those values and actively set the height, width, units, and potential depth values within the form state using `form_set_value()`.

While it seems odd to use the validation step to manipulate the form data, it is the only place that the form API allows us to do so. The net result is that we create new values in the `$form_state` collection that match up with the columns in our field. When Drupal submits the widget, it will look through the `$form_state` for variables that match the names of the columns in the field. It doesn't care that we put those values there ourselves, just that they exist is what matters. The original string still exists in the `height_width_depth` variable, but Drupal will just ignore it.

We are also going to do a little custom theming to our combined widget. Note the following lines:

```
$element['dimfield_combined_wrapper']['#theme'] = 'dimfield_combined_
wrapper';
```

```
$element['dimfield_combined_wrapper']['#attached']['css'][] = drupal_
get_path('module', 'dimfield') . '/dimfield-admin.css';
```

The first line tells the rendering system to use a theme hook named dimfield_combined_wrapper to render everything that appears under $element['dimfield_combined_wrapper']. The second tells the system to also load a particular CSS file whenever this form element is displayed. In our case we'll do something simple and just stick the two form elements—height_width_depth and units —into a wrapped set of divs:

```
function dimfield_theme() {
  return array(
    'dimfield_combined_wrapper' => array(
      'render element' => 'element',
    ),
  );
```

```
    }
    function theme_dimfield_combined_wrapper($variables) {
        $element = $variables['element'];

        $hwd = drupal_render($element['height_width_depth']);
        $units = drupal_render($element['units']);

        return <<<END
        <div class="clearfix">
        <div class="dimfield-combined">{$hwd}</div>
        <div class="dimfield-units">{$units}</div>
        </div>
END;
    }
```

All form element arrays look the same to a theme function: they are passed in as a single array called $element. We then take the two components that we know make up the entire array, render them separately, and stick them into a set of divs. The CSS file we attached earlier will make the divs appear side by side, creating a much more attractive UI. The CSS file is quite simple:

```
.dimfield-combined {
    float: left;
    margin: 0 30px 0 0;
}
```

By taking advantage of the way Drupal looks for and saves form data, we are able to develop any arbitrarily complex widget we want. We could even have a widget that displays nothing to the screen at all, but assigns a value during its validate phase based on some third party data, some other field in the same form, information from the URL, or even the time of day. Drupal will dutifully save that data, not caring how it got there as long as our widget gave it the name Drupal was expecting.

Using formatters to display our field

Now that we've defined our field type, and we've created a widget to make it editable from a form, the only piece left is to decide how to display it in user output. (User output usually means the computer screen, but it could also mean an RSS feed, printed page, or various other types of output). Drupal lets us control that display using formatters.

Formatters follow a very similar pattern to field types and widgets. There is an info hook to define what formatters are available, and then there's a series of callbacks for all of the formatters our module defines. In most cases though, there's only one callback we need worry about.

Declaring a formatter

First, let's look at the info hook given here:

```
function dimfield_field_formatter_info() {
  return array(
    'dimfield_default' => array(
      'label' => t('Default'),
      'field types' => array('dimensions'),
    ),
    'dimfield_table' => array(
      'label' => t('Show as table'),
      'field types' => array('dimensions'),
      'settings' => array('units_as' => 'column'),
    ),
  );
}
```

In the preceding snippet we define two formatters, and there's not much to define. Each formatter has an internal name defined by the array key, a human-readable label, and a list of the field types that it applies to. Just as with widgets, we can define a formatter in any module that works with any field type we want, as long as we know how to handle the data it gives us.

Single-value formatters

Formatters only have two callbacks, and most formatters will only use one. Again, let's look at the simple implementation first.

```
function dimfield_field_formatter_view($obj_type, $object, $field,
                                       $instance, $langcode, $items,
                                       $display) {
  $element = array();
  $settings = $display['settings'];

  switch ($display['type']) {
    case 'dimfield_default':
      foreach ($items as $delta => $item) {
        if ($field['settings']['num_dimensions'] == 2) {
          $output = t('@height @unit by @width @unit', array(
```

```
          '@height' => $item['height'],
          '@width' => $item['width'],
          '@unit' => dimfield_units($item['units']),
        ));
      }
      elseif ($field['settings']['num_dimensions'] == 3) {
        $output = t(
          '@height @unit by @width @unit by @depth @unit', array(
            '@height' => $item['height'],
            '@width' => $item['width'],
            '@depth' => $item['depth'],
            '@unit' => dimfield_units($item['units']),
          ));
      }
      $element[$delta] = array('#markup' => $output);
    }
    break;
}

return $element;
}
```

The `formatter_view` callback is expected to return a renderable array that the theme system can understand. In this case, we simply want a formatted string that describes the data stored in the field. As before, we get multiple field values passed to the callback at once in an array. So we simply iterate over them one by one and assign them to the `$element` variable. The `#markup` element type tells Drupal "Here's some HTML. I've already formatted it, just use it". When that element gets rendered later, in the page, the strings we generated using the `t()` function will simply get displayed with all of the appropriate data in them.

Complex formatters

There is, of course, nothing preventing us from rendering all of the values together if we want. In fact, our second formatter will do just that. Rather than a series of values one after another, we'll render all of the available values in a single table.

Then the question arises, how do we display units? As their own column? Inline on each cell? Just in the header of each dimension column? In cases like this, the best option is to let the user decide using the configuration capabilities of formatters.

Recall from a moment ago that the `dimfield_table` formatter declared a `settings` key, which was an array. That array defines all of the possible settings parameters for that formatter and their default values. In order to make use of formatter settings there are also two other hooks we need to implement: `hook_field_formatter_settings_summary()` and `hook_field_formatter_settings_form()`.

```
function dimfield_field_formatter_settings_form($field, $instance,
$view_mode, $form, &$form_state) {
  $display = $instance['display'][$view_mode];
  $settings = $display['settings'];

  $form = array();

  if ($display['type'] == 'dimfield_table') {
    $form['units_as'] = array(
      '#title' => t('Show units'),
      '#type' => 'select',
      '#options' => array(
        'column' => t('As their own column'),
        'cell' => t('In each cell'),
        'none' => t('Do not show units'),
      ),
      '#default_value' => $settings['units_as'],
      '#required' => TRUE,
    );
  }

  return $form;
}
function dimfield_field_formatter_settings_summary($field, $instance,
$view_mode) {
  $display = $instance['display'][$view_mode];
  $settings = $display['settings'];

  $summary = '';

  if ($display['type'] == 'dimfield_table') {
    if ($settings['units_as'] == 'column') {
      $summary = t('Show units as their own column');
    }
    else if ($settings['units_as'] == 'cell') {
      $summary = t('Show units in each cell');
    }
```

```
        else if ($settings['units_as'] == 'none') {
          $summary = t('Do not show units');
        }
      }

      return $summary;
    }
```

The form hook is a very simple form offering the user a select box to pick what the `units_as` setting should be: column, cell, or none. As with other settings forms, the name of the form element matches the name of the settings variable so it gets saved automatically. The summary hook, then, simply takes that setting and returns a string that Drupal can display to the user so that he knows what the current setting is.

Now let's have a look at the view hook code for the table formatter:

```
function dimfield_field_formatter_view($obj_type, $object, $field,
$instance, $langcode, $items, $display) {
  $element = array();
  $settings = $display['settings'];

  switch ($display['type']) {
    // ...
    case 'dimfield_table':
      $rows = array();
      foreach ($items as $delta => $item) {
        $row = array();
        if ($settings['units_as'] == 'cell') {
          $row[] = t('@value (%units)', array(
            '@value' => $item['height'],
            '%units' => dimfield_units($item['units']),
          ));
          $row[] = t('@value (%units)', array(
            '@value' => $item['width'],
            '%units' => dimfield_units($item['units']),
          ));
        }
        else {
          $row[] = $item['height'];
          $row[] = $item['width'];
        }
        if ($field['settings']['num_dimensions'] == 3) {
          if ($settings['units_as'] == 'cell') {
```

```
          $row[] = t('@value (%units)', array(
            '@value' => $item['depth'],
            '%units' => dimfield_units($item['units']),
          ));
        }
        else {
          $row[] = $item['depth'];
        }
      }
      if ($settings['units_as'] == 'column') {
        $row[] = dimfield_units($item['units']);
      }
      $rows[] = $row;
    }

    $header = array(t('Height'), t('Width'));
    if ($field['settings']['num_dimensions'] == 3) {
      $header[] = t('Depth');
    }
    if ($settings['units_as'] == 'column') {
      $header[] = t('Units');
    }

    $element = array(
      '#theme' => 'table',
      '#rows' => $rows,
      '#header' => $header,
    );
    break;
  }

  return $element;
}
```

In this formatter, we build up a series of rows of data consisting of height, width, and depth if applicable. Each row is an array, and then we have an array of arrays to give us a table structure. That array we assign to an element that will get rendered as a `table`, as defined by the `#theme` key. Because Drupal defines a `theme_table()` function, that data will get passed to that function when the element is rendered and returned as an HTML table.

Note also that we're changing how the table gets built based on the settings we configured a moment ago. There may or may not be a column dedicated to units, and we may or may not display the units as part of each cell. Due to the fact that a `settings` value is exclusive, we don't need to worry about those two colliding as both can never be true.

We can, of course, have much more complex formatters. To use our map example we have seen previously, a formatter could take a series of coordinate data and output them on a map using a mapping service. As long as we return a renderable array to Drupal, we can do whatever we want.

Managing non-Field fields

One of the advantages of using the Field system is that it gives us a consistent, powerful UI for all Field data that we add to an entity. However, an entity may have non-Field data on it as well. A node or artwork title, for instance, is not a Field. The `poll` module in core doesn't use Fields for the poll configuration. An entity that is being pulled from a third party system may have all sorts of data associated with it that does not live in a Field module.

Fortunately, Drupal offers a way for us to integrate that data into the Field UI. Let's go back to the artwork module from *Chapter 6, Working with Content* and integrate the title into the Field system. It takes but a single hook:

```
function artwork_field_extra_fields() {
  $extra = array();

  foreach (artwork_types() as $type) {
    $extra['artwork'][$type->type] = array(
      'form' => array(
        'title' => array(
          'label' => t('Title'),
          'description' => t('The name of the artwork'),
          'weight' => -5,
        ),
      ),
      'display' => array(
        'title' => array(
          'label' => t('Title'),
          'description' => t('The name of the artwork'),
          'weight' => -5,
        ),
      ),
    );
  }

  return $extra;
}
```

`hook_field_extra_fields()` lets us define, per entity type and per bundle, what "extra fields" the Field system should be aware of. In our case, we loop over all artwork types and declare that all of them have a title pseudo-field. That pseudo-field is present both when displaying the edit form for artwork entities (the first key) and when displaying them (the second key). In both cases the definition is the same but we could easily make them different if we want.

There are only three keys to each definition. `label` and `description` should be self-explanatory. The `weight` key defines what the default "weight" of the title pseudo-field is in relation to other Fields (or pseudo-fields) on an entity. By setting the weight to **-5**, we ensure that by default the title will be shown first.

There is no requirement that they stay there, however. Now that the Field system knows about the title field, the user can easily drag-and-drop the title to appear in between two different Fields, at the bottom of the page, or even not at all.

Finding entities and fields

Creating, editing, and deleting data is all well and good, and is a key part of any content management system. However, there is also another important feature that makes a CMS worthwhile–Searching.

In a very simple case, searching for data is easy. We have a database, we know SQL, so let's rock and roll. However, Drupal doesn't restrict data to living in an SQL database. In fact, with field storage engines a single entity could conceivably live in a variety of different places. Consider the case of an artwork that has pictures associated with it via a field that pulls images from Flickr, and additional background information from a third party collection management system. Simply resorting to SQL to find artworks matching some given criteria is not feasible, since two of those three data stores is not an SQL database. Moreover, we may not be able to predict the table structure of the one that is since Drupal creates its database dynamically.

Fortunately, Drupal provides a unified query system for searching entities and fields. Although it does not allow for searching across different data stores, it does provide a data store agnostic way of searching for entities. (Searching across different data stores is an incredibly complex problem, usually best solved by indexing all data from various data stores into a single search index such as Apache Solr.)

To demonstrate how entity and field queries work, let's start by creating a new menu item to list recently created artworks. We'll put it in the artwork module for now.

```
function artwork_menu() {
  // ...
  $items['artwork/recent'] = array(
    'title' => 'Recently added artworks',
    'page callback' => 'artwork_page_list_recent',
    'access arguments' => array('view artworks'),
    'file' => 'artwork.pages.inc',
  );

  return $items;
}
```

Just as Drupal provides a query builder for SQL databases that abstracts database-specific logic, it also provides a query builder for Entities and Fields. The API for it is a single class named, boringly enough, EntityFieldQuery.

Before we have a look at EntityFieldQuery directly, let's take a step back and consider what sorts of things we can search on. At the conceptual level, there are three "levels" of data by which we can filter:

- **Entity level data**: It is data that is common to all entities of all types. This includes the entity type itself, the bundle name, the entity ID, and the revision ID (if applicable). All entities of any type will have these items.

- **Properties**: They are those data elements that are common to all objects of a given entity type, but not to all entities. That is, they are pieces of data common to all nodes, or to all users, or to all artworks. Examples include the 'node title' and 'creator uid' for nodes, user 'login name' for user entities, and the 'artwork title' and 'creation date' for artworks.

- **Fields**: They are, of course, specific to a given bundle definition (painting or sculpture). However, they may also be shared by entities of different types.

When searching for entities, we can filter by or order by data at each of those levels. Not all combinations make sense, however, and the query will reject nonsensical combinations by throwing an exception.

Since we cannot know what the storage engine or engines are that an entity uses, that too limits the complexity of the searches we can do. For instance, we are only able to do "AND" searches, not complex conditions with OR. We also cannot search across different data stores. Nonetheless, that still leaves a huge range of use cases that can be solved very easily.

> Always use EntityFieldQuery when selectively searching for entities. Never try to query the database directly, as there is no guarantee that there is a relational database involved.

Let's start with simply showing the five most recently created artworks:

```
function artwork_page_list_recent() {
  $content = array();

  $query = new EntityFieldQuery();
  $query
    ->entityCondition('entity_type', 'artwork')
    ->propertyOrderBy('created', 'DESC')
    ->range(0, 5);
  $result = $query->execute();

  $artworks = artwork_load_multiple(array_keys($result['artwork']));
  foreach ($artworks as $artwork) {
    $content[] = artwork_page_view($artwork, 'teaser');
  }

  return $content;
}
```

We start by creating a new query object. We then call methods on it, to filter by "entity type is 'artwork'", and then "order by the 'created' property, newest first" (that is, descending order). The `range()` method, just like DB queries, takes the start position as its first parameter and the count as its second.

If we assume an SQL database, the resulting SQL will look something like the following:

```
SELECT artwork.aid AS entity_id, artwork.vid AS revision_id, artwork.
type AS bundle, 'artwork' AS entity_type
FROM
artwork artwork
ORDER BY artwork.created DESC
LIMIT 5 OFFSET 0
```

The advantage here is that, should the author of the artwork module change the table structure on us, or if artworks were stored in a non-SQL data store, the SQL query above would break horribly but the EntityFieldQuery would continue to work because Drupal builds it dynamically based on what we're searching for.

Now look at that query again. It's returning three properties, the entity id, revision id, and bundle name. All entity queries return that same data: the entity type, entity id, revision id, and bundle. Each record is keyed by its entity id, which in turn is keyed by the entity type (since it is possible to get back multiple types of entities in a single query).

Because we know exactly what that structure is, we can leverage it easily. In this case we want to fully load all artworks that we found, so we run `array_keys()` on the `$result['artwork']` array, to get an array of just those ids and then load them. Note that we're using `artwork_load_multiple()`. Rather than loading each artwork separately, and running whatever queries are needed to do so, we load them all at once. That means one or five (or fifty if we were allowing that many) results all take about the same amount of time to load.

Once we have our artwork objects, we simply get the render array representing each one using the functionality we build in Chapter 6 and merge them together, then return the resulting array. When it gets rendered we will see all of our artworks, one after another.

Now let's make one small change to our field query:

```
$query = new EntityFieldQuery();
$query
  ->entityCondition('entity_type', 'artwork')
  ->propertyOrderBy('created', 'DESC')
  ->fieldCondition('field_artist', 'value', 'Da Vinci')
  ->range(0, 5);
$result = $query->execute();
```

Here, we also filter for just those artworks that have a field named `field_artist`, the `value` column of which is exactly equal to the string `Da Vinci`. The rest of the code is the same, but we will now get fewer results. If we assume that everything is stored in the local SQL database then the query could be something like this:

```
SELECT field_data_field_artist0.entity_id AS entity_id, field_data_
field_artist0.revision_id AS revision_id, field_data_field_artist0.
bundle AS bundle, fcet.type AS entity_type
FROM
field_data_field_artist field_data_field_artist0
INNER JOIN field_config_entity_type fcet ON fcet.etid = field_data_
field_artist0.etid
INNER JOIN artwork artwork ON artwork.aid = field_data_field_artist0.
entity_id
WHERE  (field_data_field_artist0.field_artist_value = 'Da Vinci') AND
(field_data_field_artist0.deleted = 0) AND (fcet.type = 'artwork')
ORDER BY artwork.created DESC
LIMIT 5 OFFSET 0
```

Again, there's no guarantee that we're even dealing with an SQL database. Aren't you glad we're letting Drupal figure all of that out for us?

It is also possible to do more complex queries on fields, for instance, the following one:

```
$query = new EntityFieldQuery();
$query
  ->entityCondition('entity_type', 'artwork')
  ->propertyOrderBy('created', 'DESC')
  ->fieldCondition('field_artist', 'value', 'Da Vinci', 'CONTAINS',
0)
  ->range(0, 5);

$result = $query->execute();
```

In this case, instead of using a simple "is exactly equal to" comparison, we are asking for any entity whose `field_artist` field has the string "Da Vinci" in it anywhere. That allows us to match both "Da Vinci" and "Leonardo Da Vinci". The fifth parameter lets us restrict results to just those fields that have "Da Vinci" as their first instance (remember, 0-based) if they are multi-value.

There are of course corresponding `entityOrderBy()`, `propertyCondition()`, and `fieldOrderBy()` methods for building up more interesting field queries. See the inline documentation in `includes/entity.inc` for the full range of options.

Summary

We have now completed a module that touches on the three most important parts of the Field API. We've created a new field type to store data, corresponding widgets to allow users to edit it, and formatters to control how that data is displayed when the entity the field is attached to is viewed.

Although our use cases were reasonably simple, Drupal allows arbitrarily complex Widgets and Formatters. Some Widgets can interact with the URL or third party data sources to handle default values, or perhaps show a completely different set of form fields under certain conditions. Formatters can use the theme system to display data themselves or leverage JavaScript libraries to create interactive visualizations of the data stored in a field. With swappable storage engines, advanced use cases can even load data from another database or server entirely, including one that does not involve SQL.

8
Drupal Permissions and Security

Permissions lie at the center of Drupal's security paradigm. Simply put, permissions determine who can perform what action on a website. Most commonly, permissions allow users to gain access (or be denied access) to specific features, such as access to the site-wide contact form or the ability to change the author of a piece of content.

These permissions are not assigned to individual users, but instead to classes of users, defined as roles. A role is a collection of permissions. Individual users may then be assigned to one or more roles, as is appropriate to your project's business rules.

> Note: When assigning permissions to roles, the default "authenticated user" role is a special case. Any permission granted to this role will also be granted to any other role except "anonymous user". Why? This is because the act of logging in to a user account defines a user as "authenticated". Custom roles created for a site inherit the base permissions assigned to the "authenticated user" role users.
>
> Understanding this behavior is critical to site builders, making it crucial for module developers. You may need to create very specific permissions in order to satisfy the business logic that your module requires. In our discussion, we will explore common problems that can occur when permissions are too broad or too narrow.

Any module may establish new permissions. In this chapter, we will discuss best practices for security and usability when defining your module's permission options.

In this chapter, we will cover the following:

- Drupal's roles and permissions concepts
- Using `user_access()` to assert permissions
- Using `hook_permission()`
- Access control with `hook_menu()`
- Common errors in defining permissions
- Declaring your own access functions
- Securing sensitive actions with permissions
- Responding when access is denied
- Enabling permissions programmatically
- Permissions, security, and Drupal forms
- Security considerations for AJAX processing

Using user_access() to assert permissions

The `user_access()` function is the primary security element in the Drupal API. Most page requests pass through the function, as do many administrative functions and the display of certain page elements. Pages, blocks, fields, and form elements are some of the items that can be shown or hidden by wrapping their display in a `user_access()` call.

The function is quite elementary, taking only two arguments:

```
user_access($string, $account = NULL)
```

Here, `$string` is the machine readable name of the permission, and `$account` is an optional copy of a `$user` object, as returned by the function `user_load()`.

The following is a typical access check, taken from the **Menu** module:

```
$form['menu'] = array(
  '#type' => 'fieldset',
  '#title' => t('Menu settings'),
  '#access' => user_access('administer menu'),
  '#collapsible' => TRUE,
  '#collapsed' => !$link['link_title'],
);
```

The preceding code checks if the user editing a page may add a link to that page in the site's navigation menu. The permission `administer menu` indicates that the user's role is trusted enough to make structural changes to the site (for instance, like adding a link to this content on the **Main menu**, which appears on every page). The `user_access()` function returns a Boolean value, namely, if TRUE, the user may perform the requested action; if FALSE, the user may not. In the case of this form code, the form element will only be displayed if the access check returns TRUE. Otherwise, the form's default value will be retained.

Note that the preceding example does not pass an `$account` object. As a result, the `user_access()` function defaults to using the current `$user` object, that is, the user currently making the page request. The `$user` object is stored in a global variable, and so it can be accessed any time a specific `$account` is not specified.

You are not required to specify an `$account` when calling `user_access()`, and in most cases this is fine, but there are use cases where you might want to check the permission against a user other than the current logged-in `$user`.

Checking the proper user account

In most cases, permission checks are made against the current user, defined in the `$user` object. Module authors must pay careful attention to the context of their permission checks, especially when displaying information about specific users.

For example, you may wish to add a section to the user account page where a site administrator can check the roles that an individual user has. To do this we would implement `hook_user_view()` and test the global `$user` object to ensure that this is a trusted administrator, who can view this information.

First, we set up a simple check for the current user: Does he/she have the permission to view this information?

```
function example_user_view($account, $view_mode) {
  if (!user_access('view user roles')) {
    return;
  }
}
```

You will see this pattern frequently in Drupal code. Failing the access check leads to a `return` out of the function and makes the code easier to follow. Since we are only adding information to an existing page, returning no data is fine. (Later in the chapter, we will look at other ways to deal with denied permissions.)

If the current user passes this access check, we must then fetch the information we want. This information is not about the `$user` but about the `$account` being viewed. So we add the logic:

```
/**
 * Implement hook_user_view().
 */
function example_user_view($account, $build_mode) {
  if (!user_access('view user roles')) {
    return;
  }
  // Get the user's roles.
  $list = $account->roles;
  if (!empty($list)) {
    // Prepare the information for theming.
    $variables = array(
      'items' => $list,
    );
    $content = theme('item_list', $variables);
    // Attach the content to the user page according to the API.
    $account->content['summary']['output'] = array(
      '#type' => 'user_profile_item',
      '#title' => t('User roles'),
      '#markup' => $content,
      '#attributes' => array('class' => array('content-creation')),
    );
  }
}
```

When implemented, our code produces the following result on a user page:

If we had accidentally run the permission check on the $account object, then we might return the wrong permissions. For clarity, let's take a look at a more complex example. In the following snippet, we want to show a list of all content types that a user can create. Our function will begin much like the last implementation, and then get more complex.

```
/**
 * Implement hook_user_view().
 */
function example_user_view($account, $build_mode) {
  if (!user_access('view content creation permissions')) {
    return;
  }
  // Get the defined node types.
  $node_types = node_permissions_get_configured_types();
  if (empty($node_types)) {
    return;
  }
  // Make an array for the list output.
  $list = array();
  foreach ($node_types as $type) {
    if (user_access('create ' . $type . ' content', $account)) {
      // Get the human-readable name of the content type.
      $list[] = check_plain(node_type_get_name($type));
    }
  }
}
```

The preceding code snippet defines a function that pulls the permissions for the account being viewed by the current user. Our two sets of permission checks operate on different user accounts.

The important piece here is the user_access() check that we run for each node type. If we were to leave off the $account, then this check would assume that we wanted to know what content types the current user could create. Doing so would mean the same results would appear no matter which user account page we viewed.

> Note: The use of the $account object instead of the $user object is a standard practice of Drupal, and a good coding practice. In Drupal, the $user object is a global value, and it would be a mistake to pass it (sometimes by reference!) when we only mean to extract information from it. Instead, lookup functions like hook_user_view() always act on a copy called $account. This pattern occurs frequently in Drupal core, and you should follow this best practice.

To finish this example, let's add our theme function to produce the proper output.

```
if (!empty($list)) {
    // Prepare the information for theming.
    $variables = array(
      'items' => $list,
    );
    $content = theme('item_list', $variables);
    // Attach the content to the user page according to the API.
    if (!isset($account->content['example'])) {
      $account->content['example'] = array();
    }
    $account->content['example'] += array(
      '#type' => 'user_profile_category',
      '#attributes' => array('class' => array('user-member')),
      '#weight' => 5,
      '#title' => t('Content'),
    );
    $account->content['example']['output'] =  array(
      '#type' => 'user_profile_item',
      '#title' => t('Content creation permissions'),
      '#markup' => $content,
      '#attributes' => array('class' => array('content-creation')),
    );
  }
}
```

With this theme function in place, we can display the following output:

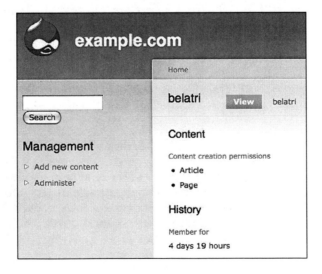

The user_access() function is very effective, and it can be used in almost all cases. Since it only takes two parameters, it may not be appropriate for all access checks, and it can never check multiple permissions at once. Later, we will look at use cases where a more complex function is needed to check permissions.

Using hook_permission()

Now that you understand the basics of Drupal's user access system, we can explore how modules can extend that system. First, a little history lesson.

Until Drupal 7, hook_permission() was known as hook_perm(). The change was made for clarity in the code, as part of a general semantic cleanup of Drupal core. (I wrote the patch, in fact.) hook_permission() also includes a number of usability improvements, which altered the format of the function's return value. These changes are substantial enough for even experienced Drupal developers to explore each element of the new hook.

The purpose of hook_permission() is to define and return an array that contains all the necessary information about your module's permissions. This includes the simple strings that can be passed to user_access(), plus a human-readable name for the permission and an optional description. Prior to Drupal 7, only the simple string was returned.

The following is an example, taken from the core **Search** module:

```
function search_permission() {
  return array(
    'administer search' => array(
      'title' => t('Administer search'),
    ),
    'search content' => array(
      'title' => t('Use search'),
    ),
    'use advanced search' => array(
      'title' => t('Use advanced search'),
    ),
  );
}
```

The module declares three separate permissions in a manner typical to Drupal modules. The first permission is for administrative configuration of the module. These sorts of permissions are rarely given to the "authenticated user" role and should never be given to anonymous users.

The second permission grants the ability to search site content using the default search form. The third permission extends the second to include an additional form for advanced searches.

> The presence of these very specific permissions may seem odd, given that there is an access content permission in the node module that grants users the ability to view site content. However, search may be considered a special case by some sites. Separating the search content permission from the access content permission adds a layer of flexibility that enables project customization.

People who complain that Drupal is too complex should consider this case for a moment. From a site builder perspective, having three extra permissions means more configuration work. However, imagine how frustrating it would be if you needed to disable search for some users but could not (or could only do so programmatically).

In cases like these, Drupal almost always embraces flexibility. The presence of multiple permissions in a core module means that someone has needed that separation for a good reason. (In the next chapter, in fact, we will discuss the reason for the bypass node access permission, which is a new feature in Drupal 7.)

Defining your module's permissions

Before writing any code for hook_permission(), it is the best practice to take out a pen and paper (or a good diagramming program), and make a chart of the actions you expect users to take. In fact, many experienced developers write this hook at the end of development, after puzzling through all the use cases in the code.

Let's consider the preceding example module. It is very direct. We want to show some information about users to trusted site administrators. Our use case looks something like the following:

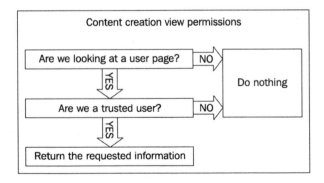

In the first case, **Are we looking at a user page?** is a question our module does not need to ask. We know through the API that using `hook_user_view()` only fires when someone is looking at a user's information. So we don't need our own permission check for that action.

What matters to us is the question **Are we a trusted user?** Here we may have to create a permission check.

We could simply use the existing `administer users` permission provided by core, but is that the best solution? In many use cases, it is likely to be. However, suppose you are building a newspaper website. In this scenario, we have "site editors" whose job is to supervise the work of others. To do so, these editors need to be able to check the content types that a user can create. However, `administer users` is a much more powerful permission, which allows the editing of user accounts and the assigning of user roles. We may not want to give that much authority and responsibility to our site editors.

In this case—in fact, in most cases—the creation of a discrete permission for each action is the best choice. Since you cannot reliably predict all the usage scenarios for your code, piling too many actions onto a single permission can limit how people can use your module. Any time you see yourself writing an `administer X` permission in the code, you should ask yourself if that permission can be made more granular.

Writing hook_permission()

For our example module, then, we need to define a permission that grants the ability to view this information about users. Our permission array is quite direct, and has three possible parts:

1. The machine-readable name of the permission. This element will be used by the module code to check `user_access()`. For our example, we use the string "view content creation permissions". By convention, this string must be in English and all lower case. It need not be a complete sentence.

2. The human-readable label for the permission. This may be the same as the machine-readable string, but should be formatted with an initial capital. You may capitalize words as needed. Unlike the machine-readable name, this string must be wrapped in `t()` so that the output may be translated. We will use "View the content creation options for registered users" because anonymous users do not have an account page to view.

3. An optional description of the permission. This string should be a complete sentence, and wrapped in `t()`. Drupal's user interface guidelines encourage you to use this element if the permission needs special clarification, especially if permission is being given to untrustworthy users who could pose a security risk. For our example, we will clearly state: "Displays the content types that a user may create on the user's profile page."

When we put these three parts together, our hook looks like the following code:

```
/**
 * Implement hook_permission().
 */
function example_permission() {
  return array(
    'view content creation permissions' => array(
      'title' => t('View the content creation options for registered
users'),
      'description' => t('Displays the content types that a user may
create on the user\'s profile page.'),
    ),
  );
}
```

> Using the `description` element is tempting, for completeness, but Drupal's UI testing discovered that it serves mostly a visual clutter for the end user.

The following screenshot shows examples of the types of permissions that benefit from a full description. This page can be found at the following path: `admin/people/permissions`

User	
Administer permissions *Warning: Give to trusted roles only; this permission has security implications.*	☐
Administer users *Warning: Give to trusted roles only; this permission has security implications.*	☐
View user profiles	☐
Change own username	☐
Cancel own user account Note: content may be kept, unpublished, deleted or transfered to the *Anonymous* user depending on the configured user settings.	☐
Select method for cancelling own account *Warning: Give to trusted roles only; this permission has security implications.*	☐

Declaring your own access functions

The `user_access()` function is a great utility function, but it cannot cover all logical use cases. It cannot, for instance, check two access permissions at the same time. You can, of course, write a statement such as:

```
if (user_access('permission one') && user_access('permission two')) {
  // perform some action...
}
```

When securing actions within your code, this approach is perfectly fine. However, menu-based access checks cannot be subject to such rules. In these cases, we need to declare our own `access callback` within the `menu` item.

For instance, let's take our last module example. Suppose that instead of displaying this information on the user profile page, we wanted to make a stand-alone page for this information. We might make a tab on the user page, using a menu callback like the following one:

```
/**
 * Implement hook_menu().
 */
function example_menu() {
  $items['user/%user/content'] = array(
    'title' => 'Content creation',
    'page callback' => 'example_user_page',
    'page arguments' => array(1),
    'access arguments' => array('view content creation permissions'),
    'type' => MENU_LOCAL_TASK,
  );
  return $items;
}
```

This would work just fine, unless we needed to check an additional permission or condition during the access check. Suppose our business rules say that only editors who may also `administer users` may view this page.

In that case, we have a problem, because the `user_access()` function cannot accept multiple permissions during a single call. In this case, we have to use the `access callback` parameters of the menu `$item`:

```
/**
 * Implement hook_menu().
 */
function example_menu()
example_menu() {
```

```
    $items['user/%user/content'] = array(
      'title' => 'Content creation',
      'page callback' => 'example_user_page',
      'page arguments' => array(1),
      'access callback' => 'example_user_access',
      'access arguments' => array('view content creation permissions',
  'administer users'),
      'type' => MENU_LOCAL_TASK,
    );
    return $items;
  }
```

For this code to succeed, we must also provide the new function
example_user_access():

```
  /**
   * Access callback that checks multiple permissions.
   *
   * Takes a list of permissions and requires that all return
   * TRUE.
   */
  function example_user_access() {
    foreach (func_get_args() as $permission) {
      if (!user_access($permission)) {
        return FALSE;
      }
    }
    return TRUE;
  }
```

> Note: When developing your module, you must rebuild the menu
> cache in order to see permission changes. You can do this by
> emptying the cache_menu table, or using the tools provided by
> Devel module or Drush.

You can even dictate more complex logic within an access control function. Suppose
we also want to prevent users from viewing pages other than their own. We would
edit the functions in the following way:

```
  /**
   * Implement hook_menu().
   */
  function example_menu() {
    $items['user/%user/content'] = array(
      'title' => 'Content creation',
```

```
      'page callback' => 'example_user_page',
      'page arguments' => array(1),
      'access callback' => 'example_user_access',
      'access arguments' => array(1,
            'view content creation permissions', 'administer users'),
      'type' => MENU_LOCAL_TASK,
    );
    return $items;
}


/**
 * Access callback that checks multiple permissions.
 */
function example_user_access() {
  global $user;
  $arguments = func_get_args();
  $account = array_shift($arguments);
  if ($account->uid != $user->uid) {
    return FALSE;
  }
  foreach ($arguments as $permission) {
    if (!user_access($permission)) {
      return FALSE;
    }
  }
  return TRUE;
}
```

In the preceding way, complex access rules may be enforced on menu callbacks.

When writing an access check outside of the menu system, it is tempting to chain together a series of IF checks to produce the logic required. Consider moving such statements into a clearly defined access function. These can improve the readability and portability of your code. If you want extra style points, consider adding a drupal_alter() function before returning TRUE or FALSE to allow other modules to rewrite your standard logic.

Responding when access is denied

In a significant change from earlier Drupal, the `drupal_access_denied()` function should no longer be called when returning a normal page context.

- Page callback functions wanting to report an **access denied** message should return `MENU_ACCESS_DENIED` instead of calling `drupal_access_denied()`

- However, functions that are invoked in contexts where that `return` value might not bubble up to `menu_execute_active_handler()` should call `drupal_access_denied()`. For more details see: http://api.drupal.org/api/function/drupal_access_denied/7

However, what does this mean in practice?

One advantage of using a menu callback is that if access is denied for the page request, Drupal automatically handles the response by running the traditional `drupal_access_denied()` function.

However, the Drupal 7 rendering engine respects more contexts than the traditional web page. Your callback function might return a JSON object, a file, or be responding as a part of a larger page (such as a form). For example, consider the following snippet of code from `contact_site_form()`:

```
// Check if flood control has been activated for sending e-mails.
  $limit = variable_get('contact_threshold_limit', 5);
  $window = variable_get('contact_threshold_window', 3600);
```

```
    if (!flood_is_allowed('contact', $limit, $window) &&
!user_access('administer contact forms')) {
    drupal_set_message(t("You cannot send more than %limit messages
in @interval. Please try again later.", array('%limit' => $limit, '@
interval' => format_interval($window))), 'error');
    drupal_access_denied();
    drupal_exit();
  }
```

The preceding code stops all processing of the contact form page if the user is suspected of spamming the form. If the user violates the threshold of allowed messages per hour, a warning message is delivered and the **Access denied** page is rendered.

Note the use of `drupal_exit()` here to stop the rest of the page execution. Since this access denied message is performed during form definition, `drupal_exit()` must be invoked to stop the rest of the rendering process.

> Note: Do not call the normal PHP `exit()` function from within Drupal code. Doing so may stop the execution of internal functions (such as session handling) or API hooks. The `drupal_exit()` function is provided to safely stop the execution of a Drupal request.

Within a normal page context, however, we should return the constant `MENU_ACCESS_DENIED` instead of `drupal_exit()`. We might do this instead of using a custom menu callback. Returning to our earlier example:

```
/**
 * Implement hook_menu().
 */
function example_menu() {
  $items['user/%user/content'] = array(
    'title' => 'Content creation',
    'page callback' => 'example_user_page',
    'page arguments' => array(1),
    'access arguments' => array('view content creation permissions'),
    'type' => MENU_LOCAL_TASK,
  );
  return $items;
}

/**
 * Custom page callback for a user tab.
 */
```

```
function example_user_page($account) {
  global $user;
  if ($user->uid != $account->uid) {
    return MENU_ACCESS_DENIED;
  }
  // ...
```

There is a subtle yet important difference between the two approaches. If we use a menu callback to assert access control, the tab link will only be rendered if the user passes the access check. If we use an access check within the page callback, the tab will always be rendered. It is poor usability to present a tab that only prints an 'access denied' message to the user. For this reason, page-level access checks should almost always be handled by `hook_menu()`.

Should I use drupal_access_denied() or a custom page?

`drupal_access_denied()` returns a version of the traditional Apache **403 access denied** page, served by Drupal. Good usability suggests that providing a friendlier error message page helps users navigate your site with ease. If you support this idea, feel free to create a custom 403 page. Drupal allows you to assign any content page as the 403 message page.

The `drupal_access_denied()` function returns the output of that page, so there is no need to code a custom 403 message into your module since one can be created and edited through the normal Drupal content interface.

Default 403 (access denied) page

http://example.com/drupal-cvs/ [   ]

This page is displayed when the requested document is denied to the current user. Leave blank to display a generic "access denied" page.

Default 404 (not found) page

http://example.com/drupal-cvs/ [   ]

This page is displayed when no other content matches the requested document. Leave blank to display a generic "page not found" page.

The settings for your 403 and 404 page are found under the **Site Information settings**.

Enabling permissions programmatically

Drupal user roles and permissions are handled through configurations in the user interface. However, there may be use cases where your module needs to set or modify permissions. There is even a module called **Secure Permissions** (`http://drupal.org/project/secure_permissions`) which disables the UI for editing roles and permissions and forces all settings to be defined in code.

If your module needs to define permissions in code, Drupal 7 provides some new hooks to make the task easier. Let's take a common example. Your module creates a page callback that should be visible by 'authenticated' but not 'anonymous' users. To activate this feature when the module is enabled, you can use `hook_enable()` as follows:

```
function example_enable() {
  $permissions = array('view example page');
  user_role_change_permissions(DRUPAL_AUTHENTICATED_USER,
                              $permissions);
}
```

This function goes into your module's `.install` file. When the module is enabled, Drupal will add the `view example page` permission to the authenticated user role.

You can (and normally should) do the reverse when the module is disabled:

```
function example_disable() {
  $permissions = array('view example page');
  $roles = user_roles();
  // Since permissions can be set per role, remove our permission from
  // each role.
  foreach ($roles as $rid => $name) {
    user_role_revoke_permissions($rid, $permissions);
  }
}
```

It is also possible to add/remove multiple permissions at the same time. To do so, we must build an array of permissions to be passed to `user_role_change_permissions()`. Suppose that our module wants to remove the default `access content` permission from the anonymous user role, while adding our new `view example page` permission. To do so, we build an array in the format `'permission name' => TRUE` or `FALSE`, for each role.

```
function example_enable() {
  $permissions = array(
    'access content' => FALSE,
    'view example page'  => TRUE,
  );
  user_role_change_permissions(DRUPAL_ANONYMOUS_USER, $permissions);
}
```

When our module is enabled, the settings for these two permissions will be changed for the anonymous user.

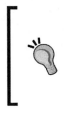

> The `user_role_change_permissions()` function is actually used by the form submit handler for the **Permissions** form. By abstracting this logic to a function, Drupal provides an easy API call for other modules. When building your modules, you should look for similar opportunities so that other developers can build off your code instead of re-implementing similar logic.

Defining roles programmatically

Just as with permissions, Drupal 7 allows roles to be set through a simple function call. The new `user_role_save()` and `user_role_delete()` functions provide the tools your module needs.

The `user_role_save()` function merely adds a new named role to the `{roles}` table and assigns it a proper role id (`$rid`). The `user_role_delete()` function removes that role from the `{roles}` table, and also cleans out any associated permissions stored in the `{role_permission}` table and any user role assignments stored in the `{users_roles}` table.

Let's say that your module allows users to moderate other user accounts. This is a powerful capability on a site, so your module automatically creates a new role that contains the proper permissions.

As in our preceding example, we will use `hook_enable()` to create the new role.

```
/**
 * Create a role for managing user accounts.
 */
function account_moderator_enable() {
  // Create the 'account moderator' role.
  user_role_save('account moderator');
}
```

After creating the role, we can also auto-assign a series of permissions:

```
/**
 * Create a role for managing user accounts.
 */
function account_moderator_enable() {
  // Create the 'account moderator' role.
  user_role_save('account moderator');
```

```
$permissions = array(
  'access user profiles',
  'administer users',
);
$role = user_role_load_by_name('acount moderator');
user_role_grant_permissions($role->rid, $permissions);
}
```

When our module is uninstalled, we should delete the role as well.

```
function account_moderator_uninstall() {
  user_role_delete('account moderator');
}
```

Securing forms in Drupal

Form handling is one of the most crucial areas of website security. Inappropriate handling of form data can lead to multiple security weaknesses including SQL injection and cross-site request forgeries (CSRF). While we cannot cover all aspects of security in a brief chapter, it is important to state some clear guidelines for Drupal module developers.

> See `http://en.wikipedia.org/wiki/CSRF` for information on CSFR, and for cross-site scripting (XSS) see `http://en.wikipedia.org/wiki/XSS`.

The Forms API

First and foremost, you should always use the Drupal Forms API when creating and processing forms in Drupal. For one, doing so makes your life easier because the Forms API contains standards for form definition, AJAX handling, required elements, validation handling, and submit handling. (See more about forms in *Chapter 5*.)

From a security standpoint, the Forms API is critical because it contains built-in mechanisms for preventing CSRF requests.

Whenever Drupal creates a form through the API, the form is tagged with a unique token called the `form_build_id`. The `form_build_id` is a random md5 hash used to identify the form during processing. This token is added by the `drupal_build_form()` routine:

```
$form_build_id = 'form-' . drupal_hash_base64(uniqid(mt_rand(), TRUE)
. mt_rand());
$form['#build_id'] = $form_build_id;
```

The form is additionally tagged with a $form['#token'] element during drupal_process_form(). The #token is used to ensure that a form request came from a known request (that is, an HTTP request that has been issued a valid session for the site). The #token value is set with drupal_get_token():

```
function drupal_get_token($value = '') {
  return drupal_hmac_base64($value, session_id().
  drupal_get_private_key(). drupal_get_hash_salt());
}
```

When Drupal processes a form, both the $form_build_id and $form['#token'] values are validated to ensure that the form request originated from the Drupal site.

> We should also note that Drupal forms default to using the POST method. While it is possible to submit Drupal forms via GET, developers are always encouraged to use POST, which is more secure. We will look at securing GET requests when we discuss AJAX handling a little later in this chapter.

Disabling form elements

In addition to the global security of a specific form, you may also wish to enable or disable specific parts of a form, either your own module's form or that provided by Drupal core (or another contributed module). In the first example of this chapter, we saw how this can be done using the user_access() function (or a similar access control function) to mark an individual form element or entire section of a form as inaccessible.

```
$form['menu'] = array(
  '#type' => 'fieldset',
  '#title' => t('Menu settings'),
  '#access' => user_access('administer menu'),
  '#collapsible' => TRUE,
  '#collapsed' => !$link['link_title'],
);
```

When the content editing form is rendered, users without the administer menu permission will not see this element of the form.

> Note that '#access' => FALSE is not the same as '#disabled' => FALSE in Drupal's Forms API. Using #disabled => FALSE will render the form element and disable data entry to that element, while '#access' => FALSE removes the element entirely from the output.

This approach is the proper way to remove form elements from Drupal. You may find yourself tempted to `unset()` certain form elements, but since Drupal forms are passed by reference through a series of `drupal_alter()` hooks, the `unset()` cannot be considered reliable. Using `unset()` also removes valuable context that other modules may be relying on when processing the `$form`.

Passing secure data via forms

As a general rule, Drupal forms do not use the traditional `hidden` form element of HTML. Since `hidden` form elements are rendered in the browser, curious users (and malicious ones) can view the elements of a form, checking for tokens and other security devices.

Since Drupal is a PHP application, it can use server-side processes to handle secret form elements, rather than relying on information passed as hidden fields from the browser.

To pass such data, a form element may be defined as `'#type' => 'value'`. Using this Forms API element prevents the data from being rendered to the browser. As an additional advantage, it also allows for the passing of complex data—such as an array—during a form request. This technique is commonly used for form elements that the user should never see such as the id of an element to be deleted during a confirmation step. Consider the following code from `aggregator.module`:

```
function aggregator_admin_remove_feed($form, $form_state, $feed) {
  return confirm_form(
    array(
      'feed' => array(
        '#type' => 'value',
        '#value' => $feed,
      ),
    ),
    t('Are you sure you want to remove all items from the feed
%feed?', array('%feed' => $feed->title)),
    'admin/config/services/aggregator',
    t('This action cannot be undone.'),
    t('Remove items'),
    t('Cancel')
  );
}
```

The form presented to the end user contains no information about the item to be deleted. That data is passed behind the scenes.

The form, as displayed to the browser, only contains the data that Drupal needs to validate the form and extract the data from its cache:

```
<form action="/drupal-cvs/admin/config/services/aggregator/remove/1"
accept-charset="UTF-8" method="post" id="aggregator-admin-remove-feed"
class="confirmation">
  <div>
    This action cannot be undone.
    <input type="hidden" name="confirm" id="edit-confirm" value="1" />
    <div class="container-inline">
      <input type="submit" name="op" id="edit-submit" value="Remove
items" class="form-submit" />
      <a href="/drupal-cvs/admin/config/services/aggregator">
        Cancel</a>
    </div>
    <input type="hidden" name="form_build_id"
            id="form-049070cff46eabd3b069f980066b7ad4"
            value="form-049070cff46eabd3b069f980066b7ad4" />
    <input type="hidden" name="form_token" id="edit-aggregator-admin-
remove-feed-form-token" value="48b0294050ef62b7d55778cf1992f326" />
    <input type="hidden" name="form_id" id="edit-aggregator-admin-
remove-feed" value="aggregator_admin_remove_feed" />
  </div>
</form>
```

The submit handler for the form picks up the data value for processing:

```
/**
 * Remove all items from a feed and redirect to the overview page.
 *
 * @param $feed
 *   An associative array describing the feed to be cleared.
 */
function aggregator_admin_remove_feed_submit($form, &$form_state) {
  aggregator_remove($form_state['values']['feed']);
  $form_state['redirect'] = 'admin/config/services/aggregator';
}
```

Running access checks on forms

While it is perfectly fine to run access checks when building a form, developers should normally not run access checks when processing a form's `_validate()` or `_submit()` callbacks. Doing so interferes with the logic of `hook_form_alter()`. For instance, if your module wishes to alter the menu form element above, so that additional users may add content items to the menu without being able to edit the entire menu, you can do so easily:

```
function example_form_alter(&$form, $form_state, $form_id) {
  if (!empty($form['#node_edit_form']) && isset($form['menu'])) {
    $form['menu']['#access'] = example_user_access(
'assign content to menu');
  }
}
```

This code changes the access callback on the `menu` form element to our own function. Since `hook_form_alter()` runs after a form is initially built, we can alter any form element in this manner.

However, form `_validate()` and `_submit()` callbacks are not run through any alter functions. This means that any access checks that run during those callbacks will always be imposed. Take for instance, the following example from Drupal's core `node.module`, that makes it impossible for normal users to change the author of a node or the time it was submitted:

```
/**
 * Perform validation checks on the given node.
 */
function node_validate($node, $form = array()) {
  $type = node_type_get_type($node);

  if (isset($node->nid) && (node_last_changed($node->nid) >
                            $node->changed)) {
    form_set_error('changed', t('The content on this page has
either been modified by another user, or you have already submitted
modifications using this form. As a result, your changes cannot be
saved.'));
  }

  if (user_access('administer nodes')) {
    // Validate the "authored by" field.
    if (!empty($node->name) && !($account = user_load_by_name(
                                    $node->name))) {
      // The use of empty() is mandatory in the context of usernames
```

```
      // as the empty string denotes the anonymous user. In case we
      // are dealing with an anonymous user we set the user ID to 0.
      form_set_error('name', t('The username %name does not exist.',
                  array('%name' => $node->name)));
    }

    // Validate the "authored on" field.
    if (!empty($node->date) && strtotime($node->date) === FALSE) {
      form_set_error('date', t('You have to specify a valid date.'));
    }
  }

  // Do node-type-specific validation checks.
  node_invoke($node, 'validate', $form);
  module_invoke_all('node_validate', $node, $form);
}
```

The inclusion of this access check may add a level of error prevention—in that users who cannot 'administer nodes' cannot alter the author without special permissions—but it does not make Drupal itself more secure. That is because the security for this form element is already set in the $form definition, so its usage here is redundant:

```
// Node author information for administrators
$form['author'] = array(
  '#type' => 'fieldset',
  '#access' => user_access('administer nodes'),
  '#title' => t('Authoring information'),
  '#collapsible' => TRUE,
  '#collapsed' => TRUE,
  '#group' => 'additional_settings',
  '#attached' => array(
    'js' => array(drupal_get_path('module', 'node') . '/node.js'),
  ),
  '#weight' => 90,
);
```

Instead, placing an access check in the validate handler forces a module author to work around the code by replacing the core node_validate() and node_submit() callbacks, which may introduce additional errors or security holes in the code.

For this reason, module authors are strongly discouraged from running access checks during form processing.

Handling AJAX callbacks securely

Drupal 7 comes with an enhanced AJAX framework that makes it easy to build interactive display elements for pages and forms. The security problem for Drupal is that AJAX callbacks take the form of menu callbacks, which unlike most Drupal forms, are essentially GET requests to the browser. This fact means that any request to an AJAX callback must be treated as malicious and that all such requests must be tested for validity before an AJAX response can be sent.

Using AJAX in forms

When using the #ajax element with the Forms API, Drupal automatically secures the AJAX callback by checking the validity of the form request. This action only works, of course, if you follow the FormsAPI correctly. Using the #ajax form element triggers the ajax_get_form() function, which uses form_build_id to test for validity:

```
function ajax_get_form() {
  $form_state = form_state_defaults();

  $form_build_id = $_POST['form_build_id'];

  // Get the form from the cache.
  $form = form_get_cache($form_build_id, $form_state);
  if (!$form) {
    // If $form cannot be loaded from the cache, the form_build_id
    // in $_POST must be invalid, which means that someone
    // performed a POST request onto system/ajax without actually
    // viewing the concerned form in the browser.
    // This is likely a hacking attempt as it never happens under
    // normal circumstances, so we just do nothing.
    watchdog('ajax', 'Invalid form POST data.', array(),
            WATCHDOG_WARNING);
    drupal_exit();
  }
// ...
```

As we saw in the preceding section that form_build_id ensured that the form request was issued by the Drupal site and was valid.

Using AJAX in other contexts

While form handling of AJAX provides both a tidy API and a security check, we are not so lucky when using other AJAX callbacks. To quote Greg Knaddison, member of the Drupal security team and author of *Cracking Drupal*, the definitive work on Drupal security:

> [I]t is often tempting when building a rich AJAX feature to slip back into creating a CSRF vulnerability via GET requests....However, because this practice of taking action in response to GET requests is not as common or standard as the form system, there is no way to provide this protection automatically or easily.

Cracking Drupal, pg 18.

To understand the point, let's look at a typical AJAX menu callback use case. Suppose we want a module that allows users to add or delete items from a list via a dynamic AJAX callback. The module might set up something like the following:

```
function example_menu() {
  $items = array();
  $items['example-ajax/%item/add'] = array(
    'title' => 'Example AJAX add to list',
    'page callback' => 'example_ajax_add',
    'page arguments' => array(1),
    'access arguments' => array('add to my list'),
    'type' => MENU_CALLBACK,
  );
  return $items;
}

function example_ajax_add($item) {
  // Do something.
}
```

Looking at the preceding code, several issues should be immediately apparent:

- The default access callback `user_access()` is probably insufficient, since we are managing a per-user list
- The permission `add to my list` provides no means to check if the user is the owner of the list being edited
- Simply trying to hide the menu item from the site navigation (through the use of the `MENU_CALLBACK` property) will not prevent other users (or even search engine crawlers) from eventually finding the page

As a result, we cannot trust the menu callback to fire any action in `example_ajax_add()` without adding some additional security checks.

First, we know that we need to check the user performing the action. From our earlier discussion, this is best handed through an access callback, so we edit our declaration:

```
'access callback' => 'example_access_ajax_add',
```

To run this check successfully, we also need to know the `$user` whose list is being updated:

```
$items['example-ajax/%item/add/%user'] = array(
```

We also need to pass the `$user` to our access callback:

```
'access arguments' => array(3),
```

So our rewritten hook looks like the following code:

```
function example_menu() {
  $items = array();
  $items['example-ajax/%item/add/%user'] = array(
    'title' => 'Example AJAX add to list',
    'page callback' => 'example_ajax_add',
    'page arguments' => array(1, 3),
    'access callback' => 'example_access_ajax_add',
    'access arguments' => array(3),
    'type' => MENU_CALLBACK,
  );
  return $items;
}
```

In our access callback, we can now check that the link references the current user. So our HTML code will look something like the following:

```
<a href="/example-ajax/3/add/10">Add to my list</a>
```

The code to generate this link would run through Drupal's `l()` function:

```
if ($user->uid > 0) {
  $output = l(t('Add to my list'), 'example-ajax/'. $item->id .'/
add/'. $user->uid);
  return $output;
}
```

In our callback, the menu system transforms 10 into a standard $user object, which we check for validity in two ways:

```
function example_access_ajax_add($account) {
  global $user;
  if (!$account->uid || $account->uid != $user->uid) {
    return FALSE;
  }
  return TRUE;
}
```

First, if user_load() returns FALSE, then the page argument is invalid. Second, if the returned $account does not match the user making the request, the request is invalid.

This is pretty good. It allows our code to check that the user making the AJAX request is the currently logged in user. However, how do we know that this request came from our server and is not a CSRF attack?

Well honestly, we don't know and we can't know. However, we can be a little paranoid and add another layer of security.

Knaddson gives us the key in *Cracking Drupal*, when he says:

> *The security team is working on an API to make [securing AJAX callback] much easier, but that API is not yet available...The system is based on the same token system used to protect Drupal forms.*

Cracking Drupal, page 18

To implement this structure, we have to add an additional argument to our page callback:

```
function example_menu() {
  $items = array();
  $items['example-ajax/%item/add/%user/%'] = array(
    'title' => 'Example AJAX add to list',
    'page callback' => 'example_ajax_add',
    'page arguments' => array(1, 3),
    'access callback' => 'example_access_ajax_add',
    'access arguments' => array(3, 4),
    'type' => MENU_CALLBACK,
  );
  return $items;
}
```

This allows us to pass a Drupal authentication token to our access callback. To make this work, we modify our link creation code to include a token:

```
if ($user->uid > 0) {
  $output = l(t('Add to my list'), 'example-ajax/'. $item->id .
'/add/'. $user->uid) .'/'. drupal_get_token($user->uid);
  return $output;
}
```

This will generate a link similar to:

```
<a href="/example-ajax/3/add/10/c4d312412df415ca0">Add to my list</a>
```

Then, in our access callback, we check the token string in addition to the user:

```
function example_access_ajax_add($account, $token = NULL) {
  global $user;
  // Check the validity of the user account.
  if ($account->uid == 0 || $account->uid != $user->uid) {
    return FALSE;
  }
  // Check the validity of the callback token.
  if (empty($token) || !drupal_valid_token($token, $account->uid)) {
    return FALSE;
  }
  return TRUE;
}
```

Drupal's token handling API performs the validation for us, and we are ensured the same protection that is given to regular Drupal forms.

> Note that this approach will only work correctly for logged-in users who are being served non-cached pages. The link we output to access this callback cannot be cached, since caching returns the same HTML output to all users.

As a general rule, you only need to worry about token handling for AJAX callbacks that perform creative or destructive actions, such as editing a list of user favorites. That is because such actions generally write to the database, and can change certain settings for your Drupal users. Simple AJAX callbacks that only read and return data do not necessarily need to be secured in this manner unless the data is user-specific.

Summary

Our coverage of Drupal's permission system should give you all the information you need to properly set the access rules for your module.

In this chapter, we have learned the basics of the permission and role system in Drupal. We have also seen how to use `user_access()` to assert permissions. We have discussed how `hook_menu()` handles access control, and also how to use `hook_permission()`.

We have seen the importance of granular permission definitions, and when to use a function other than `user_access()` to assert permission control. We discussed how to write a custom access control function, and how to respond when access is denied. We also saw how to assign and remove permissions using `hook_enable()` and `hook_disable()`.

We learnt how to manage roles programmatically along with the basics of securing Drupal forms. Lastly we looked at how to safely handle AJAX callbacks.

9
Node Access

Out-of-the-box, Drupal is a great system for creating and managing content. Users can log in and create content. Proper use of roles and permissions allows site editors to review some or all of a site's content. Site visitors can read published posts.

But what happens if you want all site visitors to view some content, but only registered users to view a select list of restricted content? If, for example, your site requires paid registration to view in-depth articles about how to build Drupal web sites, the basic permissions provided by Drupal are not enough.

There are cases where you need more advanced rules regarding which of the users (or groups of users) can create, view, edit, and delete content. To enable these rules, Drupal provides a **Node Access** system. Node Access provides an API for determining the **grants**, or permissions, that a user has for each node. By understanding how these grants work, a module developer can create and enforce complex access rules.

In Drupal 7, any module may declare node access rules. This is a change from the earlier versions, and it provides some of the most powerful tools for Drupal development.

In this chapter, we will cover:

- Node Access compared to `user_access()` and other permission checks
- How Drupal grants node permissions
- The `node_access()` function
- `hook_node_access()` compared to `{node_access}`
- Controlling permissions to create content
- Using `hook_node_access()`
- When to write a Node Access module

- The {node_access} table and its role
- Defining your module's access rules
- Using hook_node_access_records()
- Using hook_node_grants()
- Rebuilding the {node_access} table
- Modifying the behavior of other modules
- Using hook_node_access_records_alter()
- Using hook_node_grants_alter()
- Testing and debugging your module
- Using Devel Node Access

Node Access compared to user_access() and other permission checks

Unlike user_access(), using the Node Access system is not a simple case of implementing a specific permission check before executing your code.

As we saw in the last chapter, user_access() determines what code may be executed for a specific user under a given set of conditions. Drupal's Node Access system is similar, but must account for variable conditions within a given set of nodes. For example, certain users may be allowed to edit any Basic page content but not allowed to edit any Article content. This condition means that Drupal must be able to distinguish among different properties of each node.

The Node Access API is a series of interrelated functions that provide a consistent programming interface for making these types of access checks. Due to the flexible nature of Drupal however, there are multiple ways to define and implement node access control mechanisms.

How Drupal grants node permissions

As we mentioned in the introduction, there are four fundamental operations that affect nodes: Create, View, Update and Delete. Collectively, these are referred to as CRUD (where View is replaced by Read). When dealing with nodes, it is vital to know which operation is being performed.

The Node Access API allows modules to alter how the default Drupal CRUD workflow behaves. Normally, Drupal nodes are created by a single user. That user "owns" the node and, in most cases, may edit or delete the node at will. Some users, like the administrative user 1, may edit any node. But by default, Drupal has no concept of group ownership of nodes. Certain roles may be given permission to edit all nodes of a type (as shown by the core `edit any Article content` permission, for instance), but out of the box there is no provision for restricting access to view that content.

The Node Access API evolved out of the need to define a flexible, extensible set of access rules. Much has improved in Drupal 7, so experienced developers will want to review this material carefully.

Node Access permissions are checked in two instances:

- When requests to act upon an individual node are made.
- When database queries return lists of nodes that match given conditions.

In order to handle node access securely, module developers need to be mindful of both cases.

The first case is fairly simple, and is generally handled by a menu callback and the `node_access()` function. Unless your module intends to interfere with the normal handling of `node_menu()`, you may be able to skip the rest of this chapter.

However, all module developers need to understand the impact of case two. Let's highlight it here.

> Any database query involving the `{node}` table must be built dynamically and be marked as a node access query. Failure to do so can introduce security vulnerabilities on sites running your code.

To understand this rule, let's look at a simple example from Drupal core. The following query is found in `node_page_default()`, the function that provides the basic node listing page:

```
$select = db_select('node', 'n')
  ->fields('n', array('nid'))
  ->condition('promote', 1)
  ->condition('status', 1)
  ->orderBy('sticky', 'DESC')
  ->orderBy('created', 'DESC')
  ->extend('PagerDefault')
```

```
        ->limit(variable_get('default_nodes_main', 10))
        ->addTag('node_access');

    $nids = $select->execute()->fetchCol();
```

This select statement uses Drupal 7's query builder to fetch a list of published nodes which have been promoted to the front page, ordered by "stickiness" and age. Notice, however, the final element of the query: `->addTag('node_access')`.

This directive invokes the `node_query_node_access_alter()` function which allows node access rules to be applied before the query is sent to the database. Failure to use the dynamic query builder and the `node_access` tag will mean that your select statement will **bypass** Drupal's built-in security features. Doing so may grant unwanted access to view, edit, or delete content **by ignoring the permissions defined for the site**.

We won't go into the inner workings of `node_query_node_access_alter()` yet. Simply put, it ensures that any query to the {node} table properly enforces the node access rules defined for the site.

Because of how this enforcement is handled, however, module developers have a near-infinite capacity to modify how Drupal handles access to nodes. The purpose of the rest of this chapter is to explain how this system is designed and the best ways for you to leverage the Node Access API to meet your specific needs.

The node_access() function

`node_access()` is the primary access callback for node operations. It is defined in `node_menu()` as the access callback for any attempt to create, view, edit or delete a node. The function itself is one of the more complex in Drupal core by virtue of the eight separate `return` statements within the function. Understanding the logic behind these `return`s is the key to using Node Access correctly.

To begin, let's examine the documentation and initial lines of the `node_access()` function:

```
/**
 * Determine whether the current user may perform the given operation
 * on the specified node.
 *
 * @param $op
 *   The operation to be performed on the node. Possible values are:
 *   - "view"
 *   - "update"
```

```
 *    - "delete"
 *    - "create"
 * @param $node
 *    The node object on which the operation is to be performed, or
 * node type (e.g. 'forum') for "create" operation.
 * @param $account
 *    Optional, a user object representing the user for whom the
 * operation is to be performed.
 * Determines access for a user other than the current user.
 * @return
 *    TRUE if the operation may be performed, FALSE otherwise.
 */
function node_access($op, $node, $account = NULL) {
  global $user;

  $rights = &drupal_static(__FUNCTION__, array());
```

From reading over the code, we can use our knowledge of Drupal to infer some key points:

- The $op parameter indicates the node operation being requested.
- Creating nodes is a special case, even changing the $node parameter sent to the function.
- Node Access is a user-driven action. That means it matters **who** is trying to perform the operation.
- Node Access in Drupal 7 is statically cached *per user* for the duration of the page request. That means that once set, it cannot be changed until another request is sent or drupal_static_reset('node_access') is called.

> Recall our discussion of $user and $account in the previous chapter. The node_access() function accepts an $account object, but falls back to using the global $user object if one is not supplied. This feature allows for access checks to be performed for users other than the current user.

A single node may return different answers to an access request depending on *who is making the request* and *what request is being made*.

The access whitelist

The first check that `node_access()` makes is to see if the callback was invoked correctly:

```
if (!$node || !in_array($op, array('view', 'update', 'delete',
'create'), TRUE)) {
    // If there was no node to check against, or the $op was not one
    // of the supported ones, we return access denied.
    return FALSE;
}
```

This code displays a bit of paranoia not found in most of the Drupal API. Checking the validity of the inbound parameters ensures that access is *never granted by accident*. When dealing with access control, defaulting to FALSE (meaning "deny access") is the proper behavior.

Caching the result for performance

The next section of code performs three simple sanity checks, plus an optimization for the static cache:

```
// If no user object is supplied, the access check is for the
// current user.
if (empty($account)) {
    $account = $user;
}

// $node may be either an object or a node type. Since node types
// cannot be an integer, use either nid or type as the static
// cache id.

$cid = is_object($node) ? $node->nid : $node;

// If we've already checked access for this node, user and op,
// return from cache.
if (isset($rights[$account->uid][$cid][$op])) {
    return $rights[$account->uid][$cid][$op];
}

if (user_access('bypass node access', $account)) {
$rights[$account->uid][$cid][$op] = TRUE;
    return TRUE;
}
```

```
if (!user_access('access content', $account)) {
  $rights[$account->uid][$cid][$op] = FALSE;
  return FALSE;
}
```

The first *if* clause ensures that we have a proper `$account` for the check.

 Remember that even anonymous users generate a valid `$account` object and may have assigned permissions.

The second clause enforces the static cache. This is a performance optimization new to Drupal 7.

The third is a `user_access()` check new to Drupal 7 and allows super-users to pass all node access checks and perform all operations on all nodes. This permission was split off from the `administer nodes` permission of prior versions in order to more clearly indicate how node access functions. It has the added benefit of allowing more granular permissions.

The last is another `user_access()` check. It simply checks that a user may `access content` on the site. If not, then the user is always denied access to all node operations.

Invoking hook_node_access()

To this point, the code is fairly obvious and the intentions are clear: Drupal is running basic security checks against known values. At this point, the core node module begins querying other modules about the access status of the node. The next piece invokes `hook_node_access()` to check for access rules:

```
// We grant access to the node if both of the following conditions
// are met:
// - No modules say to deny access.
// - At least one module says to grant access.
// If no module specified either allow or deny, we fall back to the
// node_access table.
$access = module_invoke_all('node_access', $node, $op, $account);
if (in_array(NODE_ACCESS_DENY, $access, TRUE)) {
  $rights[$account->uid][$cid][$op] = FALSE;
  return FALSE;
}
elseif (in_array(NODE_ACCESS_ALLOW, $access, TRUE)) {
  $rights[$account->uid][$cid][$op] = TRUE;
  return TRUE;
}
```

Here we see a distinct difference between Drupal 7 and Drupal 6 (and earlier): any module may respond to this access check. Prior to Drupal 7, only modules that defined a node type could respond, using the old `hook_access()` function. This constraint made it difficult for module developers to modify the business logic for `node_access()`. This is a major change in the Drupal API, and one which we will explore in some depth.

> The constants `NODE_ACCESS_DENY` and `NODE_ACCESS_ALLOW` are set by `node.module`. We will look at these later in the chapter.

Notice also the note in the comments: `If no module specified either allow or deny, we fall back to the node_access table`. The execution order of Node Access hooks matters. When we consider the logic for our business rules, we must remember that other modules may also have a stake in the access rights to a node.

So far, we're up to five return statements in the code.

Access to a user's own nodes

The next clause is an exception for handling nodes created by the current user:

```
// Check if authors can view their own unpublished nodes.
if ($op == 'view' && !$node->status && user_access('view own
unpublished content', $account) && $account->uid == $node->uid &&
$account->uid != 0) {
    $rights[$account->uid][$cid][$op] = TRUE;
    return TRUE;
}
```

Drupal assumes that unpublished content should not be visible to users. However, the `view own unpublished content` permission exists to allow authenticated users to see their content even if it has not been published. Unless a third-party module intervenes, only users with this permission, `bypass node access` or user 1 may view unpublished content.

Invoking the node access API

Now that Drupal has accounted for that special case, the code falls through to the `{node_access}` table for checking permissions.

```
// If the module did not override the access rights, use those set
// in the node_access table.
if ($op != 'create' && $node->nid) {
```

```
      if (module_implements('node_grants')) {
        $query = db_select('node_access');
        $query->addExpression('1');
        $query->condition('grant_' . $op, 1, '>=');
        $nids = db_or()->condition('nid', $node->nid);
        if ($node->status) {
          $nids->condition('nid', 0);
        }
        $query->condition($nids);
        $query->range(0, 1);

        $grants = db_or();
        foreach (node_access_grants($op, $account) as $realm => $gids) {
          foreach ($gids as $gid) {
            $grants->condition(db_and()
              ->condition('gid', $gid)
              ->condition('realm', $realm)
            );
          }
        }
        if (count($grants) > 0) {
          $query->condition($grants);
        }
        $result = (bool) $query
          ->execute()
          ->fetchField();
        $rights[$account->uid][$cid][$op] = $result;
        return $result;
      }
      elseif (is_object($node) && $op == 'view' && $node->status) {
        // If no modules implement hook_node_grants(), the default
        // behavior is to allow all users to view published nodes,
        // so reflect that here.
        $rights[$account->uid][$cid][$op] = TRUE;
        return TRUE;
      }
    }
```

Here we get to the heart of the Node Access API. The key is in the function `node_access_grants()`, which defines the permissions for the current user for the current operation. Modules respond to this function using `hook_node_grants()`, which we will examine in detail a little later.

This clause is primarily a query builder function, designed to create the proper join from the {node} table to the {node_access} table and then return the result of that query. Understanding how that query is constructed – and how the {node_access} table is populated – is the key to understanding Node Access.

> **Dealing with unpublished content**
>
> For experienced module authors, one major difference between Drupal 7 and previous versions is that hook_node_grants() is now invoked for unpublished content. Great care must be taken to prevent exposing unpublished content to users.

If the Node Access API does not assert rules, this clause will default to allowing access to content. But notice that the function does not end here.

```
elseif (is_object($node) && $op == 'view' && $node->status) {
    // If no modules implement hook_node_grants(), the default
    // behavior is to allow all users to view published nodes,
    // so reflect that here.
    $rights[$account->uid][$cid][$op] = TRUE;
    return TRUE;
  }
}


  return FALSE;
}
```

At the very end of the function, notice the final return FALSE; statement. From a security standpoint, this catch-all ensures that we never grant access by accident. Whenever writing an access check, FALSE should be your default return.

hook_node_access() compared to {node_access}

For module developers, the two key points to the node_access() function are the behaviors of the two hook invocations: hook_node_access() and hook_node_grants(). Because of the fundamental difference between how the two hooks are implemented, for the rest of the chapter, we will refer to a *node access module* as one that implements hook_node_grants() and writes to the {node_access} table. A module that implements hook_node_access() will be referred to as an *access control module*.

hook_node_access() is the simpler of the two systems. It is a self-contained hook that allows individual access control modules to pass judgment on a node. Note, however, that in Drupal core its use is limited to only three of the four node operations: Create, Update and Delete. We can see this clearly in node.module's implementation:

```
/**
 * Implements hook_node_access().
 */
function node_node_access($node, $op, $account) {
  $type = is_string($node) ? $node : $node->type;

  if (in_array($type, node_permissions_get_configured_types())) {
    if ($op == 'create' && user_access('create ' . $type . ' content',
$account)) {
      return NODE_ACCESS_ALLOW;
    }

    if ($op == 'update') {
      if (user_access('edit any ' . $type . ' content', $account) ||
(user_access('edit own ' . $type . ' content', $account) && ($account-
>uid == $node->uid))) {
        return NODE_ACCESS_ALLOW;
      }
    }

    if ($op == 'delete') {
      if (user_access('delete any ' . $type . ' content', $account)
|| (user_access('delete own ' . $type . ' content', $account) &&
($account->uid == $node->uid))) {
        return NODE_ACCESS_ALLOW;
      }
    }
  }

  return NODE_ACCESS_IGNORE;
}
```

Because hook_node_access() fires before checking the {node_access} table, it is used to define the default behavior for node permissions. This behavior is very useful for items like creating and editing content according to node type, but it can be very limiting when defining the rules for viewing a node. For that reason, Drupal core never asserts a value on the View operation for a node.

Instead, core returns the NODE_ACCESS_IGNORE constant, which indicates that access to the View operation should be handled by the {node_access} table.

By default, the {node_access} table contains a single record:

nid	gid	realm	grant_view	grant_update	grant_delete
0	0	all	1	0	0

This row allows the node access system to generate a default JOIN from the {node} table to the {node_access} table that will always return TRUE.

However, if your site is not running any node access modules (that is, no modules that implement hook_node_grants()), then no JOIN will be required. In this case, all nodes will be returned.

If you install a node access module, however, you will immediately be prompted to rebuild content access permissions for the site.

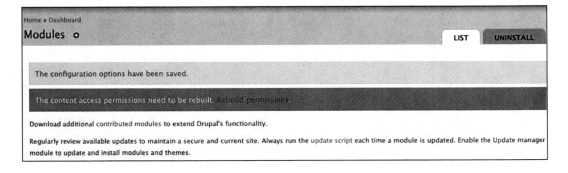

Rebuilding the permissions will update the {node_access} table with the rules defined by the module(s) you have installed. When we activate the example module we will be building in this chapter, here is the result:

```
+-----+-----+---------------+-------------+---------------+---------------+
| nid | gid | realm         | grant_view  | grant_update  | grant_delete  |
+-----+-----+---------------+-------------+---------------+---------------+
| 255 |  2  | role_access   |      1      |       1       |       1       |
| 277 |  2  | role_access   |      1      |       1       |       1       |
| 278 |  2  | role_access   |      1      |       1       |       1       |
| 278 |  3  | role_access   |      1      |       1       |       1       |
| 279 |  2  | role_access   |      1      |       1       |       1       |
| 280 |  2  | role_access   |      1      |       1       |       1       |
| 281 |  2  | role_access   |      1      |       1       |       1       |
| 281 |  3  | role_access   |      1      |       1       |       1       |
| 282 |  2  | role_access   |      1      |       1       |       1       |
| 283 |  2  | role_access   |      1      |       1       |       1       |
| 284 |  2  | role_access   |      1      |       1       |       1       |
| 285 |  2  | role_access   |      1      |       1       |       1       |
| 285 |  4  | role_access   |      1      |       1       |       1       |
| 286 |  2  | role_access   |      1      |       1       |       1       |
| 287 |  2  | role_access   |      1      |       1       |       1       |
| 287 |  4  | role_access   |      1      |       1       |       1       |
| 288 |  2  | role_access   |      1      |       1       |       1       |
| 289 |  2  | role_access   |      1      |       1       |       1       |
| 289 |  4  | role_access   |      1      |       1       |       1       |
| 290 |  2  | role_access   |      1      |       1       |       1       |
| 291 |  2  | role_access   |      1      |       1       |       1       |
| 292 |  2  | role_access   |      1      |       1       |       1       |
| 292 |  3  | role_access   |      1      |       1       |       1       |
| 293 |  1  | role_access   |      1      |       1       |       1       |
| 294 |  2  | role_access   |      1      |       1       |       1       |
| 295 |  2  | role_access   |      1      |       1       |       1       |
| 296 |  2  | role_access   |      1      |       1       |       1       |
| 296 |  3  | role_access   |      1      |       1       |       1       |
+-----+-----+---------------+-------------+---------------+---------------+
```

Note that the {node_access} table uses the node id (**nid**) as its primary key. As a result, it can only be used to check access for content that has already been created. This means that node access modules cannot assert permissions for the Create operation. To do so, your module must implement hook_node_access() and respond to the 'create' operation.

Rebuilding the access permissions will also trigger node_query_node_access_alter() to begin rewriting node queries for the View, Update, and Delete actions.

However, modules that only implement hook_node_access() do not write records to the {node_access} table, nor do they impose query altering logic. As a result, we might consider hook_node_access() to be an easier (and often more efficient) approach to solving the problem of node access.

When using a node access module, Drupal will add a JOIN statement to every node query. This can have minor performance implications for your site if you have large amounts of content.

Using hook_node_access()

Drupal 7 replaces the old `hook_access()` function with `hook_node_access()`. This change was one of the many improvements to come from a work session at DrupalCON Szeged in 2008, and credit goes to Larry Garfield (Crell) for implementing these changes.

`hook_node_access()` allows any module to have a say in how node access is handled. It does not require database storage, or the use of the rest of the Node Access API. Further, it may be applied to any of the four basic CRUD operations.

The hook passes three parameters:

- `$node`, the complete node object being acted upon, or a node type string in the case of the Create operation.
- `$op`, the operation being performed.
- `$account`, the user requesting access to the node for this action.

All three of these parameters will always be populated, and your hook should respond according to the specific operation being performed. There are three possible return values for each request:

- `NODE_ACCESS_ALLOW`

  Indicates that the operation should be permitted. This is an explicit allow, and at least one module must return this value for the operation to be validated by `hook_node_access()`.

- `NODE_ACCESS_DENY`

  Indicates that the operation should not be permitted. This is an explicit deny, and if issued, it will cancel any `NODE_ACCESS_ALLOW` directives issued by other modules.

- `NODE_ACCESS_IGNORE`

  The default return statement. This value indicates that your module has no stake in whether to allow or deny the operation being requested.

A sample access control module

For example, suppose we have the following editorial rule on our site: *Any authenticated user may post Articles provided he or she has been a member of the site for more than two days.* (This rule prevents people from creating an account just to post spam the site; it also might afford a "cooling" off period before people reply to other posts.)

The basic permission 'create Article content' does not allow for this use case, but a quick module using `hook_node_access()` can. Let's call it the Delay module.

Assuming we have written our module's `delay.info` file, we can create the following file:

```php
<?php

/**
 * Implement hook_node_access().
 *
 * Only allow posts by users with accounts more than two days old.
 */
function delay_node_access($node, $op, $account) {
}
```

Now we can implement our custom logic controls. First, ignore all operations other than `create`.

```php
function delay_node_access($node, $op, $account) {
  if ($op != 'create') {
    return NODE_ACCESS_IGNORE;
  }
}
```

> The proper reply when your module does not wish to assert permission to a node is NODE_ACCESS_IGNORE. Failure to return this value is an API error.

Second, we ignore all content types other than 'article':

```php
if ($op != 'create' || $node != 'article') {
  return NODE_ACCESS_IGNORE;
}
```

Next, we need to check the information about the user performing the action. Registration time data is stored in `$account->created` as a Unix timestamp, so it can be compared to the current time easily.

```php
// Drupal stores the page request in the constant REQUEST_TIME.
if (empty($account->created) || $account->created > (REQUEST_TIME
- (48 * 3600))) {
  return NODE_ACCESS_DENY;
}
```

And we are done, right? Well, we have properly enforced our rules, which is a deny statement for users who do not pass the time threshold. However, we have not completed our function, since the API requires a return statement from every module, so we must add a final note that indicates our indifference to other rules.

```
return NODE_ACCESS_IGNORE;
```

Now we are done. In one simple module, in just sixteen lines of code (six of which are comments), we have changed the rules for content creation on our site. Here is the entire module (except for the delay.info file):

```php
<?php
/**
 * Implement hook_node_access().
 *
 * Only allow posts by users with accounts more than two days old.
 */
function delay_node_access($node, $op, $account) {
  if ($op != 'create' || $node != 'article') {
    return NODE_ACCESS_IGNORE;
  }
  // Drupal stores the page request in the constant REQUEST_TIME.
  if (empty($account->created) || $account->created > (REQUEST_TIME
- (48 * 3600))) {
    return NODE_ACCESS_DENY;
  }
  return NODE_ACCESS_IGNORE;
}
```

That's how simple and powerful `hook_node_access()` can be.

A second access control module

Now, let's take a look at a slightly more complex example. Suppose we want users to be able to create content normally, but instead of editing content by type, we want them to be able to edit all content created by users who have the same roles that they do.

Before we write that code, let's rough out our logic a bit. For the 'Update' operation, follow these rules:

1. Get the role(s) of the user trying to edit the content.
2. Get the role(s) of the user who is the content author.
3. If the roles match, allow the user to edit the content.
4. If the roles do not match, deny editing access.

It is a good idea to write out such rules and review them with the project sponsor, because doing so can reveal the implications of applying the logic you have defined. In this case, rule #4 becomes key, because we will explicitly deny access to edit content, even for users who might have the `edit any Article content` permission. Doing so might lead to confusion for some users, so we should ensure that this is the rule that we want.

> We should point out, from a security perspective, that these rules will place all 'authenticated users' into the same group. This behavior may be desirable, or it may open a risk that all registered site users can edit all content. For the purpose of our demonstration module, let's assume that this behavior is desired, and that users who need their content protected will be given an additional role.

Since this is the behavior we want, the functionality is pretty easy to enforce. Let's create a `role_edit.module` file for this behavior. Our module starts out much like the Delay module.

```php
<?php
/**
 * Implement hook_node_access().
 *
 * Allow users to edit all nodes created by their peers.
 */
function role_edit_node_access($node, $op, $account) {
  if ($op != 'update') {
    return NODE_ACCESS_IGNORE;
  }
  // Return the default response.
  return NODE_ACCESS_IGNORE;
}
```

Since we only care about the Update operation, we ignore all other cases.

The roles for our active user are in the `$account->roles` property and easily accessible. To find the roles of the node's owner, however, we must load the user based on the $node->uid.

```php
$owner = user_load($node->uid);
```

For exact role matching, we can now do an `array_diff()` on the two user's roles.

```php
$diff = array_diff($account->roles, $owner->roles);
```

If the $diff array is empty, then the two users have the same roles and can be considered peers.

```
if (empty($diff)) {
   return NODE_ACCESS_ALLOW;
}
```

Finally, we want to change our default return value, since our rule #4 indicated we want strict access control enforced. So if the diff returns a value, we deny access:

```
return NODE_ACCESS_DENY;
```

And that's the entire module. 17 lines of code:

```php
<?php
/**
 * Implement hook_node_access().
 *
 * Allow users to edit all nodes created by their peers.
 */
function role_edit_node_access($node, $op, $account) {
  if ($op != 'update') {
    return NODE_ACCESS_IGNORE;
  }
  $owner = user_load($node->uid);
  $diff = array_diff($account->roles, $owner->roles);
  if (empty($diff)) {
    return NODE_ACCESS_ALLOW;
  }
  return NODE_ACCESS_DENY;
}
```

If we wanted to optimize this code, we could add in two additional checks. The first simply checks for a user id match, and removes the need for the `array_diff()`:

```
if ($account->uid == $node->uid) {
   return NODE_ACCESS_ALLOW;
}
$owner = user_load($node->uid);
```

The second would use `drupal_static()` to avoid running `user_load()` multiple times for the same user id.

```
$owners = &drupal_static(__FUNCTION__);
if (!isset($owners[$node->uid])) {
   $owners[$node->uid] = user_load($node->uid);
}
```

> On node listing pages, this hook will often be called multiple times.
> You may be able to optimize your code by using `drupal_static()` to
> remove repeated queries to the database. Using the Devel module can
> help you find redundant queries that would benefit from static caching:
> `http://drupal.org/project/devel`

Now our module is 23 lines of optimized code:

```php
<?php
/**
 * Implement hook_node_access().
 *
 * Allow users to edit all nodes created by their peers.
 */
function role_edit_node_access($node, $op, $account) {
  if ($op != 'update') {
    return NODE_ACCESS_IGNORE;
  }
  if ($account->uid == $node->uid) {
    return NODE_ACCESS_ALLOW;
  }
  $owners = &drupal_static(__FUNCTION__);
  if (!isset($owners[$node->uid])) {
    $owners[$node->uid] = user_load($node->uid);
  }
  $diff = array_diff($account->roles, $owners[$node->uid]->roles);
  if (empty($diff)) {
    return NODE_ACCESS_ALLOW;
  }
  return NODE_ACCESS_DENY;
}
```

We could possibly optimize this further by statically storing the `$diff` results, but that is probably unnecessary and adds little to our example.

The same types of logic could be applied to the Delete operation for nodes as well.

View operations and access control modules

While `hook_node_access()` can be applied to all CRUD operations, it is very rarely applied to the View operation and Drupal core never does so. Module authors are strongly encouraged to always return NODE_ACCESS_IGNORE for the View operation so that the Node Access API may function as expected.

The reasoning behind this rule is that advanced access rules are more likely to be applied to the View operation; many sites only require access restrictions on who can view content because only editors and administrators may create content.

If you implement hook_node_access() on the View operation, you are likely to alter the expected node access behavior in ways that make debugging difficult for the site owner and other module developers. Therefore, only node access modules should assert rules on the View operation; access control modules should refrain from doing so.

If you think you must enforce View rules in hook_node_access(), please clearly document that you have done so on your module's project page and in an accompanying README.txt file.

When to write a node access module

Clearly, hook_node_access() is a very powerful function. As we have seen, many common use-cases can be solved in just a few lines of code. So it is important for module developers to consider when to use hook_node_access() to implement access control as opposed to a complete node access module.

Since access control modules should not respond to the View operation, node access modules become necessary any time you need to use access rules to restrict access to the nodes that a user may view. The reason for this has to do with how Drupal builds its access controls when listing nodes. hook_node_access() is only effective for running access checks against individual nodes – a fact made clear by the fact that the $node object is passed as a parameter.

However, hook_node_access() is no use to us when generating a list of nodes, for three reasons:

- It provides no means to alter a node listing query to produce a proper list of accessible nodes.
- Running an individual lookup function for every node on a page can be resource intensive.
- An implementation of hook_node_access() can overrule the behavior defined by other modules, which may not be desirable.

While it is tempting to solve all your access needs with hook_node_access(), doing so limits the flexibility of your module. hook_node_access() is recommended for single use-case modules, particularly those written for a specific site or project.

Writing a complete node access module, on the other hand, is a more complex task, and one that we will examine in detail in the rest of this chapter. The advantages to writing a node access module are:

- Node access modules can work in conjunction with other modules to provide flexible access control rules.

- Node access rules set by one module may be modified by any other module, whereas `hook_node_access()` implementations cannot.

- Node access modules typically address common usage scenarios and are therefore re-usable by more people. While this is not a technical advantage, it is a great reason to contribute code to the Drupal project.

The {node_access} table and its role

The primary difference between access control modules and node access modules is the use of the {node_access} table. When a node access module is installed, database queries for the {node} table can be JOINed to the {node_access} table in order to delimit the list of returned values.

By default, the {node_access} table contains a single record which allows all content to be viewed by all users (except those who cannot `access content`, as we saw when looking at the `node_access()` function).

When a node access module is enabled, however, this default record is removed, and node queries will be modified appropriately. Let's look again at a sample query-builder function that returns a simple list of published nodes:

```
$select = db_select('node', 'n')
    ->fields('n', array('nid'))
    ->condition('promote', 1)
    ->condition('status', 1)
    ->orderBy('sticky', 'DESC')
    ->orderBy('created', 'DESC')
    ->extend('PagerDefault')
    ->limit(10)
    ->addTag('node_access');

$nids = $select->execute()->fetchCol();
```

When executed, the following query is passed to the database:

```
SELECT n.nid FROM node n WHERE n.promote = 1 AND n.status = 1 ORDER BY
n.sticky DESC, n.created DESC LIMIT 0, 10;
```

The above query means:

Select the first ten distinct node ids for published and promoted nodes, ordered by "stickiness" and age.

If we have a node access module enabled, however, hook_query_alter() will fire the node_query_node_access_alter() function, which will rewrite the query by adding a conditional JOIN to the node access table.

 Drupal 7's database API uses the add_tag() method to register hook functions. The value passed to the method – here node_access – informs the name of the alter hook. Query alters take the format hook_query_TAG_NAME_alter().

Our sample node access query looks like so after it has been processed by node_query_node_access _alter():

```
SELECT DISTINCT(n.nid) FROM node n INNER JOIN node_access na ON n.nid
= na.nid WHERE (n.promote = 1) AND (n.status = 1) AND (((na.gid =
0) AND (na.realm = 'all')) OR (((na.gid = 2) AND (na.realm = 'role_
access'))) AND na.grant_view >= 1) ORDER BY n.sticky DESC, n.created
DESC LIMIT 0, 10;
```

In plain English, here's what it means:

Select the first ten distinct node ids for published and promoted nodes, ordered by "stickiness" and age, provided that one of the following conditions is true: 1) The default 'all users may view all nodes' rule is still in effect; or, 2) At least one of the current user's access grants allows access to view the node.

That's a whole lot to take in, so we'll unpack it some more.

When node_query_node_access_alter() runs, it asks a few basic questions before altering the query. These are:

- Can this user access all content?

  This request is carried out by the node_access_view_all_nodes() function, which checks to see if any node access modules are enabled, what the user's permissions are, and if access is granted by the default 'view all content' record. If TRUE, then the alter query exits without changing the query.

- Can this user `bypass node access`?

  New in Drupal 7, the `bypass node access` permission has been split from the `administer nodes` permission. This permission allows super-users to ignore all node access rules (including those enforced by `hook_node_access()`). Normally, this permission is only retained by user 1, but on some sites, select roles should always be allowed to view all nodes.

- What node access permissions does this user have?

  Here, the function calls `node_access_grants()` to determine what node access permissions the user account has been granted. These grants are returned by your module's `hook_node_grants()` function. Each returned grant is used to create a new OR clause in the final node access query.

  > Note that we said *OR clause*. This is crucial. Node access in Drupal is still a permissive system. If you are using multiple node access modules and one grants access, that access cannot be taken away by another node access module's grants. There are, however, ways to enforce "deny" grants through either `hook_node_access()` or `hook_node_grants_alter()`, which we will discuss later.

- What action are we performing?

  The last question checks the operation being performed (View, Update, or Delete) in order to add the proper access clause against the `grant_view`, `grant_update`, or `grant_delete` columns of the `{node_access}` table.

Unlike `hook_node_access()`, the query runs against the `{node_access}` table and does not care which individual node we are trying to view, update, or delete. Instead, the node access system here provides a layer of abstraction so that listing queries can be properly filtered according to the site's access rules.

{node_access} table schema explained

The `{node_access}` table works by storing the necessary information for running a proper JOIN to the `{node}` table based on the conditions described above. To fully understand how the above query example works (and to plan your node access module), let's examine the structure of the table itself.

The {node_access} table contains six columns, each with a specific role in the API.

- nid is an integer and is the foreign key to the {node} table, used as the JOIN field for SELECT statements.

- gid is an integer and represents the grant id declared by a node access module. All gids are paired with an appropriate realm, as defined by the module.

- realm is a string (maximum 255 characters) that indicates the name of the access rule assigned by a module. Modules may define multiple realms, and each realm may have multiple gids. Taken together, a realm/gid pair creates a specific access **grant** for the given node id.

- grant_view is an integer that provides a Boolean value indicating that the grant in this row allows the node to be viewed by users with the proper permission.

- grant_update is an integer that provides a Boolean value indicating that the grant in this row allows the node to be edited by users with the proper permission.

- grant_delete is an integer that provides a Boolean value indicating that the grant in this row allows the node to be deleted by users with the proper permission.

Taken together, each row of the {node_access} table defines a rule set for a node. A node may have more than one rule set. Note that the {node_access} table itself does not care about the publication status of the node. When defining your modules's realms, you should take into account how to handle access to unpublished content.

> Because they can write multiple records to the {node_access} table and add JOINs to most node queries, node access modules can be resource intensive. In order to keep performance high, sites that plan to use node access modules should generally allow for 5-10% additional processing power for the database server.

Defining your module's access rules

Now that we understand how Drupal limits access to nodes, we are ready to explore the API for module developers. Before we write any code, however, we should write out the access rules we wish to enforce and review them for accuracy and potential trouble.

For our test module, we want to leverage Drupal's role system to create tiers of users. Each member of a role will only be able to View, Edit, or Delete content created by other members of that role. Some users, however, may not be allowed to Edit or Delete content, so our module needs to separate the three permissions properly.

Written out, here is what our rule set looks like:

1. All users will be assigned to one or more roles.
2. All nodes will be assigned grants based on the role(s) of the node author.
3. Users will be assigned individual grants for the View, Update, and Delete actions based on their assigned roles and permissions.
4. Users with the proper permission will be able to View, Update, and Delete a node, regardless of its publication state.
5. If the author of a node changes, the grants for that node will change.
6. If the author of a node is assigned new roles, the grants for the author's nodes will not be altered unless the nodes are updated.

These rules all seem pretty straightforward, except for rule #6. To be honest, we put in rule #6 to prevent us from having to write additional code to handle this case, which would merely complicate our example. However, when writing a node access module, you need to keep in mind all the variables that may affect how your rule sets are enforced.

Remember:

- Node access rules are recalculated and stored every time a node is saved
- User access grants are calculated for every page request
- Node access rules must be rebuilt for the entire site any time a node access module is added or removed
- Node access grants may be different for each of the three operations – View, Update, and Delete – even for the same user

Your module needs to be aware of the greater context in which its rules operate. So writing out the expected behavior of the module – and posting that definition in a README file and as online and module help documentation – is a key part to writing a good node access module.

Based on the rules and guidelines above, we have a good idea how to write our module. Let's call it Role Access and get to work.

Creating the role access module

We begin with the standard module `.info` file and a stub `.module` file, as shown below:

```
; $Id$
name = Role Access
description = Limit content access by user role.
core = 7.x
files[] = role_access.module
```

Save this as `role_access.info` inside a `/sites/default/modules/role_access/` directory.

Then create a stub `role_access.module` file:

```php
<?php

// $Id$

/**
 * @file
 * Role access module file.
 *
 * Provides a simple content access scheme based on the
 * author's role.
 */
```

Now we are ready to begin building our module. The code in the next sections will all add to this base file.

Using hook_node_access_records()

Enforcing rules with a node access module takes two parts. The first is *writing your module's rules to the* {`node_access`} *table*. This action is performed with the `hook_node_access_records()` function. This function is called every time a node is created or updated. It is your module's responsibility to respond appropriately to this hook.

 When creating or updating nodes, modules should never perform direct database queries to {`node_access`}. Doing so breaks the API because other modules can no longer rely on the expected behavior of the node access system.

When `hook_node_access_records()` fires, it passes a single parameter, the `$node` object being acted upon. Our module must respond based on the information in the `$node` object or be able to derive its rules from that information.

 This last statement may seem obvious, but bears repeating. If your business rules rely on special information not found in the default `$node` object, it is your responsibility to add that data using `hook_node_load()`. We will look at this in more detail later in this chapter.

For Role Access, we need to know the roles assigned to the user who authored the node.

```
/**
 * Implement hook_node_access_records().
 *
 * We want to store a row for each role assigned
 * to the author of the content.
 *
 */
function role_access_node_access_records($node) {
  // First get the user record. Note that we avoid using $user here,
  // since that is the global $user object.
  $account = user_load($node->uid);

  // Now, get the roles array from the $account object.
  $roles = array_keys($account->roles);
```

Here we use the Drupal API to grab the roles assigned to the node author. The use of `array_keys()` in the last line means that we will be given a simple array of role ids. These role ids will be used as the grant ids that we store in the {node_access} table. A typical `$roles` result will look like this if we `var_dump()` its value:

```
array(2) {
  [0]=> int(2)
  [1]=> int(4)
}
```

From here, we are required to build a well-formed $grants array which defines the rules for our module. This array matches the schema of the {node_access} table and adds a 'priority' key. For our module, we return an array element for each role:

```
// Initialize a $grants array.
$grants = array();

// Iterate through the $roles and get our grants.
// We use the role id as the grant id, so let's name it that way for
clarity.
foreach ($roles as $grant_id) {
  $grants[] = array(
    'realm' => 'role_access', // The name of our module.
    'gid' => $grant_id,
    'grant_view' => 1,
    'grant_update' => 1,
    'grant_delete' => 1,
    'priority' => 0, // If not zero, other grants are ignored.
  );
}
// Return our grants.
return $grants;
}
```

Inspecting the output of this code shows us:

```
$grants[0] = array(
  'realm' => 'role_access',
  'gid' => 2,
  'grant_view' => 1,
  'grant_update' => 1,
  'grant_delete' => 1,
  'priority' => 0,
),
$grants[1] = array(
  'realm' => 'role_access',
  'gid' => 4,
  'grant_view' => 1,
  'grant_update' => 1,
  'grant_delete' => 1,
  'priority' => 0,
);
```

Note that we do not need to identify the node itself. The API handles that for us.

A few things to consider when returning your node grants.

- Your module may assert one or more 'realms' as appropriate to your business logic.

- The 'realm' must be a string unique to your module. Namespace your grant with the name of the module. If you only store one grant, use the name of the module as the realm.

- The three grants are each checked separately to determine permissions. This means that you may define all three grants (view, update and delete) in a single statement.

- The 'priority' element is deprecated for Drupal 7. It can be used to discard the grants set by other modules. However, this is best done through the new `hook_node_access_records_alter()`. (See `http://drupal.org/node/686858` for details.)

- Your grants declarations must be integers (0 or 1) and not Boolean TRUE or FALSE. Drupal 7's database layer uses stricter variable typing than Drupal 6 and below, so be sure to update your legacy code.

- The {node_access} table does not distinguish between published and unpublished nodes. Only trusted users should be given permission to access unpublished content.

We have now established our rules in the database. Let's examine the second part of the node access system.

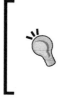

> Right now, if we save a node with our module in this form, nothing happens. Why? Because the Node Access API assumes that your module also implements `hook_node_grants()`. Without that hook, your records will not be stored. Drupal does this to save database overhead associated with storing unused records.

Using hook_node_grants()

For every page request involving nodes, Drupal queries the enabled modules for the node access grants that are in force for the current user. Modules respond to this query using `hook_node_grants()`.

Unlike `hook_node_access_records()`, which is node-centric, `hook_node_grants()` is user-centric. The hook passes two parameters:

- `$account` – the user object of the person viewing the page.

- `$op` – the operation being performed (view, update or delete).

Note that we do not have access to the $node object here. This is because the node access API is used to provide advanced filtering of queries, both for single nodes and for groups of nodes. This level of abstraction is what makes node access work.

So our Role Access module must determine what permissions our current user has. This is a fairly simple operation, since user roles are attached to the $account object:

```
/**
 * Implement hook_node_grants().
 */
function role_access_node_grants($account, $op) {
  // Get the user roles.
  $roles = array_keys($account->roles);

  // Error checking.
  if (empty($roles)) {
    return array();
  }

  // Initialize a $grants array.
  $grants = array();

  // Iterate through the roles.
  foreach ($roles as $grant_id) {
    $grants['role_access'][] = $grant_id;
  }

  // Return the grants.
  return $grants;
}
```

Again, we are expected to return a $grants array. This array is keyed by the **realm(s)** of our module. Each realm may then declare an array of grant ids.

These values are then concatenated for all modules on the site, and a final $grants array is constructed. This array is used to alter queries to the {node} table in order to enforce our node access rules.

These grants **must** match those provided in hook_node_access_records(), otherwise, the grants will fail and the operation will be denied.

Security considerations

The above code works just fine. But there is a potentially dangerous flaw in its logic: we do not account for variations of the different operations. As written, the module gives View, Update, and Delete access to all nodes based on user role. This could be a huge problem if we don't want some roles to delete content.

One way to correct this issue is to leverage the core permission system to establish additional rules that our module implements. We can assign specific permissions to allow each role access to the various operations.

If you recall *Chapter 8, Drupal Permissions and Security,* implementing `hook_permission()` gives us an easy way to do this.

```
/**
 * Implement hook_permission().
 *
 * Define our modules permissions as follows:
 *   -- view role access content
 *   -- update role access content
 *   -- delete role access content
 *
 * Naming these properly helps avoid conflicts with other modules.
 * Note that we name these based on the $op value passed by
 * hook_node_grants(). This allows us to use string concatenation
 * when doing our access check.
 */
function role_access_permission() {
  return array(
    'view role access content' =>  array(
      'title' => t('View role-restricted content'),
      'description' => t('Allow users to view content assigned by
role.'),
    ),
    'update role access content' =>  array(
      'title' => t('Edit role-restricted content'),
      'description' => t('Allow users to edit content assigned by
role.'),
    ),
    'delete role access content' =>  array(
      'title' => t('Delete role-restricted content'),
      'description' => t('Allow users to delete content assigned by
role.'),
    ),
  );
}
```

Once we have these permissions in place, we can simply enforce them inside `hook_node_grants()`. We must add the permission logic to our `foreach` loop.

```
function role_access_node_grants($account, $op) {
  // Get the user roles.
  $roles = array_keys($account->roles);

  // Error checking.
  if (empty($roles)) {
    return array();
  }

  // Initialize a $grants array.
  $grants = array();

  // Iterate through the roles.
  foreach ($roles as $grant_id) {
    // Check the permission callback!
    if (user_access($op . ' role access content')) {
      $grants['role_access'][] = $grant_id;
    }
  }

  // Return the grants.
  return $grants;
}
```

Now we have a mechanism for restricting the access rules based on the operation being performed. Our recommended configuration looks like this:

PERMISSION	ANONYMOUS USER	AUTHENTICATED USER	ADMINISTRATOR	EDITOR	WRITER
Role Access					
View role-restricted content Allow users to view content assigned by role.	☑	☑	☑	☑	☑
Edit role-restricted content Allow users to edit content assigned by role.	☐	☐	☑	☑	☑
Delete role-restricted content Allow users to delete content assigned by role.	☐	☐	☑	☐	☐

Rebuilding the {node_access} table

One of the trickier parts of the node access system is rebuilding the {node_access} table. When you first install a node access module, you will notice a warning at the top of the configuration page, prompting you to rebuild permissions.

As a site administrator, you should always rebuild permissions when prompted to do so. As a module developer, you are responsible for ensuring that those permissions are rebuilt correctly.

In our example module code, we avoided this issue by relying on data that is always present in the $node object, the user's identity, from which we can derive the user's roles. However, if your module relies on data not stored by Drupal core or contributed modules – both of which should be listed as dependencies[] in your module.info file – then it is your responsibility to store the data necessary to rebuild the {node_access} table properly.

For example, let's look quickly at the Domain Access module. This module stores information about its grants in the {domain_access} table, which mirrors much of the data in {node_access}. The table schema is as follows:

```
$schema['domain_access'] = array(
    'fields' => array(
      'nid' => array('type' => 'int', 'unsigned' => TRUE, 'not null'
=> TRUE, 'default' => 0),
      'gid' => array('type' => 'int', 'unsigned' => TRUE, 'not null'
=> TRUE, 'default' => 0),
      'realm' => array('type' => 'varchar', 'length' => '255', 'not
null' => TRUE, 'default' => '')),
    'primary key' => array('nid', 'gid', 'realm'),
    'indexes' => array(
      'nid' => array('nid')),
  );
```

Domain Access keeps track of two separate **realms**, but sets all three **grant** operations to TRUE for each node. So this table stores just the data necessary to rebuild the node access table.

To ensure that your data is present during rebuild, your module should implement hook_node_load(). This will ensure that the data required by your implementation of hook_node_access_records() is available to you.

> It is important to load this data in hook_node_load() rather than inside hook_node_access_records() for the following reason. Other modules may wish to act based on your data – particularly modules that implement hook_node_access_records_alter(). While hook_node_load() allows the $node object to be altered and extended, hook_node_access_records() does not. So it is your module's responsibility to ensure that the data used by your node access logic is loaded onto the $node object properly.

Since the Role Access module can always access $node->uid to derive its data, we won't worry about data storage for our module.

Modifying the behavior of other modules

Our choice of Role Access as a sample module was deliberate for two reasons: first, we can ignore the data storage issue discussed above; second, the role system gives us a good opportunity to look at how other modules may modify the behavior of node access modules.

If you saved and installed the Role Access code to this point, you will see that it works just fine, but with two potential issues.

- For most sites, anonymous users are not allowed to create content but they are allowed to view content. Since Role Access restricts the View operation to users with the same role, this would mean that anonymous users cannot view any content.

- All custom roles are also tagged as authenticated users (role id 2). This means that any content created by someone in an 'administrator' role would also be tagged for authenticated users. This seems too permissive.

We could write some logic into the Role Access module to handle these use cases, but it may also be the case that the default functionality is proper. So rather than edit the module or create some special module settings and exception handling, in Drupal 7 we can write a simple extension module that will modify the behavior of the parent module.

Using the new `hook_node_access_records_alter()` and `hook_node_grants_alter()`, we can fundamentally alter how any other node access module behaves. To do so, we will create the Role Access Extend module to implement our optional behaviors.

Using hook_node_grants_alter()

When using node access alter hooks, we must decide: Should we alter what is saved in the database {`node_access`} or should we alter how the user interacts with the stored data? Since we might want to turn this module off, the best solution is to leave {`node_access`} alone and instead alter the grants on page load. We do this with the new Drupal 7 `hook_node_grants_alter()`.

`hook_node_grants_alter()` is a very powerful hook. After Drupal has gathered all the node access permissions set by your site's modules, this hook fires and allows a module to modify the cumulative `$grants` array by reference. In structure, the hook looks much like `hook_node_grants()`. It passes `&$grants`, plus the requesting user's `$account` object and the requested `$op`.

To make our first rule work, we need to control the View operation and decide which user roles may view content as if they were in the authenticated user role. First, we create our `role_access_extend.info` file, and then we create a `role_access_extend.module`.

```php
<?php

// $Id$

/**
 * @file
 * Role Access Extend
 * Additional configuration options for Role Access.
 */
```

We know that we need a configuration option to allow anonymous users to view content as authenticated users. Rather than create a new setting, we can again leverage the permission system:

```php
/**
 * Implement hook_permission().
 */
function role_access_extend_permission() {
  return array(
    'view role access as authenticated user' =>  array(
```

```
      'title' => t('View role-restricted content as authenticated
user'),
      'description' => t('Allow anonymous users to view content
created by authenticated users. Lack of this permission removes access
for users in custom roles.'),
    ),
  );
}
```

So now we have a new permission setting:

PERMISSION	ANONYMOUS USER	AUTHENTICATED USER	ADMINISTRATOR	EDITOR	WRITER
Role Access					
View role-restricted content Allow users to view content assigned by role.	☑	☑	☑	☑	☑
Edit role-restricted content Allow users to edit content assigned by role.	☐	☐	☑	☑	☑
Delete role-restricted content Allow users to delete content assigned by role.	☐	☐	☑	☐	☐
Role Access Extend					
View role-restricted content as authenticated user Allow anonymous users to view content created by authenticated users. Lack of this permission removes access for users in custom roles.	☑	☐	☐	☐	☐

We can then use `hook_node_grants_alter()` to modify the permissions that anonymous (and other users) have. To do so, we have to understand the format for the $grants array that is passed to our hook.

Drupal gathers these grants with the `node_access_grants()` function, which combines all module grants into a single associative array of arrays. The $grants array keys are the realms of access control; and the array associated to these keys indicate the grant ids that are active for that realm. A `var_dump()` of a typical $grants array looks like so:

```
array(1) {
  ["role_access"] => array(1) {
    [0] =>  int(2),
    [1] =>  int(4),
  }
}
```

We may alter any element of this array, adding or removing items that suit our business rules. Remember, however, that the resulting array will be used to write a JOIN query to the {node_access} table. It may help to read the above array in that context. A standard node query might run a simple SELECT:

```
SELECT title, nid FROM node WHERE status > 0 ORDER BY sticky, created
LIMIT 10;
```

When the node access grants are applied, the query will be executed as:

```
SELECT n.title, n.nid FROM node n INNER JOIN node_access na ON n.nid =
na.nid WHERE (na.realm = 'role_access' AND na.gid = 2) AND n.status >
0 ORDER BY sticky, created LIMIT 10;
```

As a module author, it is your responsibility to understand how these queries will be rewritten so that your code can produce the desired results.

 Remember that the grant ids are the array *values*, not the array *keys* for your node access realm!

Now that we know how the query will be affected, we can write the code to add the grant necessary to make anonymous users act like authenticated users.

```php
/**
 * Implement hook_node_grants_alter().
 */
function role_access_extend_node_grants_alter(&$grants, $account, $op)
{
  // We only act on the 'view' operation.
  // If our grant is not present, do nothing.
  if ($op != 'view' || !isset($grants['role_access'])) {
    return;
  }

  // Get the defined role id for 'authenticated user'.
  $rid = DRUPAL_AUTHENTICATED_RID;

  // Check the permission and set the grant.
  if (user_access('view role access as authenticated user')) {
    $grants['role_access'][] = $rid;
  }
}
```

This code will grant anonymous users with the proper permission access to View content as if they were authenticated.

> **Security warning!**
>
> Be very careful with any code that provides this type of privilege escalation. For instance, if we failed to check that $op == 'view' we would be giving anonymous users permission to View, Update and Delete all content on the site!

The above example is great, but what if we want to restrict custom roles to only view content created by people in those roles? That is, we might need to remove the ability to View content as an authenticated user. With a slight modification to the code, we can do so:

```
/**
 * Implement hook_node_grants_alter().
 */
function role_access_extend_node_grants_alter(&$grants, $account, $op)
{
  // We only act on the 'view' operation.
  // If our grants is not present, do nothing.
  if ($op != 'view' || !isset($grants['role_access'])) {
    return;
  }
  // Check the permission.
  $access = user_access('view role access as authenticated user');

  // Get the defined role id for 'authenticated user'.
  $rid = DRUPAL_AUTHENTICATED_RID;

  // Check authenticated users.
  if ($account->uid > 0) {
    // Users with more than one role should have 'authenticated users'
    // removed.
    if (count($account->roles) > 1 && in_array($rid, $grants['role_
access']) && !$access) {
      // The grants array is in the order $grants[$realm][$key] =>
      // $value, so flip it, unset, and flip back.
      $grants['role_access'] = array_flip($grants['role_access']);
      unset($grants['role_access'][$rid]);
      $grants['role_access'] = array_flip($grants['role_access']);
    }
  }
```

```
    // Check anonymous users.
    else if ($access) {
      $grants['role_access'][] = $rid;
    }
  }
}
```

With this code in place, we can easily assign the proper permissions to allow roles to view content as if they were authenticated users.

Using hook_node_access_records_alter()

This is great! Using very little code, we have made a major change to the business logic of the Role Access module, something that was nearly impossible prior to Drupal 7.

We still have a problem, however. Since all custom roles are also given the 'authenticated user' role, we are storing grants in the {node_access} table that may be too permissive. It may be that we do not want to store the records at all. So we have another hook we can use, in conjunction with a new permission.

First, we edit `role_access_extend_permission()`:

```
/**
 * Implement hook_permission().
 */
function role_access_extend_permission() {
  return array(
    'view role access as authenticated user' =>  array(
      'title' => t('View role-restricted content as authenticated
user'),
      'description' => t('Allow anonymous users to view content
created by authenticated users. Lack of this permission removes access
for users in custom roles.'),
    ),
    'assign role access as authenticated user' =>  array(
      'title' => t('Save role-restricted content as authenticated
user'),
      'description' => t('Save new and updated content so that
authenticated users have permissions. <em>Normally this is set to
off.</em>'),
    ),
  );
}
```

This permission will inform our use of `hook_node_access_records_alter()`.

`hook_node_access_records_alter()` is almost identical to `hook_node_access_records()`. The function passes the `&$grants` array by reference, plus the `$node` being acted upon.

```
/**
 * Implement hook_node_access_records_alter().
 *
 * If a user saves content, make sure that an access record for the
 * 'authenticated user' role should actually be stored.
 */
function role_access_extend_node_access_records_alter(&$grants, $node)
{
```

If we run a `var_dump()` on the typical `$grants` being passed to this function, we see an array that should seem familiar:

```
array(2) {
  [0]=>
  array(6) {
    ["realm"]=> string(11) "role_access"
    ["gid"]=> int(2)
    ["grant_view"]=> int(1)
    ["grant_update"]=> int(1)
    ["grant_delete"]=> int(1)
    ["priority"]=> int(0)
  }
  [1]=>
  array(6) {
    ["realm"]=> string(11) "role_access"
    ["gid"]=> int(5)
    ["grant_view"]=> int(1)
    ["grant_update"]=> int(1)
    ["grant_delete"]=> int(1)
    ["priority"]=> int(0)
  }
}
```

What we need to do is make sure that the realm '**role_access**' only returns grant id 2 if the user's role allows it. So we run a check for the user's permissions and modify the `$grants` array as needed.

```
// We cannot use the global $user here; we want the creator/editor
of the content.
$account = user_load($node->uid);
```

```
  // Check the permission.
  $access = user_access('assign role access as authenticated user',
$account);

  // Get the defined role id for 'authenticated user'.
  $rid = DRUPAL_AUTHENTICATED_RID;

  // Now add the role.
  if ($access) {
    $grants['role_access'][] = array(
      'realm' => 'role_access',
      'gid' => $rid,
      'grant_view' => 1,
      'grant_update' => 1,
      'grant_delete' => 1,
      'priority' => 0,
    );
  }
  // Or take it away.
  else {
    foreach ($grants as $key => $grant) {
      if ($grant['realm'] != 'role_access') {
        continue;
      }
      if ($grant['gid'] == $rid) {
        unset($grants[$key]);
      }
    }
  }
}
```

When this code runs, our $grants will be modified as needed, and the records sent
to the {node_access} table will reflect our new permissions. Another var_dump()
looks like so:

```
array(1) {
  [1]=>
  array(6) {
    ["realm"]=> string(11) "role_access"
    ["gid"]=> int(5)
    ["grant_view"]=> int(1)
    ["grant_update"]=> int(1)
    ["grant_delete"]=> int(1)
    ["priority"]=> int(0)
  }
}
```

Now we have an advanced rule set that gives us a great deal of flexibility, and you have two new hooks in your Drupal toolkit.

Testing and debugging your module

Testing and debugging node access modules presents a particular challenge in Drupal, largely because most access rules are user-based. That fact, combined with user 1's ability to bypass all access checks, means that you cannot test node access module through the browser while logged in as user 1. Nor can you test while logged in as any user who has the `bypass node access` permission, since that permission causes the entire node access system to be ignored, granting the user View, Update, and Delete permission to all nodes.

While we don't have space to write up a Simpletest suite for our module here, there are a few simple tricks you can remember to make your development (and support!) life easier.

- Never test as user 1 or a user who can `bypass node access`.
- You can use `hook_node_load()` and `hook_node_view()` to append your modules rule set to the node object for display. If you do so, be sure only to display this information to trusted users.
- Remember to examine the contents of `{node_access}` after a node is saved. Be sure the rules in the table reflect the logic of your code.
- Be sure that the data you need to store your rules is loaded onto the `$node` object so you can safely rebuild `{node_access}` when you need to.
- Be sure to test access to both published and unpublished content.

These guidelines will help, but there is a better, faster, and easier way to debug your working code.

Using Devel Node Access

The Devel Node Access module is part of the Devel module suite (`http://drupal.org/project/devel`). The module is maintained by salvis (`http://drupal.org/user/82964`) and gives you a browser-based view into how node access rules are being enforced on your site.

node	realm	gid	view	update	delete	explained
						node_access entries for nodes shown on this page
Populus	role_access	2	1	1	1	• *authenticated users* with the permission *View role-restricted content* may *view* this content • *authenticated users* with the permission *Edit role-restricted content* may *update* this content • *authenticated users* with the permission *Delete role-restricted content* may *delete* this content
Populus	role_access	4	1	1	1	• *editors* with the permission *View role-restricted content* may *view* this content • *editors* with the permission *Edit role-restricted content* may *update* this content • *editors* with the permission *Delete role-restricted content* may *delete* this content
Et Haero Diam Melior	role_access	2	1	1	1	• *authenticated users* with the permission *View role-restricted content* may *view* this content • *authenticated users* with the permission *Edit role-restricted content* may *update* this content • *authenticated users* with the permission *Delete role-restricted content* may *delete* this content

The key to Devel Node Access is its own internal hook system, which allows node access modules to declare a readable summary of their rules. Writing this hook is good practice, since it helps you articulate what your module does.

Using hook_node_access_explain()

hook_node_access_explain() is a function that should be responded to only by the module that sets the grants returned by hook_node_access_records(). So for our sample, we will implement it in the base Role Access module.

The hook passes one argument $row, which is an object representing one row from the {node_access} table. Your module should inspect the data, and respond with information if the $row belongs to it.

```
/**
 * Implement hook_node_access_explain().
 */
function role_access_node_access_explain($row) {
  // If not our grant, ignore.
  if ($row->realm != 'role_access') {
    return NULL;
  }
```

```
    // Get a list of user roles.
    $roles = user_roles();
    // Get our permission definitions.
    $permissions = role_access_permission();

    // Initiate a results variable, for theming the output.
    $results = array();
    // Check each access rule.
    foreach (array('view', 'update', 'delete') as $op) {
      if (in_array($row->gid, array_keys($roles))) {
        $results[] = t('%roles with the permission %perm may %op
this content', array('%role' => $roles[$row->gid], '%perm' =>
$permissions[$op . ' role access content']['title'], '%op' => $op));
      }
    }
    // Prepare for theming. The $results are already secure, having run
    // through t().
    $variables = array(
      'items' => $results,
      'title' => '',
      'type' => 'ul',
    );
    // Return a nicely themed list.
    return theme('item_list', $variables);
}
```

By providing this hook, both the developer and module users can enable Devel Node Access to see how node access rules are being enforced.

Using the Devel Node Access by user block

The Devel Node Access module also provides a block which displays the results of the node_access() function. This block can help you sort through the reason(s) why access has been granted or denied. It presents a table, showing the ten most recent site visitors and their access to a specific node.

username	create	view	update	delete
admin	YES: bypass node access	YES: bypass node access	YES: bypass node access	YES: bypass node access
dutiwrecl	YES: by *node (permissions)*	YES: node access	YES: by *node (permissions)*	YES: by *node (permissions)*
uicuswe	NO: no reason	YES: node access	NO: node access	NO: node access
slabres	NO: no reason	YES: node access	NO: node access	NO: node access
phauetr	NO: no reason	YES: node access	NO: node access	NO: node access
cruramitege	NO: no reason	YES: node access	NO: node access	NO: node access
drutakimoc	NO: no reason	YES: node access	NO: node access	NO: node access
guthet	NO: no reason	YES: node access	NO: node access	NO: node access
chepri	NO: no reason	YES: node access	NO: node access	NO: node access
seprobug	NO: no reason	YES: node access	NO: node access	NO: node access

Access permissions by user

In the preceding case, the user **dutiwrecl** has been granted editing permissions by the node module. Other users may view the content because a node access module (in this case Domain Access, `http://drupal.org/project/domain`) has granted access.

If you review our discussion of how the `node_access()` function operates, you can quickly see how handy this developer's utility can be.

Summary

This has been a long chapter, and we hope you found it rewarding. Understanding and using node access is one of the most powerful tools in the Drupal API. We have covered a wide array of topics, but the key points to remember are:

- How access to a node is determined
- To always use dynamic query syntax for node lists and to tag node queries with add_tag('node_access')
- The differences between `hook_node_access()` and writing a node access module
- How to alter Create, View, Update and Delete access to individual nodes
- The three major operations controlled by the Node Access API
- How to filter listing queries using the Node Access API

- How to write your own node access module
- How to modify existing node access modules
- The importance of storing the data required by your rule set and loading it with hook_node_load()

With an understanding of these elements and the debugging tools provided by Devel Node Access, you should be able to implement the access rules required for any Drupal project.

10
JavaScript in Drupal

JavaScript is used in Drupal like in most other web applications. It is used to power features such as the overlay, autocomplete, drag and drop, and so on. This chapter will focus on the JavaScript integration into Drupal and how to use the JavaScript helpers.

Some of the important topics this chapter will cover are:

- How to add JavaScript to pages through Drupal
- Altering JavaScript added to a page by Drupal core and other modules
- Using the helper functions built into Drupal
- Working with theming and translations in JavaScript
- Working with AJAX and Drupal

By the end of this chapter you should have the base knowledge to work with JavaScript within Drupal.

JavaScript inside Drupal

JavaScript is an integral part of Drupal providing dynamic features, a unique administration experience, and a library of JavaScript for module developers to use. The jQuery JavaScript framework comes bundled with Drupal along with several jQuery plugins. JavaScript is provided using the **Library API** which is available for modules to take advantage of.

Along with jQuery 1.4.4 the following plugins are provided by Drupal:

- jQuery UI 1.8.6
- jQuery Cookie, a simple, lightweight utility plugin for reading, writing, and deleting cookies

- jQuery Form, a plugin to easily and unobtrusively upgrade HTML forms to use AJAX
- iQuery Once, which filters out all elements that had the same filter applied to them previously
- jQuery BBQ, a back button and query library
- Farbtastic, a color wheel

Adding JavaScript

Most of the JavaScript written for Drupal utilizes jQuery but it is not a requirement. When JavaScript is added to the page there are some things to be aware of.

Drupal sets jQuery up to use its no conflict mode. This means that the $ variable is relinquished so Drupal can work with other JavaScript libraries that may use the $ variable. More detail is available at http://api.jquery.com/jQuery.noConflict.

In the absence of $ there are two methods for writing JavaScript that use jQuery. The first is to use jQuery in any place where you may have used the $. For example:

```
jQuery().ready(function() {
    ...
});
```

The other way is to wrap your code in an anonymous function and choose an alias. For example:

```
(function($) {
    $().ready(function() {
        ...
    });
})(jQuery);
```

In this case jQuery is passed in with the alias of $. Technically, $ can be replaced with a different valid alias of your choice. This works for JavaScript within a file or when placed inline on the page.

Drupal has the ability to preprocess JavaScript files where multiple files are converted into fewer files. Preprocessing provides a performance improvement for end uses as they have fewer files to download. For the preprocessor to create valid JavaScript it is recommended that at places where optional JavaScript semicolons are allowed, they should be used. In the preceding example, the semicolon after the closing (jQuery) is an example of where to use the optional semicolons.

Adding JavaScript and CSS files to .info files

The simplest method to add JavaScript and CSS to a page is by adding them to the .info files for a module. When JavaScript and CSS files are specified in a .info file they are added to all pages and configured to use preprocessing (more on that later). An example that adds a script and CSS file looks like:

```
scripts[] = foo.js
stylesheets[screen][] = bar.css
```

Each of these is a file and the path is relative to the root of the module. The `scripts` property is an array of script files. The `stylesheets` property is an array of media types and each media type is an array of CSS files.

Using drupal_add_js()

The most common method of adding JavaScript to a page is by using the function `drupal_add_js()`. This utility function provides the ability to add files (both external to Drupal and within the file system), add inline JavaScript, and pass variables between PHP and JavaScript.

Typically Cascading Stylesheets (CSS) are used alongside JavaScript. Drupal provides a function to add CSS to a page that works in a fashion similar to `drupal_add_js()`. It's called `drupal_add_css()`. The APIs between the two functions are almost identical. The feature set differs in that CSS doesn't have variables to pass in from PHP and stylesheets have media and Internet Explorer options.

Through the examples in this chapter we will create a Hello World module that displays **Hello World** in various ways using JavaScript. The function definition for `drupal_add_js()` provides two arguments with varying values depending on what you are doing with it. The definition is:

```
function drupal_add_js($data = NULL, $options = NULL)
```

As we work through the Hello World module we will examine the different variances and possible values which can be passed into `drupal_add_js()`.

Adding JavaScript files

Adding a file is the default behavior of `drupal_add_js()` and `drupal_add_css()`. Adding a JavaScript file and a CSS file to a page would look like the following:

```
drupal_add_js('path/to/hello_world.js');
drupal_add_css('path/to/hello_world.css');
```

This provides for adding a file in the simplest form. In the case of adding a file, the first argument is always the path to the file. Paths to the files within the Drupal installation are relative to the base path of the site. When these files are displayed in the browser the base path will be added to the path of the file within Drupal.

Since modules can live in more than one place within the file system, the function `drupal_get_path()` can be used to get the path of the module providing the file. Rewriting the examples above to point to the module's location in the file system dynamically, we would write:

```
$path = drupal_get_path('module', 'hello_world');
drupal_add_js($path . '/hello_world.js');
drupal_add_css($path . '/hello_world.css');
```

 For more information on using `drupal_get_path()` with modules, themes, and other systems within Drupal, see the API documentation at `http://api.drupal.org/api/function/drupal_get_path/7`.

In this simple example, we are only passing in the `$data` argument, in this case the file name, because Drupal defaults to adding files. The second argument is called `$options` and can accept either a string with the type JavaScript or CSS being added, or an array of options. Adding this JavaScript in more detail could be re-written as:

```
$path = drupal_get_path('module', 'hello_world');
drupal_add_js($path . '/hello_world.js', 'file');
drupal_add_css($path . '/hello_world.css', 'file');
```

While dealing with files, the second argument can be set to `'file'` for files internal to the Drupal filesystem or at a relative path URL, and `'external'` for files outside the Drupal installation.

The `$options` argument can be used to set several other options for each file including `weight`, `group`, `every_page`, `scope`, `defer`, `preprocess`, and `caching`.

JavaScript files are rendered based on group, whether they are on every page, and then by weight. The JavaScript groups are `JS_LIBRARY`, `JS_DEFAULT`, and `JS_THEME`. Within each group files are sub-grouped by whether `every_page` is set to true. Scripts on every page are listed before files on some pages. Finally, within each sub-group files are ordered by weight.

When a JavaScript library or plugin is used, it should be added with a group of
`JS_LIBRARY`, so that it is added to the page before the JavaScript that uses the library
or plugin. When two libraries are added to the page that are dependent on each
other, they can be added with the same group with one followed by the other in the
order they should be included or with two different weights. To illustrate this, the
following code adds `mylibrary.js` to the page as a library before `hello_world.js`.

```
$path = drupal_get_path('module', 'hello_world');
$options = array(
    'group' => JS_LIBRARY,
);

drupal_add_js($path . '/mylibrary.js', $options);
drupal_add_js($path . '/hello_world.js');
```

In our example you will notice that we can leave out the default settings. In this case
`'file'` is default so it does not need to be added to either of the calls.

For JavaScript included in ever page there is an option of every_page that should be
set to true. When this is set to true for a script it impacts preprocessing (more on that
later) and the order the script is included. Within a group files flagged as being on
every page are included before files that are not included in every page.

JavaScript within a group and within the sub-group of being or not being included in
every page are ordered by weight. The default weight is 0. Files with a lower weight
are listed before files with a higher weight.

> Libraries that rely on `drupal.js` need to be aware of the weight set for
> `drupal.js`. The weight set for `jquery.js` is -20, and the weight for
> `drupal.js` is -1.

The `scope` that a file can be added to is either the `'header'` or `'footer'`. The
default value is `'header'` and places the JavaScript at the head of the page. The most
common places to include the JavaScript are in the header or footer. Custom scopes
for JavaScript to be placed can be defined in a theme or module. In cases where
custom scopes have been defined, the scopes provided in the theme or module can
be used in addition to `'header'` and `'footer'`.

`Defer` is an option for the script tag in HTML, supported by Internet Explorer. It tells
the browser that the script can defer execution until after the page has been rendered.
This is useful for scripts that do not need to execute or be available when the page is
rendered. In Drupal this is set to TRUE or FALSE.

The preprocessing and caching properties go hand in hand. Preprocessing is the feature Drupal provides to aggregate the files added to the page into fewer files. Preprocessing of files is based on group and if a page is included in every page. For example, files grouped as JS_LIBRARY on every page are all grouped into one preprocessed file. Files grouped as JS_LIBRARY that are not on every page are grouped into another preprocessed file. Each group and subgroup of every_page is a different preprocessed file. This is done to minimize the amount of JavaScript sent to the user and to take advantage of browser based caching. When cache is set to FALSE files are not preprocessed since preprocessed files are cached.

Putting this together, a JavaScript file set to defer with caching and its preprocessing disabled, with a group set to be added after drupal.js would look like the following:

```
$path = drupal_get_path('module', 'hello_world');
$options = array(
    'group' => JS_LIBRARY,
    'cache' => FALSE,
    'preprocess' => FALSE,
    'defer' => TRUE,
);
drupal_add_js($path . '/mylibrary.js', $options);
```

Adding CSS files

CSS files are added in a similar manner to JavaScript files. The API to drupal_add_css() differs only in the options that can be passed in via the second argument. The options for CSS files are weight, group, every_page, media, basename, browsers, and preprocess. Just like drupal_add_js(), 'file' is used for files internal to Drupal or using a relative path to Drupal and 'external' is used for CSS files that are external to Drupal and they have a full URL.

There are three groups provided as constants by Drupal:

- CSS_SYSTEM is for system files and libraries
- CSS_DEFAULT is the module CSS files should use
- CSS_THEME comes after the other options and is used for theme CSS

CSS has different media that it's applied to. For example, stylesheets with a media of screen are only applied when the page is rendered for screens. Other cases, like printing, ignore the stylesheet. The default value is 'all'.

The following code adds a system CSS file which is not preprocessed and is only used for screen:

```
$path = drupal_get_path('module', 'hello_world');
$options = array(
    'group' => CSS_SYSTEM,
    'media' => 'screen',
    'preprocess' => FALSE,
);
drupal_add_css($path . '/hello_world.css', $options);
```

Passing variables from PHP to JavaScript

Drupal provides a means of passing variables from PHP to JavaScript using `drupal_add_js()`. Many applications want to pass configuration information to JavaScript that runs on a page. This function is the means in Drupal to pass that information easily.

Drupal calls the variables passed from PHP to JavaScript settings. A simple example of a setting that passes the text "Hello World!" from PHP to JavaScript would look like:

```
drupal_add_js(array('helloWorld' => "Hello World!"), 'setting');
```

 Variable names in the PHP portion of Drupal are in lowercase with an underscore separating words. In JavaScript they should be in lowerCamelCase. For more information see the coding standard at `http://drupal.org/coding-standards`.

JavaScript can access this at `Drupal.settings.helloWorld`. For example the following JavaScript would display the "Hello World" as a pop-up:

```
alert(Drupal.settings.helloWorld);
```

Settings are unlike other uses of `drupal_add_js()`. They are added to the page in the header with a weight of `JS_LIBRARY`. There are no other options besides specifying that it is a setting, as shown in the following example:

```
drupal_add_js(array('hello_world' => "Hello World!"), 'setting');
```

Settings should be added in a way that respects the namespacing of other settings added to the page. Passing multiple settings should be done in a nested array. For example:

```
$settings = array(
    'helloWorld' => array(
            'display' => 'alert',
            'message' => 'Hello World!',
    ),
);
drupal_add_js($settings, 'setting');
```

In this example, the message is available at `Drupal.settings.helloWorld.message`. Keeping all the settings in `Drupal.settings.helloWorld`, keeps the settings for this module separate from the settings added by other modules.

Adding inline JavaScript

JavaScript can be added inline on the page using the `inline` option. An example that alerts "Hello World!" would look like:

```
drupal_add_js('alert("Hello World!");', 'inline');
```

The options accessible to inline JavaScript are `defer`, `group`, `every_page`, `weight`, and `scope`. Inline JavaScript is not cached by the browser and cannot be preprocessed. Inline JavaScript that is added, which defers until after the browser has loaded with a weight of `JS_THEME` would look like this:

```
$options = array(
    'type' => 'inline',
    'group' => JS_THEME,
    'defer' => TRUE,
);
drupal_add_js("alert('Hello World!')", $options);
```

> API Documentation for `drupal_add_js()` is available at
> `http://api.drupal.org/api/function/drupal_add_js/7`

Adding inline CSS

CSS can also be added inline and the API is similar to the one for JavaScript. To add inline CSS it would look like this:

```
drupal_add_css("body { color: #ffffff; }", 'inline');
```

The second argument can contain an array of options to be used including group, scope, and preprocess. Once CSS is added, with a weight of CSS_THEME set to not preprocess, it will look like:

```
$options = array(
    'type' => 'inline',
    'group' => CSS_THEME,
    'preprocess' => FALSE,
);
drupal_add_css("body { color: #ffffff; }", $options);
```

> API Documentation for drupal_add_css() is available at
> http://api.drupal.org/api/function/drupal_add_css/7

Using the Library API

Drupal 7 provides a Library API where libraries and plugins of JavaScript and CSS can be defined and programmatically added later. jQuery and the other libraries provided with Drupal are all defined using the system modules implementation of hook_library(). We can use farbtastic, a jQuery color picker included with Drupal, as an example. Included in farbtastic is a JavaScript file and a CSS file. To add farbtastic to a page it would look as follows:

```
drupal_add_library('system', 'farbtastic');
```

This will not only add JavaScript and CSS, but will also add any dependent libraries. An example of this can be seen in the overlay module where drupal_add_library() adds the overlay. A call is made to add the parent overlay JavaScript that looks like this:

```
drupal_add_library('overlay', 'parent');
```

In the function overlay_library(), parent is set to have jQuery BBQ and jQuery UI core as dependencies to the overlay parent. This means those two libraries will be added to the page before the overlay. Drupal knows the library chain of dependencies, so you don't have to.

> API documentation about drupal_add_library() is available at
> http://api.drupal.org/api/function/drupal_add_library/7.

Defining a library with hook_library

When a module has a library or plugin it wants to use or make available to other libraries, it should define it as a library using `hook_library()`. Since we have a JavaScript file and CSS file in our Hello World module, we can add it as a library in the following way:

```
/**
 * Implements hook_library().
 */
function hello_world_library() {
    $path = drupal_get_path('module', 'hello_world');
    $libraries = array();
    $libraries['hello_world_library'] = array(
      'title' => 'Hello World',
      'website' => 'http://example.com',
      'version' => '1.0',
      'js' => array(
            $path . '/hello_world.js' => array(),
      ),
      'css' => array(
            $path . '/hello_world.css' => array(),
      ),
      'dependencies' => array(
                    array('system', 'ui.dialog'),
      ),
    );
    return $libraries;
}
```

The `title`, `website`, and `version` properties are used to define meta data about the libraries. This is important when looking for information, documentation, and checking for updates to a library.

The `js`, `css`, and `dependencies` do all the work. If any dependencies are defined, they are added before the JavaScript and CSS defined here. Then the JavaScript and CSS are added with the key for each line being the first argument for either `drupal_add_js()` or `drupal_add_css()` and the value being the `options` argument for each of the corresponding functions.

Drupal has three special dependencies that are added which do not need to be defined. They are `jquery.js`, `jquery.once.js`, and `drupal.js`. These are added to the page when the first call to `drupal_add_js()` is made or when `drupal_add_library()` is first called.

From here onwards, when we want to use the hello world library, we would add it with the following call:

```
drupal_add_library('hello_world', 'hello_world_library');
```

The first argument is the module that defined the library and the second argument is the key for the library defined.

 API documentation about hook_library() is available at http://api.drupal.org/api/function/hook_library/7.

Altering information in hook_library

Drupal provides a hook_library_alter() function, where modules can intercept the libraries defined by hook_library() and either act or make changes to them. A simple example could be another module providing a more recent version of the hello_world.js script. For the example the module will be called Hello World Update. In the file hello_world_update.module we have the following implementation of hook_library_alter():

```
/**
 * Implements hook_library_alter().
 */
function hello_world_library_alter(&$libraries, $module) {
  if ($module == 'hello_world' &&
      isset($libraries['hello_world_library'])) {
    // Verify existing version is older than the one we are
    // updating to.
    if (version_compare($libraries['hello_world_library']['version'],
'2.0', '<')) {
      // Update the existing Hello World to version 2.0.
      $libraries['hello_world_library']['version'] = '2.0';
      $libraries['hello_world_library']['js'] = array(
        drupal_get_path('module', 'hello_world_update') . '/hello_
world_2.0.js' => array(),
      );
    }
  }
}
```

The two arguments passed in are the libraries defined by a module and the name of the module. In this case we check to see if the version already defined is older than the version provided by this module. If so, we replace the JavaScript call with a different one.

API Documentation for `hook_library_alter()` is available at `http://api.drupal.org/api/function/hook_library_alter/7`

Using renderable arrays

A Drupal **Renderable Array** is the way much of the output for a Drupal page is represented before it is rendered into HTML. Theme functions, discussed in *Chapter 3, Drupal's Theme Layer*, can return either a Drupal Renderable Array or HTML to output. If a Renderable Array is returned it will be rendered into HTML by `drupal_render()`. If you are familiar with the Form API from previous versions of Drupal you've seen the Renderable Arrays. They are the arrays from Form API extrapolated to other uses. The Renderable Array for a form element might look like this:

```
$form['options'] = array(
    '#type' => 'textfield',
    '#title' => t('Author name'),
    '#maxlength' => 25,
    '#attached' => array(
       'css' => array(
         drupal_get_path('module', 'hello_world') . '/example.css',
    ),
      'js' => array(
        "alert('Hello World!')" => array('type' => 'inline'),
    ),
  );
```

The `#attached` property on a renderable or form array can be used to add JavaScript, CSS, and libraries. The keys are as follows:

- `js` is for JavaScript
- `css` is used for CSS
- `library` is used to add libraries

For each item in a sections array, like `js`, the key is the data and the options are the value. If the value is omitted, the default options are assumed.

Using renderable arrays and attaching the JavaScript, CSS, and libraries is important in several places throughout Drupal where caching of individual elements happen. An example is with blocks which can be cached. A common use case is when JavaScript is added to a block. If the JavaScript is added within the content of the block using `drupal_add_js()` it will be added when the block is not cached. Cached blocks do not rebuild the content so `drupal_add_js()` will not be called.

If a renderable array is used instead with attached JavaScript, the renderable array is cached which contains the calls to the JavaScript. When the cached content is rendered and JavaScript, CSS, then the libraries included in the renderable array will be added to the page.

An example that adds JavaScript and CSS to the output of a block would look like the following:

```
$output['content'] = array(
  '#value' => 'The content of the block.',
  '#attached' => array(
    'css' => array(
      drupal_get_path('module', 'hello_world') . '/example.css',
    ),
    'js' => array(
      "alert('Hello World!')" => array('type' => 'inline'),
    ),
  ),
);
```

Altering JavaScript

JavaScript added to a page has a last chance to be altered before being rendered to the output page. Just before the JavaScript is rendered in HTML it is passed through `hook_js_alter()`. A module that implements `hook_js_alter()` has a last chance to act on or change the JavaScript.

An example of this would be if a module wants to swap out the compressed version of jQuery with an uncompressed version. This would be helpful for debugging purposes. In the example, we will call the module jQuery Uncompressed. In the jquery_uncompressed.module file `hook_js_alter()` would look like the following:

```
/**
 * Implements hook_js_alter().
 */
function jquery_uncompressed_js_alter(&$javascript) {
  $path = drupal_get_path('module', 'jquery_uncompressed')
  $javascript['misc/jquery.js']['data'] = $path . '/jquery.
uncompressed.js';
}
```

The `$javascript` array passed in contains all the JavaScript to be added to the current page. This hook is called just before JavaScript is rendered to be added to the page. This is the last point to alter it.

The keys to the array, to find what you're looking for, are dependent on the type of JavaScript that was added.

- File and external JavaScript is identified by the path to the file that was passed in for its location.

- Settings are available at $javascript['settings'].

- Inline JavaScript is not easily identifiable. Each time an inline script is added to a page it is added with a numeric value starting at 0. If two inline scripts were added to a page, they would be added at $javascript[0] and $javascript[1]. The numbers are based on the order in which they were added to a page, which is unreliable.

 API Documentation for hook_js_alter() is available at
http://api.drupal.org/api/function/hook_js_alter/7

Altering CSS

CSS can be altered in a similar manner to JavaScript using hook_css_alter(). An array containing all the CSS about to be added to the page is passed though hook_css_alter() as a last opportunity to make changes before the CSS is rendered into HTML and added to the page. An example use of the hook_css_alter() would be to remove the system.css file provided by core, as seen here:

```
/**
 * Implements hook_css_alter().
 */
function example_css_alter(&$css) {
  unset($css[drupal_get_path('module', 'system') . '/system.css']);
}
```

Identifying items in the array passed in for CSS files is similar to JavaScript files. The key for internal and external files is the path to the file used when it was originally added. Like inline JavaScript, inline CSS is added using numeric keys in the order the CSS was added.

 API Documentation for hook_css_alter() is available at
http://api.drupal.org/api/function/hook_css_alter/7

Drupal specific JavaScript

Within Drupal there are numerous helper functions. These range from systems like theming and translation to utility functions that parse JSON.

Themeable presentation

The entire presentation inside of Drupal is customizable through the theme system, and JavaScript is no different. Drupal provides a system for theming the presentation generated by the JavaScript that can be overridden within JavaScript in a theme. We can start with an example, `hello_world.js`, that is added by a module that looks like this:

```
(function($) {
  $().ready(function() {
    $('#hello-world').html('<h2>Hello World!</h2>');
  });
})(jQuery);
```

When the page is loaded, the html inside the div with the ID `hello-world` will be replaced with `<h2>Hello World!</h2>`. What if a theme wants the wrapper to be an `h3` tag instead of an `h2` tag? This is where Drupal JavaScript theming comes in.

A module should provide a theming function within the `Drupal.theme.prototype` namespace. Then, the module would call `Drupal.theme()` to access the theme function. This system allows a theme to provide an override function within the `Drupal.theme` namespace. The following example illustrates this.

```
(function($) {
  Drupal.theme.prototype.hello = function(text) {
    return '<h2>' + text + '</h2>';
  }
  $().ready(function() {
    $('#hello-world').html(Drupal.theme('hello', 'Hello World!'));
  });
})(jQuery);
```

`Drupal.theme()` will call the `Drupal.theme.prototype.hello()` function and pass in all the arguments, but the first one. This is useful because the theme can provide an override function. If a module provides a `hello_world.js` file as the one above, and a theme provides a JavaScript file with the following function, the output will be changed.

```
(function($) {
  Drupal.theme.hello = function(text) {
    return '<h3>' + text + '</h3>';
  }
})(jQuery);
```

`Drupal.theme()` will call `Drupal.theme.hello()` instead of `Drupal.theme.prototype.hello()`. The theme can override the presentation in JavaScript this way.

Translatable strings

All the text inside the Drupal interface is translatable. The text within JavaScript can be translated as well. Inside the PHP code for Drupal the `t()` function is used for translations. Inside JavaScript the `Drupal.t()` function is used to handle translations.

Continuing the Hello World module we can extend it to handle, say "hello" to different cities, where the "hello" part is translatable.

```
(function($) {
  Drupal.theme.prototype.hello = function(text) {
    return '<h2>' + Drupal.t('Hello @city', {'@city': text}) + '</
h2>';
  }
  $().ready(function() {
    $('#hello-world').html(Drupal.theme('hello', 'Chicago'));
  });
})(jQuery);
```

The part we are interested in is where it says:

```
Drupal.t('Hello @city', {'@city': text})
```

Here the string `'Hello @city'` is a translatable string. The `@city` part is dynamic and will be filled in by the value of `text`. This setup enables translations to modify the string and still pass the dynamic portions through.

There are three ways variables can be passed through `Drupal.t()` depending on the first character of the variable:

- Variables beginning with a `!` are inserted as is, with no modification.
- When a variable begins with an `@` symbol the value is passed through `Drupal.checkPlain()`, a function that converts the string to plain text. HTML markup is converted to text that can be displayed.
- `%` at the beginning of a variable will cause the variable to be passed through `Drupal.checkPlain()` and `Drupal.theme('placeholder')`.

Behaviors

If you're familiar with writing jQuery, you know that the code you want to execute as early as possible in a page load is wrapped in something like the following:

```
$(document).ready(function() {
    ...
});
```

When the document is ready the code wrapped inside this function will be executed. This is a common pattern for jQuery-based JavaScript. Drupal provides a system that wraps and extends this concept called **behaviors**. Behaviors are attached and detached from a section of content. The most common usage is to attach a behavior to an entire page.

Rewriting our Hello World example seen previously to use behaviors would look as follows:

```
(function($) {
  Drupal.theme.prototype.hello = function(text) {
    return '<h2>' + Drupal.t('Hello @city', {'@city': text}) +
'</h2>';
  }
  Drupal.behaviors.helloWorld = {
    attach: function(context, settings) {
      $('#hello-world', context).html(Drupal.theme('hello',
'Chicago'));
    }
  }
})(jQuery);
```

The behavior is at `Drupal.behaviors.helloWorld` and has an `attach` function to attach the behavior to the page. When the document is ready, Drupal calls all the `attach` functions for all behaviors. It passes in the context, the document, and the settings, which on page load is the value of `Drupal.settings`.

On the surface this looks like an unintuitive method as compared to the more common pattern used in jQuery. The behaviors pattern provides a lot more. For example, when content retrieved through AJAX is added to the page, it is passed through the `attach` functions for all the behaviors. The `context` is the content being added that was obtained from the AJAX request and the `settings` is either settings that were returned with the AJAX request or the settings within `Drupal.settings`.

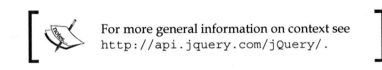

For more general information on context see `http://api.jquery.com/jQuery/`.

Along with the ability to attach behaviors is the ability to detach a behavior. A typical structure for a behavior is:

```
(function($) {
  Drupal.behaviors.example = {
    attach: function(context, settings) {
      . . .
    }
    detach: function(context, settings, trigger) {
      . . .
    }
  }
})(jQuery);
```

For example, when an AJAX-based JavaScript removes content from a section of the page before adding new content to the section, the `detach` functions for the behaviors are called on the content being removed. This provides an opportunity for behaviors to act on this content one last time.

An example of this is initiated by the Drupal AJAX system. Before a form is sent, via AJAX to Drupal, `detach` is called on all the behaviors. This provides an opportunity for behaviors that make changes to the form, that should not be sent to Drupal, to be removed. When the new content is brought into the page the behaviors are attached again.

AJAX helpers

Included in Drupal is an AJAX library that integrates Drupal, jQuery, and AJAX. This system provides a set of properties for forms and functions, to use in Drupal callbacks, which quickly and easily build AJAX into Drupal modules. Using the helper functions and properties AJAX can be built into Drupal pages rather than bolted into the pages.

Adding AJAX to forms

A common use of AJAX is dynamically updating forms, based on input, to other parts of the form. When one element in the form is updated, other elements change or are populated with information based on a change. For an example, we can look at an option list form element that updates a markup element.

We start with an implementation of hook_menu() to define the form page, as seen here:

```
/**
 * Implements hook_menu().
 */
function hello_world_menu() {
  $items = array();
  $items['hello_world/simple_form_example'] = array(
    'title' => 'Hello World: Simple AJAX Example',
    'page callback' => 'drupal_get_form',
    'page arguments' => array('hello_world_simple_form_example'),
    'access callback' => TRUE,
  );

  return $items;
}
```

We follow this by creating a form callback called hello_world_simple_form_ example(). This creates the form to insert into the page.

```
function hello_world_simple_form_example($form, &$form_state) {
  $form = array();
  $form['hello_city'] = array(
    '#title' => t("Choose a city"),
    '#type' => 'select',
    '#options' => array(
      t('World') => t('World'),
      t('Chicago') => t('Chicago'),
      t('New York') => t('New York'),
```

```
        t('Los Angelas') => t('Los Angelas'),
    ),
    '#ajax' => array(
      'callback' => 'hello_world_simple_form_callback',
      'wrapper' => 'ajax_markup_div',
    ),
  );

  $form['ajax_markup'] = array(
    '#prefix' => '<div id="ajax_markup_div">',
    '#suffix' => '</div>',
    '#markup' => t('Hello World'),
  );

  if (!empty($form_state['values']['hello_city'])) {
    $form['ajax_markup']['#markup'] = t("Hello !city", array('!city'
=> $form_state['values']['hello_city']));
  }
  return $form;
}
```

Here we have two form elements of `hello_city` and `ajax_markup`. The `hello_city` element has a `#ajax` property, which is new to Drupal 7. It defines a callback, which is an internal Drupal callback function, and a wrapper. This is the wrapper on the page that will be updated by the response to the AJAX request.

The second element, called `ajax_markup`, is a markup form element. This element holds HTML. We initially populate the markup with 'Hello World'. For this element to be updated we need to add a wrapper to it. In this case the wrapper is a `div` with the same ID that we set as the wrapper in the `#ajax` part of the `hello_city` element.

After the form is set up there is an `if` statement for the case when a value is available on `$form_state` for the `hello_city` element. When the form is initially created, there won't be a value. When the AJAX request is made, it will be passed through this form with the values from the form. When that happens the `if` statement will be executed causing the `ajax_markup` element to be updated.

This will be followed by the execution of the callback defined by the `#ajax` property on the `hello_world` element. That function looks like this:

```
function hello_world_simple_form_callback($form, $form_state) {
  return $form['ajax_markup'];
}
```

The callback function `hello_world_simple_form_callback()` passes the `$form` and `$form_state` variables after they have gone through `hello_world_simple_form_example()`. In this case we are returning the form element that is being replaced.

Drupal knows this is a renderable array and renders it to the appropriate value. Drupal sends the updated HTML back to the page where the Drupal AJAX handlers retrieve the changes and replace the wrapper.

AJAX automatically applied

AJAX can be automatically applied to elements on a page. This is done by applying the `use-ajax` class to an element on a page. A typical use would be to apply the `use-ajax` class to a link within a page to trigger an AJAX action. Links are commonly used because the page the link points to might be for the cases when JavaScript is disabled as a fallback.

In the following example we are going to provide a link that, when clicked, will add "Hello World" to a `div` within the page. To start, we have two menu callbacks that we add to `hello_world_menu()`. One item for the page we are generating and the other is the callback URL used for AJAX or when JavaScript is disabled.

```
$items['hello_world/link'] = array(
  'title' => 'Hello World: Link',
  'page callback' => 'hello_world_link',
  'access callback' => 'user_access',
  'access arguments' => array('access content'),
);
$items['hello_world_link_callback'] = array(
  'page callback' => 'hello_world_link_response',
  'access callback' => 'user_access',
  'access arguments' => array('access content'),
);
```

The first menu item is to our page where the link is located and where the AJAX will add content. The second menu item is the callback that will handle the AJAX request or the page request, when JavaScript is unavailable.

```
function hello_world_link() {
  drupal_add_js('misc/ajax.js');
  $link = l(t('Say Hello'), 'hello_world_link_callback/nojs/',
array('attributes' => array('class' => array('use-ajax'))));
  return '<div>' . $link . '</div><div id="saying-hello"></div>';
}
```

The page callback where the link lives, starts by using `drupal_add_js()` to add `misc/ajax.js`. This JavaScript does the work to automatically make the AJAX work. This is followed by a link with a callback to `hello_world_link_callback/ nojs/`. The first part of this link is the callback where the AJAX request is handled. The `/nojs/` at the end is special. When JavaScript is not available it is passed to the response function so it knows it was called to be a full page load. When JavaScript is available it is replaced with `/ajax/`. This is passed into the callback function so it knows it was called via an AJAX request.

What makes this link become an AJAX link is the class being added with the name `use-ajax`. The JavaScript file we added at the beginning, `ajax.js`, looks for links with this class and converts them into AJAX.

```
function hello_world_link_response($type = 'ajax') {
  if ($type == 'ajax') {
    $output = t("Hello World!");
    $commands = array();
    $commands[] = ajax_command_append('#saying-hello', $output);
    $page = array('#type' => 'ajax_commands', '#ajax_commands' =>
$commands);
    ajax_deliver($page);
  }
  else {
    return t("Hello World in a new page.");
  }
}
```

When the callback to handle the request is called, the type of action is passed in. When no JavaScript is available, `nojs` is passed in. When the request is AJAX, `ajax` is passed in. This can be used in the callback functions logic to properly respond to each case.

In this case we use an `if` statement. When the request is AJAX, we respond in one way and when JavaScript is not available we respond differently.

When the request is an AJAX callback we start by creating the response text of "Hello World!". This is followed by creating an array to hold commands we want Drupal to execute and adding a command to it.

A **command** is an action we want the JavaScript to perform when it receives the AJAX response. The commands provide ways in which jQuery can manipulate the content of the page with the responded data. In this case the command used is the `ajax_command_append()`. This command accepts a jQuery selector and content. The content is appended to the selector. This Drupal function utilizes the `jQuery.append()` function.

Once the response is set up it is inserted into a renderable array. The type is `ajax_commands`, which will know how to render the AJAX command that was created in the callback. To send the AJAX response properly `ajax_deliver()` is used. This function properly formats the response for the JavaScript on the receiving side.

Additionally, Drupal tracks the JavaScript and CSS files within a page. If a new file is added within an AJAX request that is not already loaded in the page the new file is sent as part of the response and added to the page along with the rest of the response.

For cases when JavaScript is not available in the initial page view and the link is followed, it is treated as a full page request and the user is sent to a new page. This page lives at the same callback that built the AJAX response. The difference is `nojs` is passed into the callback so it knows the response is not in AJAX. In this case the `else` is executed generating a different message for the new page.

AJAX commands

Drupal provides several AJAX commands that can add or alter content in a page using jQuery methods. In the previous section we covered `ajax_command_append()`. Here are all the possible commands that can be used.

ajax_command_after

When `ajax_command_after()` is used, `jQuery.after()` is the method used to add content to the page. The arguments are `$selector`, `$content`, and `$settings`. `$selector` is the jQuery selector on the page and `$content` is the content to add after the selector. `$settings`, the third argument, is a set of settings used by the behaviors for this single command.

ajax_command_alert

The alert command is a core JavaScript command. `ajax_command_alert($text)` is used to alert returned text. The text is presented in an alert box.

ajax_command_append

This command is similar to `ajax_command_after`. Instead of adding the content after the selector it appends it to the end of the selector. The interface to the function is the same as `ajax_command_after()` with the `$selector`, `$content`, and `$settings` arguments. `$selector` is the jQuery selector on the page, `$content` is the content to append to the selector, and `$settings` is used by behavior for just this one command.

ajax_command_before

To add content before an element use `ajax_command_before()`. It utilizes `jQuery.before()` to add content before a selector. Again the `$selector`, `$content`, and `$settings` arguments are used.

ajax_command_changed

To note that something within a page has changed `ajax_command_changed($selector, $asterisk)` can be used. Elements found on the page with the given jQuery selector will have the `ajax-changed` class applied to them. `$asterisk` is an optional CSS selector, that resides inside `$selector`. This is used to optionally append an asterisk to that element.

ajax_command_css

`ajax_command_css()` uses the `jQuery.css()` command to update the CSS within the page. This command takes in `$selector` and `$argument` arguments. For example, changing a page's background color would look as follows:

```
$commands[] = ajax_command_css('body', array('background-color' =>
'#FFFFFF'));
```

ajax_command_data

jQuery provides a 'data' command to store data within a page outside of element attributes. The `ajax_command_data()` function enables Drupal AJAX to add and update data inside jQuerys data cache. The three arguments are:

- `$selector`, the jQuery element selector
- `$name`, the name of the data item being accessed
- `$value`, the value for the item

ajax_command_html

`ajax_command_html()` utilizes `jQuery.html()` to update the html for a given selector. The arguments are `$selector` (the jQuery selector), `$html` (the HTML to update the selector to use), and `$settings` (optional settings for this command to use).

ajax_command_prepend

To add content at the beginning of an element use the `prepend` command. This utilizes `jQuery.prepend()` to add the content. The arguments for `ajax_command_prepend()` are `$selector`, `$content`, and `$settings`.

ajax_command_remove

The remove command removes elements from a page. The single argument is the selector to be removed. `jQuery.remove()` is utilized to remove the elements from the page.

ajax_command_replace

The ajax_command_html replaces the html content within an element. For cases where the entire element needs to be replaced `ajax_command_replace()` should be used. It takes advantage of `jQuery.replaceWith()` to replace the entire element. The three arguments are `$selector`, `$html`, and `$settings`. `$html` is the full html the selector will be replaced with. For example, take the html:

```
<div class="container">
  <div class="inner">Hello World!</div>
</div>
```

An `ajax_command_replace()` looks like the following:

```
$commands[] = ajax_command_replace('.inner', '<h2>Goodbye World!
</h2>';
```

This will update the html to look like the following:

```
<div class="container">
  <h2>Goodbye World!</h2>
</div>
```

ajax_command_restripe

The restripe command tells Drupal to restripe a table. This is useful when content inside the table has been altered. The only argument is the jQuery selector for the table.

ajax_command_settings

`ajax_command_settings()` is used to add settings to the response. The first argument is the settings to be sent with the response. If only the first argument is given, or the second argument is FALSE, then the setting will only be used for the response. If the second argument, the `$merge` argument, is set to TRUE the settings will be merged into `Drupal.settings`.

 For more information on the jQuery APIs visit `http://api.jquery.com`.

Summary

We have covered the basic principles and commands of using JavaScript and jQuery within the context of Drupal. We started by adding JavaScript to a page as a file, inline, and as a setting. We continued by looking at adding complete libraries with dependencies and altering JavaScript right before the page was rendered.

Drupal provides helper functions and libraries which are useful in creating Drupal modules. We covered how these libraries and some of the more commonly used elements work.

11
Working with Files and Images

Drupal 7 introduced a new API for files and images, bringing the functionality of popular contributed modules like `Imagecache` and `Imagefield` into core for the first time. In this chapter, we will build two modules that take advantage of this new functionality. Some of the concepts we will cover are:

- Understanding Drupal's `public` and `private` filesystems
- Associating files and images with content
- Implementing a stream wrapper for custom file handling
- Programmatically manipulating images using image styles and effects
- Understanding Drupal's new **Image Styles** functionality
- Implementing your own image effects for use with **Image Styles**

By the time you are done with this chapter, you should have a good understanding of how to manipulate files and images using Drupal, including some methods for retrieving remote files and images.

The Twitpic and watermark modules

In this chapter, we will be building the `Twitpic` module. This module will enable you to interact with images stored on the **Twitpic** website (http://twitpic.com) and integrate them with Drupal in a variety of ways. It provides a stream wrapper that allows developers to pull images from Twitpic by referring to them with a custom URI, and offers a demo of how Drupal's Image API can be used to manipulate these images.

We will also be creating a second module, which allows users to add a simple text watermark to images. Users will be able to configure the watermark so that it displays custom text in a specified color. This effect will be available for use in **Image Styles**, the Drupal 7 implementation of the `Imagecache` module.

Files in Drupal

When you installed Drupal for the first time, you probably got the following error and wondered why you needed to create *three directories for files*:

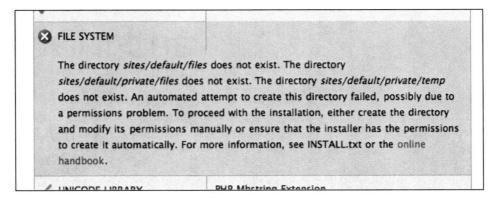

Drupal defines three types of file storage, namely, public, private, and temporary. Public files are available to the world at large for viewing or downloading. This is where things such as image content, logos, and downloadable files are stored. Your public file directory must exist somewhere under Drupal's root, and it must be readable and writeable by whatever 'user' your web server is running under. Public files have no access restrictions. Anyone, at anytime, can navigate directly to a public file and view or download it.

Private files are not available to the world for general download. The private files' directory should reside outside Drupal's root directory. However, it will still be writeable by the web server user. Isolating private files this way allows developers to control who can and can't access them as they wish. For instance, you could write a module that only allows users who have a specific role, to access PDFs in the private filesystem.

It is very important that private files live outside of Drupal's web root, despite the fact that by default they do not. In order for private files to be useful, they must be readable to the user your web server runs as. However, if these files are then under Drupal's web root, they will be readable to anybody. Proper testing is extremely important for properly securing private files. For more information on how to properly secure your private file system, see the following site: `http://drupal.org/node/344806`

Temporary file storage is typically only used by Drupal for internal operations. When files are first saved by Drupal, they are first written into the temporary file area so they can be checked for security issues. After they have been deemed safe, they are written to their final location.

Each of the directories in the preceding error message reflects the default location for each type of file. You can change these default locations after your installation is complete by logging in as administrator and visiting `admin/config/media/file-system` as seen in the following image:

Home » Administer » Configuration » Media
File system ○

Public file system path

    sites/default/files

A local file system path where public files will be stored. This directory must exist and be writable by Drupal. This directory must be relative to the Drupal installation directory and be accessible over the web.

Private file system path

A local file system path where private files will be stored. This directory must exist and be writable by Drupal. This directory should not be accessible over the web.

Temporary directory

    /tmp

A local file system path where temporary files will be stored. This directory should not be accessible over the web.

Default download method

⊙ Public local files served by the webserver.

This setting is used as the preferred download method. The use of public files is more efficient, but does not provide any access control.

[Save configuration]

You can also indicate whether the default download method should be public or private. (After installation it is public.)

File API

In Drupal 6, most file handling functionality was provided through a rough core API combined with contributed modules such as `Filefield`. Drupal 7 provides a more robust and consistent API that allows developers to interact with files in a standard set of functions that perform tasks like creating, opening, moving, and deleting files.

In order for files to be associated with nodes and other Drupal content, they must have a record in Drupal's `file` table. Each record identifies a file with a unique ID as well as associated metadata like file size and mime-type.

Many File API functions, such as `file_copy()` and `file_move()`, take a file object as one of their arguments. The file object is a PHP standard class containing the metadata from the `files` table, and these API functions manage updating the information in the `files` table when files are moved or deleted. This is one reason it is so important to use these API functions for files associated with content—if you don't, the `files` table will be inconsistent and your files may not show up properly.

If you need to work with files outside the context of Drupal content, there is a separate set of functions in the File API with `unmanaged` in their name. For instance, where `file_copy()` will update the files table and copy your file, `file_unmanaged_copy()` will just copy the file.

 For a full list of the functions available in the File API, refer to the API documentation at:
`http://api.drupal.org/api/group/file/7`

Here is a simple example of how this works. A common task while building a Drupal site is importing data from another source and turning it into nodes. This will not only include textual information like the title and body, but also images. These images may live in a local directory, or they may live out on a website you're importing from.

Let's look at how we can grab a file from an external site, save it to the default file system, and attach it to a node we create. For this example, you will be working with the field `image` in the article content type.

First we need to get a file and save it:

```
$image = file_get_contents('http://drupal.org/files/issues/druplicon_
2.png');
$file = file_save_data($image, 'public://druplicon.png',FILE_EXISTS_
REPLACE);
```

> In order to open files from remote locations, PHP must have the `allow_url_fopen` setting enabled in your `php.ini`. For more information see: `http://us2.php.net/manual/en/filesystem.configuration.php#ini.allow-url-fopen`

This is pretty straightforward. Using the PHP function `file_get_contents()`, we grab an image of Drupal's mascot, the Druplicon, and save it into the variable `$image`. We then save it locally using the Drupal API function `file_save_data()`, which returns a file object `file_save_data()`, and takes three arguments. The first argument is the contents of the file, as a string. `file_get_contents()` returns a string, so this works out well.

The second argument specifies the location where the file should be saved. This destination should be represented as a URI, using one of the system's registered stream wrappers. We will discuss stream wrappers in more detail later in the chapter, but for now, just know that you can refer to any of Drupal's file system types using a custom URI scheme, namely, `public://`, `private://`, or `temp://`. This will read or write the file into the appropriate file system without the developer needing to know the details of where the files are physically located. Here we are saving our file to the public file system.

The third argument specifies what `file_save_data()` should do when a file already exists with the same name as the file we're trying to save. There are three constants defined to indicate the possible actions that Drupal can take:

- `FILE_EXISTS_REPLACE`: The new file should overwrite the existing file.
- `FILE_EXISTS_RENAME`: Rename the new file by appending an incrementing number to the new file's name until no collision occurs. For example, if `druplicon.png` and `druplicon_1.png` already existed, then the new file would be `druplicon_2.png`.
- `FILE_EXISTS_ERROR`: Don't do anything and just return `FALSE`.

The default option is `FILE_EXISTS_RENAME` but we have specified that the file should be replaced if it exists.

After the file is saved, a file object is returned. This object contains the `fid` or file ID, as well as associated metadata. Now that we have saved the image, we can create a node and attach the image to it:

```
$node = new stdClass;
$node->type = 'article';
node_object_prepare($node);
```

```
$node->title = 'The World of Crell';
$node->language = LANGUAGE_NONE;
$node->body[LANGUAGE_NONE]['0']['value'] = 'GAHHHH!';
$node->field_image[LANGUAGE_NONE]['0']['fid'] = $file->fid;
node_save($node);
```

As discussed in *Chapter 6, Working with Content*, a node is an object and fields are properties of the object, indexed by language. In terms of this example, the highlighted line is the most important one. All we need to do, is to associate our file with the image field, is add the `fid` of our returned file object to a `fid` property of the field's instance. When the node is saved, Drupal will extract all the appropriate information from the `files` table and add it to the image field.

That's it! After running this code, you can visit your site's front page and you should see something like the following:

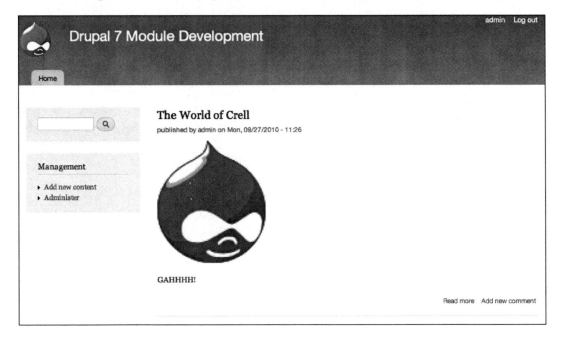

This simple example shows how easy it is to manage files in Drupal, and should provide a good jumping off point for further exploration.

As mentioned earlier in the chapter, Drupal 7's File API uses PHP stream wrappers. It also introduces the ability for developers to create their own PHP stream wrappers and integrate them with Drupal file handling. Let's take a look at what stream wrappers are and how developers can use them.

Stream wrappers

If you've been writing PHP for very long, you have most likely needed to work with local or remote files at some point. The following PHP code is a common way to read a file into a variable that you can do something with:

```
$contents = ";
$handle = fopen("/var/www/htdocs/images/xyzzy.jpg", "rb");
while (!feof($handle)) {
  $contents .= fread($handle, 8192);

}

fclose($handle);
```

This is pretty straightforward. You get a handle to a local file using `fopen()` and read 8 KB chunks of the file using `fread()` until `feof()` indicates that you've reached the end of the file, at which point you `fclose()` the handle. The contents of the file are now in the variable `$contents`. In addition to local files, you can also access remote files through `fopen()` like this:

```
$handle = fopen("http://drupal.org/files/issues/druplicon_2.png",
"rb");
```

`Data` that you can access this way is streamable, meaning you can open it, close it, or seek to an arbitrary place in it. Stream wrappers are an abstraction layer on top of streams that tell PHP how to handle specific types of data. When using a stream wrapper, you refer to the file just like a traditional URL—`scheme://target`. Often the target will be the path and filename of a file either located locally or remotely, but as we will see in our sample code, it can be any data that uniquely identifies the data you are trying to access.

The above examples use two of PHP's built in stream wrappers. The second uses the `http://` wrapper for accessing websites using the `http` protocol, and the first uses the `file://` wrapper for accessing files on local storage. `file://` is the default scheme when one is not specified, so in this case simply passing the file's path works fine.

PHP also allows developers to define their own wrappers for schemes that PHP does not handle out of the box, and the Drupal File API has been built to take advantage of this. For instance, Drupal defines the `private` scheme to allow Drupal developers to interact with files in Drupal's private file system. Let's look at how this works by creating a scheme to retrieve images from a remote website.

Creating a stream wrapper

In this example we are going to create a stream wrapper to retrieve photos from Twitpic, an image hosting service for Twitter users. Twitpic defines a REST API to retrieve photos from the URL `http://twitpic.com/show/<size>/<image-id>` where size is either `mini` or `thumb`, and image-id is a unique identifier you can retrieve from a photo's URL, as seen in the following screenshot:

> The full Twitpic API is defined at `http://twitpic.com/api.do`

So you can retrieve the thumbnail of this photo from the URL `http://twitpic.com/show/thumb/7nyr2`. This makes it very easy to refer to photos from Twitpic in your code. However, if this URL format should change, then you could end up with a lot of code to clean up. We can mitigate this by writing a stream wrapper that encapsulates this logic in one place. This stream wrapper will use the format `twitpic://<image-id>/<size>`.

There are two things that we need to do to create a custom stream wrapper in Drupal. First, we need to create a custom class which implements our functionality, then we need to register the class using `hook_stream_wrappers()`.

PHP defines a set of functions that stream wrappers can implement, as listed at `http://www.php.net/manual/en/class.streamwrapper.php`. Drupal expanded on that list and created an interface called `DrupalStreamWrapperInterface`. Any stream wrapper class used in Drupal must implement this interface or else it will not register properly.

In some cases you may not need some of this functionality provided by the interface. For instance, in our example, we are only reading photos from Twitpic without offering the ability to write data anywhere, so functions like `stream_write()` and `stream_mkdir()` don't apply. In these cases we simply return `FALSE`.

> For the full implementation details of `DrupalStreamWrapperInterface`, refer to `http://api.drupal.org/api/drupal/includes--stream_wrappers.inc/7`. You may also want to refer to PHP's prototype stream wrapper class at `http://php.net/manual/en/streamwrapper.stream-open.php`.

`DrupalStreamWrapperInterface` is quite extensive, with over 20 functions to be defined by the implementing classes. Every stream wrapper should implement each of PHP's file handling functions. As mentioned earlier, many of these simply `return FALSE`. Others simply pass through to matching PHP functionality. (`stream_eof()` simply calls and returns the results of `feof($handle)`.)

Since the class is so large, you may want to put it into a separate file to improve readability and maintainability of your code. You can do this by creating a new file in your module's directory, and adding it to the `files[]` array in your `module.info` file as shown:

```
files[] = twitpicstreamwrapper.inc
```

In order to keep things simple, we will only discuss the most noteworthy parts of the class shown in the following code. The full code listing can be downloaded from the Packt website.

```
/**
 * Twitpic Stream Wrapper
 *
 * This class provides a complete stream wrapper implementation.
 */
class TwitPicStreamWrapper implements DrupalStreamWrapperInterface {

  /**
   * Instance URI as scheme://target.
   */
  protected $uri;

  /**
   * A generic resource handle.
   */
  public $handle = NULL;
```

```php
/**
 * Overrides getExternalUrl().
 *
 * Return the HTML URL of a Twitpic image.
 */
function getExternalUrl() {
  // Get image_id and size from the URI into an array.
  $target = file_uri_target($this->uri);
  $options = array_combine(
    array('image_id', 'size'),
    explode('/', $target)
  );

  // If no size is specified, default to thumb.
  if (empty($options['size'])) {
    $options['size'] = 'thumb';
  }

  // Create the URL
  $url = 'http://twitpic.com/show/' . $options['size'] . '/' .
$options['image_id'];
  return $url;
}

/**
 * Support for fopen(), file_get_contents(),etc.
 */
public function stream_open($uri, $mode, $options, &$opened_path) {
  $allowed_modes = array('r', 'rb');
  if (!in_array($mode, $allowed_modes)) {
    return FALSE;
  }

  $this->uri = $uri;
  $url = $this->getExternalUrl();

  $this->handle = ($options & STREAM_REPORT_ERRORS) ? fopen($url,
$mode) : @fopen($url, $mode);
  return (bool)$this->handle;
}
}
```

A read-only stream wrapper like ours needs to perform two main functions. First, it needs to translate a URI like `twitpic://y6vvv/thumb` to a URL or path that can be opened and read. Second, it needs to be able to open a file handle to this resource so that developers can get the necessary data.

To manage the first requirement, we have implemented `getExternalURL()`. Any class implementing `DrupalStreamWrapperInterface` is required to override this function with their own implementation. This code is pretty straightforward; we just parse the object's URI, set some appropriate defaults, and return an appropriately structured Twitpic API URL:

```
function getExternalUrl() {
  // Get image_id and size from the URI into an array.
  $target = file_uri_target($this->uri);
  $options = array_combine(
    array('image_id', 'size'),
    explode('/', $target)
  );
```

Note the use of `file_uri_target()` to retrieve the target information from the URI. This is a helper function provided by the Drupal File API to make it easier to parse stream wrapper URIs. You can also call `file_uri_scheme()` to retrieve the scheme from a URI.

The `stream_open()` function is similarly straightforward. This will get called when a developer tries to open a resource handled by our stream wrapper using PHP functions like `fopen()` or `file_get_contents()`.This function takes four arguments, and needs to return FALSE or a handle to our resource.

The first argument is our wrapper's URI. The second argument, `$mode`, indicates whether the stream should be opened for reading and/or writing, as well as other flags. Any mode can have `b` appended to it, to indicate that the file should be opened in binary mode. (So where `r` indicates read-only, `rb` indicates read-only in binary mode.)

```
$allowed_modes = array('r', 'rb');
if (!in_array($mode, $allowed_modes)) {
  return FALSE;
}
```

We are implementing a read-only scheme, so if we get any mode other than `r` or `rb` we return FALSE.

The third argument is a bitmask of options defined by PHP. The one we're dealing with here is STREAM_REPORT_ERRORS, which indicates whether or not PHP errors should be suppressed (for instance if a file is not found). The second is STREAM_USE_PATH, which indicates whether PHP's include path should be checked if a file is not found. This is not relevant to us, so we ignore it. If a file is found on the include path, then the fourth argument $opened_url should be set with the file's real path.

Looking at the rest of the code for stream_open(), we can see how this comes together:

```
$this->uri = $uri;
$url = $this->getExternalUrl();
```

We save our URI into a protected property, and then call getExternalURL() to translate it into an actual Twitpic URL that we can grab a photo from. We can then fopen() this URL and set our internal handle.

```
if ($options && STREAM_REPORT_ERRORS) {
  $this->handle = fopen($url, $mode);
}
else {
  $this->handle = @fopen($url, $mode);
}
```

If STREAM_REPORT_ERRORS is not set, we suppress fopen() errors by prepending @, which indicates to PHP that errors should not be reported. It is always good coding practice to properly handle the options available to your stream functions if they are applicable to your user case.

In addition to creating an implementation of DrupalStreamWrapperInterface, modules that define their own stream wrappers must register them with Drupal's stream wrapper registry by implementing hook_stream_wrappers(). This hook returns an associative array defining some information about our stream wrapper, as shown in the following code:

```
/**
 * Implement hook_stream_wrappers().
 */
function twitpic_stream_wrappers() {{
  return array(
    'twitpic' => array(
      'name' => 'Twitpic photos',
      'class' => 'TwitpicStreamWrapper',
      'description' => t('Photos from the Twitpic hosting service.')
```

```
        'type' => STREAM_WRAPPERS_READ_VISIBLE,
    ),
  );
}
```

The array is keyed on our wrapper's scheme, in this case `twitpic`. Each scheme must in turn define another associative array with the following keys:

- `name`: A short descriptive name for our wrapper.

- `class`: The name of your PHP class that implements Drupal's stream wrapper interface.

- `description`: A sentence or two describing what this wrapper does.

- `type`: A constant indicating what type of stream wrapper this is—readable and/or writeable, local or remote, among other things. These are defined in `includes/stream_wrappers.inc` and can be reviewed at: `http://api.drupal.org/api/drupal/includes--stream_wrappers.inc/7`

Note that in our example we have defined our wrapper as `STREAM_WRAPPERS_READ_VISIBLE`. This means it is read only, but visible in Drupal's UI. An example of a wrapper that is not visible in the UI is Drupal's `temp://` scheme, which is for internal use only (it is set to `STREAM_WRAPPER_HIDDEN`).

This is all that is needed to implement your own custom stream wrapper. It may seem like a lot, but once you understand what needs to be implemented, it is really quite simple.

Now that your stream wrapper is finished, you will be able access photos from Twitpic as easily as any other remote source using Drupal's File API. Now that we can do this, let's look at some of the ways in which Drupal's Image API can be used to modify and manage images.

In this example we have mostly focused on the Drupal-specific part of writing stream wrappers. For more general documentation on stream wrappers see `http://us2.php.net/manual/en/intro.stream.php`

Images in Drupal

Just as the contributed `Filefield` module largely handled file handling in Drupal 6, two modules—`Imagefield` and `Imagecache`, largely handled image handling. `Imagefield` was used for attaching images to nodes, and `Imagecache` was used to create derivations of those images by resizing or cropping them. This was very popular for things like creating square thumbnails in a grid for image galleries. The functionality of both modules has been brought into core for Drupal 7, along with an improved API for managing this functionality from code.

Image API

The Drupal 7 Image API provides a variety of functions to manipulate images. By default, Drupal uses the GD image management library that is included with PHP. However Drupal also offers the ability to switch to a different library if needed. For instance, a contributed module could implement the `ImageMagick` library for developers who needed support for additional image types such as TIFF, which GD does not support.

Working with images is similar to working with files. You get an image object by opening a local image using `image_load()`, and then pass this object to one of the image manipulation functions provided by Drupal. Once you've performed the desired modifications to your image, you save it using `image_save()`.

 Image API functions can only access files on your local file system. You can still use stream wrapper schemes like `public://` and `private://` to refer to files, but remote file systems will not function properly.

The following Drupal functions are available for image manipulation:

- `image_crop()`: Crop an image to specified dimensions.
- `image_desaturate()`: Convert an image to grayscale.
- `image_resize()`: Resize an image to specified dimensions. This can affect the image's aspect ratio.
- `image_rotate()`: Rotate an image to the specified number of degrees.
- `image_scale()`: Resize an image to specified dimensions without affecting the image's aspect ratio.
- `image_scale_and_crop()`: Combine scale and crop in one operation.

> For full details of these and other functions available in the Image API
> refer to http://api.drupal.org/api/group/image/7

Let's take a look at how to we might integrate some of these functions with our
Twitpic module. First, let's make create a hook_menu() implementation that we
can use to trigger our code.

```
/**
 * Implement hook_menu().
 */
function twitpic_menu() {
  $items = array();

  $items['twitpic/munge/%'] = array(
    'title' => 'Munge a Twitpic image',
    'description' => 'Displays a Twitpic image, munged in various ways
(cropped, rotated, etc).',
    'page callback' => 'twitpic_image_munge',
    'access arguments' => array('access_content'),
    'type' => MENU_CALLBACK,
  );

  return $items;
}
```

When the URL twitpic/munge is requested, this hook will call the function
twitpic_image_munge(), which takes two arguments. The first is the ID of
the Twitpic image we want to manipulate, and the second is an operation to be
performed. The allowed operations are rotate, scale, and desaturate. These
arguments will be automatically passed to twitpic_image_munge() when
appended to the URL, as discussed in *Chapter 5, Building an Admin Interface*.

Let's look at the callback function now:

```
/**
 * Munge an image from Twitpic by applying a resize, crop or
 * rotate to it.
 *
 * @param $id
 *    The image's ID, as extracted from its original URL.
 * @param $operation
 *    An operation to perform on the image. Can be 'rotate',
 *    'scale', or 'desaturate'.
```

```
  */
  function twitpic_image_munge($id, $operation = 'rotate') {
    // If we get a disallowed operation, just return.
    $operations = array('rotate', 'desaturate', 'scale');
    if (!in_array($operation, $operations)) {
      return;
    }

    $twitpic_uri = 'twitpic://' . $id . '/thumb';
    $local_uri = 'public://' . $id . '.jpg';
    $twitpic_image = file_get_contents($twitpic_uri);
    $local_path = file_unmanaged_save_data($twitpic_image,      $local_
uri, FILE_EXISTS_REPLACE);
    $local_image = image_load($local_path);

    switch ($operation) {
      case 'scale':
        image_scale($local_image, NULL, 50, FALSE);
        break;

      case 'desaturate':
        image_desaturate($local_image);
        break;

      case 'rotate':
        image_rotate($local_image, 45, 0x7D26CD);
        break;
    }

    $local_uri = drupal_tempnam('public://', $id);
    image_save($local_image, $local_uri);

    return theme('image', array('path' => $local_uri));
  }
```

The first thing we do is to define our allowed operations, and return if the operation passed in doesn't match one of them. This allows us to fail gracefully in that situation. Then we put together the Twitpic URI and grab a local copy of the Twitpic image using `file_get_contents()` as we did earlier in the chapter. For the purposes of this example, we just hardcode the size to `thumb`, but you could easily add that as an additional argument, if you wish to do so.

After this setup, we start getting into the meat of the function.

```
$local_path = file_unmanaged_save_data($twitpic_image, $local_uri,
FILE_EXISTS_REPLACE);
  $local_image = image_load($local_path);
```

Since we are not associating this file with any other content within Drupal, we have no need for it to be entered into the `files` table. Therefore, we use `file_unmanaged_save_data()` as opposed to `file_save_data()`, in order to prevent unnecessary records from being written.

Once the file is saved, we call `image_load()` to get back `$local_image`, a Drupal image object that we can pass on to the image manipulation functions. Like the file object, an image object contains a variety of information about the image that has been loaded, including its height and width, mime-type, and a handle to the image.

Now that we have an image object, we can mess with it using Drupal's API functions. For the purposes of this experiment, we just hardcode some sample manipulations in, to see the kind of things you can do.

```
switch ($operation) {
  case 'desaturate':
    image_desaturate($local_image);
    break;

  case 'scale':
    image_scale($local_image, NULL, 50, FALSE);
     break;

  case 'rotate':
    image_rotate($local_image, 45, 0x7D26CD);
    break;
}
```

As you can see, we have three possible manipulations depending on the operation passed in through the URL. All of these functions work directly on our image object, `$local_image` which is passed by reference, so we don't need to worry about return values.

The first example, `image_desaturate()`, is the simplest. It just converts the image to grayscale, with no configuration arguments.

The scale case uses `image_scale()`, which takes four arguments. The first two are the target height and width of the new image. Since `image_scale()` preserves an image's aspect ratio, you actually only need to provide one of these, and you can leave the other one NULL, as we've done in the example. If you provide both values, one of them may end up smaller than specified because of the calculations needed to preserve the image's aspect ratio. The last argument specifies whether or not `image_scale()` should upscale an image when you provide a height and/or width that is larger than the original. This typically results in a lower quality pixilated image, so we have specified FALSE.

Finally, the `rotate` case uses `image_rotate()`, which takes two arguments. The first is the number of degrees the image should be rotated to, and the second specifies an optional background color that should be used to fill in any space left behind by the rotation. This color should be specified using the color's hex value. In this example, we rotate 45 degrees and fill the background with purple.

Finally we need to save and display the resulting image:

```
  $local_uri =drupal_tempnam('public://');
image_save($local_image, $local_uri);

  return theme('image', array('path' => $local_uri));
}
```

We create a local filename using `drupal_tempnam()`, which just generates a random filename we can use when given a path. It may seem tempting to use information like the file's Twitpic ID or the operation to be performed in the file's name. However, in this example, these items are passed in through the URL, and this cannot be trusted. It is possible to create a security problem if you are not very careful using user-submitted data in filenames, and thus it is best to avoid that, if at all possible.

We can now pass this path, along with our modified image object, to `image_save()`, to save our image to the public filesystem. Once saved, it is a simple matter to call the theme function for images, to generate the necessary HTML for our image to be displayed. The following is an example of what you would see when requesting `twitpic/munge/7nyr2/rotate`:

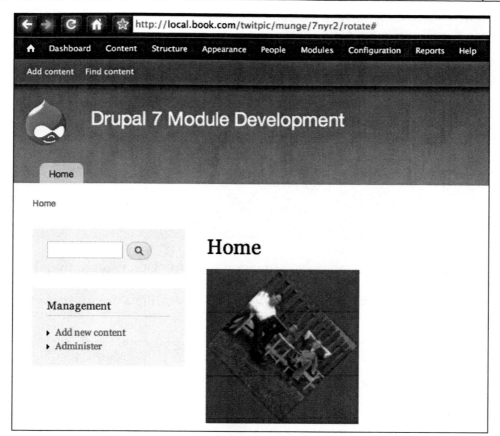

This is all very cool, but sometimes it might be nice to pre-create some manipulations for repeated use, or even a set of manipulations to be executed in order. This is what Image Styles are for, and we'll look at that now.

Image Styles

`Image Styles` is the Drupal 7 core replacement for the popular `Imagecache` module, which has been around since Drupal 5. `Image Styles` is a collection of manipulations which can be saved as a group to be applied to images. Once saved, these styles can be easily used as formatters for Image fields, or they can be used in code by calling a theme function as we did above with our hand-crafted images.

You can create an image style by visiting `admin/config/media/image-styles` where you will see the following screen:

> Home » Administer » Configuration » Media
>
> **Image styles** ○
>
> Image styles commonly provide thumbnail sizes by scaling and cropping images, but can also add various effects before an image is displayed. When an image is displayed with a style, a new file is created and the original image is left unchanged.
>
> ✦ Add style
>
> | STYLE NAME | SETTINGS | OPERATIONS |
> |---|---|---|
> | thumbnail | Default | edit |
> | medium | Default | edit |
> | large | Default | edit |

Drupal ships with three commonly used image styles in place, namely, thumbnail, medium and large. Each of these scales an image to a specific size. If you want to create a new style, you can click **Add style**, and after entering a unique name for your style, you will see the following screen:

> **Edit *test* style** ○
>
> Style *test* was created.
>
> **Preview**
>
> original (view actual size)   test (view actual size)
>
> 600px   600px
>
> 800px   800px
>
> **Image style name** *
>
> test
>
> The name is used in URLs for generated images. Use only lowercase alphanumeric characters, underscores (_), and hyphens (-).
>
> | EFFECT | OPERATIONS |
> |---|---|
> | There are currently no effects in this style. Add one by selecting an option below. | |
>
> Select a new effect ⬍   Add
>
> Update style

This is where you can start adding new manipulations (or, in Drupal parlance, 'effects') to your image. As you can see from the drop-down menu shown, all of the standard Drupal effects are available to be used. When you select an effect and click on the **Add** button, you may get a configuration form that allows you to specify options for that effect. Typically these configuration options will match the arguments of the associated functions. So the **Desaturate** effect does not have a configuration form, but the **Scale** effect does, as shown:

Add *Scale* effect ⊙

Scaling will maintain the aspect-ratio of the original image. If only a single dimension is specified, the other dimension will be calculated.

Width

[   ] pixels

Height

[   ] pixels

☐ Allow Upscaling

Let scale make images larger than their original size

(**Add effect**) Cancel

Once the appropriate options are entered and saved, the styles screen will be updated with a live preview of what the new effect will look like. As you add more and more effects, this live update will continue to reflect them. You can also adjust the order in which the effects are applied, since this can vastly affect the resulting image. Rotating before a crop results in an image that is different from one that is cropped before rotating.

This may seem like a lot of configuration information for a book focused on coding, but it provides the context for what we're about to do. As you can see, all of Drupal's built in effects are available for use in a style, but what if you need an effect that isn't listed? For instance, a common effect is to add a text watermark to your images. Let's look at how we might do that.

Creating image effects

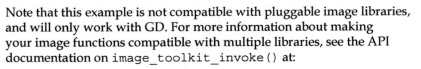

Note that this example is not compatible with pluggable image libraries, and will only work with GD. For more information about making your image functions compatible with multiple libraries, see the API documentation on `image_toolkit_invoke()` at:

`http://api.drupal.org/api/function/image_toolkit_invoke/7`

We will begin with the assumption that you have created a standard module `.info` file with all the information needed for a module named `watermark`. The first step in creating a new image effect is implementing `hook_image_effect_info()`.

```
/**
 * Implements hook_image_effect_info().
 */
function watermark_image_effect_info() {
  $effects = array();

  $effects['watermark'] = array(
    'label' => t('Watermark'),
    'help' => t('Add a watermark to an image.'),
    'effect callback' => 'watermark_effect',
    'form callback' => 'watermark_form',
    'summary theme' => 'watermark_summary',
  );

  return $effects;
}
```

This kind of hook should look pretty familiar by now. It is very similar to `hook_menu()`, which was discussed in *Chapter 5, Building an Admin Interface*. We create an associative array of the effects that we are defining, and return it to the caller. The array is keyed by a unique identifier, in our case, `watermark`. This array contains the following information about our image effect:

- `label`: The label that will be used in the effects drop-down on the styles page. This text will also be used after you have added your effect, if you have not defined a summary theme below.

- `help`: A text description of what your effect does.

- `effect callback`: A function that will be called to actually execute your effect on an image. This function name indicates where your image manipulation code will go.

- form callback: If your effect allows users to enter configuration data (such as the width and height fields in the previous scale example), then this indicates the function that defines your configuration form. This value is optional. If your effect does not require any configuration information, then this key is not necessary.

- summary theme: After your effect is added to a style, you can create a theme callback which returns customized text to be displayed on the styles admin screen. For instance, the rotate effect displays the number of degrees that the user entered. This value is also optional. If you don't provide it, your effect will display the value you provided in the label key.

As you can see, we have defined three callbacks that we need to create. First, we will look at our configuration form. It would be nice for users to be able to specify what text they would like on watermarked images, so we will offer the option to enter custom text as well as give them an option to indicate what color it should be.

```
/**
 * Form structure for the watermark configuration form.
 *
 * @param $data
 *   The current configuration for this watermark effect.
 */
function watermark_form($data) {
  $form['text_color'] = array(
    '#type' => 'textfield',
    '#default_value' => (isset($data['text_color'])) ? $data['text_color'] : '#FFFFFF',
    '#title' => t('Text color'),
    '#description' => t('The color of the text to be used for this watermark. Use web-style hex colors (#FFFFFF for white, #000000 for black).'),
    '#size' => 7,
    '#maxlength' => 7,
    '#element_validate' => array('image_effect_color_validate'),
  );

  $form['text'] = array(
    '#type' => 'textfield',
    '#default_value' => (isset($data['text'])) ? $data['text'] : 'Drupal loves kittens!',
    '#title' => t('Watermark text'),
    '#description' => t('Text to be written on the image.'),
    '#size' => 30,
    '#maxlength' => 60,
```

```
    );

    return $form;
}
```

Effect form callbacks return partial Form API structures. You only need to provide the fields you would like users to enter, and Drupal will take care of the submission details. We have defined two form elements to hold our configuration options, namely, `text_color` and `text`. In general these are pretty standard Form API arrays, but there a couple of things to point out.

Your form callback also takes a single argument — `$data` — which is an associative array containing the current values of our form options, if any. You should use this information to fill your `form` elements with the user's current options or, if they are empty, to fill in sane defaults. We have set the default color here to be white, and the default text to **Drupal loves kittens!**

One final thing to note is that we are using the `#element_validate` property to specify an array of callbacks, which will be used to validate this specific element. This is a Form API property we haven't seen before, but you can use it in any form element definition. Drupal contains the function `image_effect_color_validate()` to verify that hex colors are properly entered, and we take advantage of this function by specifying it here.

Now let's make a customized message based on the user's options, to be displayed in the image style's effect listing. This just allows us to give a little more detail to the user, and makes it more obvious what our effect is doing.

```
/**
 * Theme callback for image watermark effect summary output.
 *
 * @param $variables
 *    An associative array containing configuration data.
 */
function theme_watermark_summary($variables) {
  $data = $variables['data'];
  return t('with color @textcolor', array('@textcolor' => $data['text_
color']));
}
```

As you can see we just return the text we're using along with the color that has been configured. This gets appended to the label we specified in our initial effect declaration.

Finally we can make the modification to our image:

```
/**
 * Image effect callback; add a text watermark to an image.
 *
 * @param $image
 *   An image object returned by image_load().
 * @param $data
 *   An array of attributes to use when performing the
 *   watermark effect.
 * @return
 *   TRUE on success. FALSE on failure.
 */
function watermark_effect(&$image, $data) {
  $data['text_color'] = str_replace('#', '', $data['text_color']);
  $red = hexdec(substr($data['text_color'], 0, 2));
  $green = hexdec(substr($data['text_color'], 2, 2));
  $blue = hexdec(substr($data['text_color'], 4));

  $color = imagecolorallocate($image->resource, $red, $green, $blue);
  imagestring($image->resource, 5, 5, 5, $data['text'], $color);
}
```

From a Drupal perspective, the important thing is that our effect callback, `watermark_effect()`, takes two arguments. The first is an image object just like we've encountered earlier, which contains a resource handle we can pass to GD functions for modification. The second is the data array just like the one passed to our configuration form callback, containing an associative array of user submitted configuration information. This array is keyed on the field names as specified in the form callback above. We use the information in `$data` to properly format our text.

Beyond that this functionality is pretty straightforward. Most of the code is concerned with properly formatting the color information. In the first four lines we convert the hex color submitted by the user (found in `$data['text_color']`) to the RGB decimal values which we will need later. We do this by parsing each individual hex value of the string and using `hexdec()` to convert them to their decimal equivalent.

The rest of the code relates to the image creation functionality from the GD image library. We will cover this briefly but for more details refer to the GD documentation at:

```
http://in2.php.net/manual/en/book.image.php
```

Once we have the color values, we use `imagecolorallocate()` to create a color identifier representing this color. Finally we can call `imagestring()`, a GD function that plots text on a string. Without going into too much detail, the following are the arguments this function takes:

- A handle to the image (in this example the resource property of the image object)
- A font size from 1-5 (5 being the largest)
- The x and y coordinates of where the text should be plotted with (0, 0) being the top left corner of the image
- The text to be plotted, in this example, the `$data['text']` as submitted by the user through our configuration form
- The color identifier we created with the user-submitted color choice

You should now be able to install this module and have the option to watermark an image on the **Image Styles** admin screen, as shown in the following screenshot:

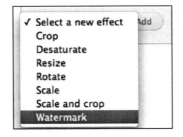

You can now add this effect, alone or in combination with other effects to a new image style. This image style can then be applied to images in nodes by adjusting the display settings in the administration screens for the node's content type. The following image shows our previous example node with a user-configured watermark applied to the image:

Pretty cool right? However, sometimes it would be nice to be able to ship some preconfigured image styles with your module. For instance, a popular Drupal contributed module is the Pirate module, which translates your entire website to pirate-speak on **Talk Like A Pirate Day**. It might be cool for the Pirate module to be able to ship a totally preconfigured image style that adds the YAR! watermark to images. Rather than having to create this image style themselves, administrators could simply install the module and it would be all set up for them. Not only that, but because this style is in code, it is more easily deployable between development environments. Thankfully, this is quite easy to do and will provide our final demonstration of Drupal 7's Image API.

Creating image styles from a module

At this point in your Drupal experience, you can probably guess what is involved in creating an image style in your module—a hook and an associative array. The hook is `hook_image_default_styles()` and the array is a simple definition of the components of your style.

> For those familiar with views in Drupal 6, this is very similar to exporting views to code using `hook_views_default_view()`.

```
/**
 * Implements hook_image_default_styles().
 */
function watermark_image_default_styles() {
  $styles = array();

  $styles['yar'] = array(
    'effects' => array(
      array(
        'name' => 'watermark',
        'data' => array(
          'text_color' => '#000000',
          'text' => 'YAR!'
        ),
        'weight' => 0,
      ),
    ),
  );

  return $styles;
}
```

This is about as simple as Drupal hooks get, especially given everything that has already been covered previously in this chapter. Our implementation of `hook_image_default_styles()` returns `$styles`, an associative array of image style definitions, keyed on a unique string. This string will act as the style's name and will be displayed on the image styles admin page.

Each style definition is a set of image effects, along with their effect-specific settings, if any. The keys this array can contain are as follows:

- `name`: The unique name of the effect we're implementing.
- `data`: An optional array of configuration settings. These should be keyed on the same text string that are used in the form callback defined by the effect. Note that default values defined in the form callback will NOT be honored if you do not include them. You will have to enter them by hand here.
- `weight`: An optional weight, used to control effect ordering when multiple effects are included in a single style. As is Drupal standard, lower weights 'float to the top' and higher weights 'sink to the bottom'.

That is really all there is to it. If you load the image styles listing, you will now see your style listed (you may need to clear the Drupal cache first).

Image styles commonly provide thumbnail sizes by scaling and cropping images, but can also add various effects before an image is displayed. When an image is displayed with a style, a new file is created and the original image is left unchanged.

✦ Add style

STYLE NAME	SETTINGS	OPERATIONS
thumbnail	Default	edit
medium	Default	edit
large	Default	edit
yar	Default	edit

One nice aspect about image styles defined by a module is that they are protected from being changed or modified by end users (or accidentally broken by the developers themselves). This is implemented in two ways. First, in order to modify the settings of a style implemented through `hook_image_default_styles()`, you must specifically take the extra step of saying you want to override it. Take a look at the following screen:

Edit *yar* style ○

This image style is currently being provided by a module. Click the "Override defaults" button to change its settings.

Preview

original (view actual size)   yar (view actual size)

600px   600px

800px   800px

Image style name
yar
This image style is being provided by *watermark* module and may not be renamed.

EFFECT	WEIGHT	OPERATIONS
Watermark		

(Override defaults)

As you can see, there is a large warning indicating that in order to change this module's settings, you must click the **Override defaults** button. This can help prevent users from inadvertently changing your image settings, thus throwing off the content and theme of your site. Once the defaults have been overridden, the user will be able to modify the settings as they wish.

This leads us to the second useful aspect of implementing your styles in code—no matter how much a style is modified; it can always be reverted back to its original state with the click of the mouse. Observe the change on the style list after a user has overridden a default style:

yar	Overridden	edit	revert

As you can see, this style has been marked as **Overridden** and it has gained a **revert** link! Clicking the **revert** link takes you to a confirmation screen, and if you agree to revert, the style's settings will be reset back to their original state as defined in the module.

Default styles are very simple to implement, but as you can see they bring along with them an enormous amount of functionality that can dramatically improve your workflow. If you spend a lot of time configuring image settings or moving configuration between sites, there is really no reason not to implement your styles in a module using `hook_image_default_styles()`.

Summary

The new File and Image APIs in Drupal 7 not only make management and maintenance of these assets much easier, they are also great fun to play around with and amazingly easy to use. By now you should be comfortable with the central concepts of file management in Drupal. You should know the difference between Drupal's public and private file systems, and understand how Drupal associates file metadata with the files they represent in the `files` table. You should also have a good understanding of stream wrappers and how they are implemented in Drupal 7. Finally you should know how to use the Image API to crop or otherwise modify images, and how to save these modifications as Image Styles for use in your content.

Many of the examples in this chapter are just shells, and could easily be improved upon or expanded. For instance, it would be reasonably easy to expand the watermark module so that it can position the watermark based on user choice, or outline it for easier readability against different backgrounds. Experimentation is encouraged!

Earlier we discussed how pre-defined image style settings can improve workflow and maintainability. In the next chapter we kick that concept up a notch by learning how to create completely pre-configured Drupal installations using install profiles.

12
Installation Profiles

This chapter will focus on creating installation profiles. Previous chapters covered building modules and features into Drupal. This chapter will cover bundling modules and themes with an installer that configures Drupal for a specific purpose.

Here are some important topics that we will cover in this chapter:

- Starting a new installation profile
- Bundling modules and themes in a distribution
- Creating a `.profile` file to store installation tasks
- Enabling modules in the install process
- Configuring the default blocks
- Running the installer without using the interactive wizard

By the end of the chapter you should have the basic knowledge to create your own installation profile and Drupal distribution.

Introducing installation profiles

Installation profiles are the way to plug into and customize the Drupal installation process. With installation profiles, additional forms and steps can be added to the installer, modules can be enabled, blocks can be set up, default settings can be configured, and the Drupal site can be customized.

An installation profile is useful when you repeat the same install tasks regularly. These tasks can be automated, which is perfect for setting up a Drupal distribution or for situations where you build out the same base site repeatedly.

Drupal distributions

Distributions provide out-of-the-box functionality without the need to download and install anything but the distribution itself. Without a distribution, you typically need to download Drupal and additional modules and themes that you need for the site to operate. Then you need to spend time running through a normal Drupal installation process, followed by time spent configuring the site. With a 'distribution', you download it, run it through the installer, and you have a functioning and a configured site. Distributions build on installation profiles by providing everything you need in one place.

Setting up a distribution

Distributions consist of Drupal core, additional modules and themes, and an installation profile to configure the site. While going through creating an installation profile, we are also going to walk through the steps needed to create a full-fledged distribution.

Standard and minimal profiles

Drupal comes pre-packaged with the standard and minimal installation profiles. The standard installation profile installs a common set of core modules. This is similar to the installation profile packaged with Drupal 6. The minimal installation profile installs only the required modules along with the block and `dblog` modules.

Creating a profile directory

Profiles are located in the `/profiles` directory, off the base of the Drupal site. To create a new profile, create a directory alongside the standard and minimal profiles provided by core. The name should be the machine-readable name of the install profile you are creating. Throughout this chapter we will build an installation profile with the name **store**.

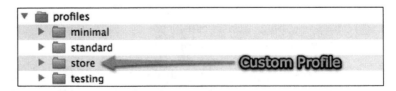

 Modules, themes, and profiles cannot share the same machine-readable name. This name should be a unique namespace for the Drupal installation.

Profile modules and themes

While modules and profiles can be stored in the /sites/all folder, as described in *Chapter 2*, modules and themes bundled with a profile have a special place where they can reside. In the profile they may have their own modules and themes directories:

```
▼ 📁 profiles
    ▶ 📁 minimal
    ▶ 📁 standard
    ▼ 📁 store
        ▶ 📁 modules   ⟵──────── Modules bundled with Profile
        ▶ 📁 themes    ⟵──────── Themes bundled with Profile
    ▶ 📁 testing
```

Storing the modules and themes within the profile enables distributions to be packaged together in one part of Drupal, and allows the standard module and theme overriding system to work.

Since modules and themes can be stored in more than one place there is an order to how Drupal chooses which source to use for a module. Modules and themes in the /sites/all folder are chosen over those in the profile folder, and modules and themes in a site specific folder are chosen over those in the /site/all folder.

Drupal.org Bundled Distributions

The drupal.org packaging system is capable of taking an installation profile with some additional configuration and creating a downloadable distribution. Details are available at http://drupal.org/node/642116.

Creating profiles

Profiles consist of a .info file and a .profile (pronounced "dot-profile") file. This is similar to how modules are structured, as described in *Chapter 2*.

The .info file for a profile looks just like a .info file for a module and contains the same information.

```
name = Example Store
description = "An example store installation profile."
version = VERSION
core = 7.x
files[] = store.profile
files[] = store.install.inc
files[] = store.install
```

The name and description fields from the store.info file are used in the first step of the installer, as seen in the following image:

If there is only one profile present in the /profiles directory, Drupal will automatically select that profile and move on to the next step.

The .profile file serves two purposes. First, it enables customizations to the installation process. These changes include adding tasks to the installer, such as adding a custom form, or altering the default installation tasks.

The second purpose of the .profile file is to act as a custom module for the site. After the installation is complete, the profile acts as any other module on the site, except that it cannot be disabled. It can run Drupal hooks, alter forms, and do anything else a normal module can do.

Enabling modules

Just like modules can be dependencies of other modules, modules can be set as dependencies of a profile. All dependent modules will be enabled as part of the install process. The difference between module dependencies and profile dependencies is that profile dependencies can be disabled without disabling the profile.

To add a dependency to a profile, use the dependencies field in the .info file. Here is an example from our store.info file of the modules we want enabled:

```
dependencies[] = block
dependencies[] = comment
dependencies[] = contact
dependencies[] = contextual
dependencies[] = dashboard
dependencies[] = help
dependencies[] = image
dependencies[] = menu
dependencies[] = path
dependencies[] = taxonomy
dependencies[] = dblog
dependencies[] = search
dependencies[] = shortcut
dependencies[] = toolbar
dependencies[] = overlay
dependencies[] = field_ui
dependencies[] = file
dependencies[] = rdf
```

> By default, the field, field SQL storage, filter, list, node, number, options, system, text, and user modules are enabled. Any other modules you want enabled need to be listed in the .info file for the profile.

> **Ensuring profile dependencies**
>
> Since dependencies of profiles can be disabled, profiles that rely on dependencies should ensure that a module is enabled before acting on it. The function module_exists() can be used to test if a module is both installed and enabled. For more details on module_exists() see http://api.drupal.org/api/function/module_exists/7.

The install task system

The Drupal installer is task based. Tasks consist of steps to collect information and act on it. For example, three of the core tasks are to collect the database configuration details, write the database configuration to the `settings.php` file, and install the modules. Drupal core provides a set of default tasks for the installer to run that an installation profile can add to or alter. The two hooks that provide access to the install tasks are:

- `hook_install_tasks()`: This allows the profile to add tasks at the end of the default tasks
- `hook_install_tasks_alter()`: This allows the profile to alter all the tasks including those provided as defaults by the installer

 For the first step of the installer, an installation profile is selected. This step cannot be altered by an installation profile.

Choosing an install task or using hook_install

Since profiles operate as a module, they can have a `.install` file containing a `hook_install()` which will be called when the profile is installed. This leaves two choices of where to perform configuration tasks.

There are two main differences between these two types of tasks:

- The profile `hook_install()` is run before custom install tasks and the site configuration form.
- Tasks in the installer can have forms, utilize the Batch API, and more. `hook_install()` can only run as a callback in a single page load.

 For complete documentation regarding `hook_install()` visit the API documentation at `http://api.drupal.org/api/function/hook_install/7`.

Anatomy of an install task

There are five properties to describe each task step to the installer. `hook_install_tasks()` describes each step to the installer as a keyed array. The key is a unique name to a callback function that executes the task. The properties of each item describing the task are as follows:

- `display_name`: A human readable name to display for this task. This is used in the user interface to inform a user as to the step they are on.

- `display`: tells the installer whether or not to display the task. This is used to provide fine-grained control over the display of the task in the installer. It is useful for tasks that may display only under certain conditions. The value is a Boolean and the default value is whether or not the "display_name" key is set.

- `type`: Specifies the type of task to be run. There are three types of tasks the installer can execute. The `normal` type of task will execute a callback function and optionally return some html. The `form` type brings up a form using the Form API. The `batch` type will return a Batch API definition.

- `run`: Tells the installer when to run the task. The default setting is `INSTALL_TASK_RUN_IF_NOT_COMPLETED`, which tells the installer to run the task once in the install process when reached in the list of install tasks. Alternately, `INSTALL_TASK_RUN_IF_REACHED` tells the installer to run the task on every page load if the task is reached in the list of tasks and `INSTALL_TASK_SKIP` tells the installer to skip the task.

- `function`: An optional parameter to set a callback function other than the key name. This is useful if you want to call the same callback function on more than one step.

Creating a task

Let's create two tasks for the `store` profile. The tasks will create two content types and fill in default settings for our site-wide contact form.

We start by defining the task to create the two content types. This will be done in `store_install_tasks()`, the profiles implementation of `hook_install_tasks()` which goes in `store.profile`:

```
/**
 * Implements hook_install_tasks().
 */
function store_install_tasks() {
  $tasks = array();
  $tasks['store_create_content_types'] = array(
    'type' => 'normal',
  );
  return $tasks;
}
```

In this case we set the array key to `store_create_content_types`, which is the callback function for this task. The `type` is set to `normal`, meaning this is a task that is run, and may return HTML.

Then in our profile, we create the function `store_create_content_types()` as follows:

```
function store_create_content_types(&$install_state) {
  $types = array(
    array(
      'type' => 'page',
      'name' => st('Page'),
      'base' => 'node_content',
      'description' => st("Use <em>pages</em> for your static content,
such as an 'About us' page."),
      'custom' => 1,
      'modified' => 1,
      'locked' => 0,
    ),
    array(
      'type' => 'product',
      'name' => st('Product'),
      'base' => 'node_content',
      'description' => st('Use <em>products</em> for items in the
store.'),
      'custom' => 1,
      'modified' => 1,
      'locked' => 0,
    ),
  );

  foreach ($types as $type) {
    $type = node_type_set_defaults($type);
    node_type_save($type);
    node_add_body_field($type);
  }
}
```

In this case the function has one variable passed, it being `$install_state`. This is a variable passed through the entire install process and each of the tasks. It contains the state and all relevant information that needs to be passed around the installer.

The content of this function defines two content types. It also makes sure that all the default information is filled in, and saves the types creating two new content types.

Next, let's create a form to enter in default contact information for the site-wide contact form. In this case we expand the `store_install_tasks()` function to add a task for the form.

```
/**
 * Implements hook_install_tasks().
 */
function store_install_tasks() {
  $tasks = array();
  $tasks['store_create_content_types'] = array(
    'type' => 'normal',
  );
  $tasks['store_configure_contact_form'] = array(
    'display_name' => t('Default site contact information'),
    'type' => 'form',
  );
  return $tasks;
}
```

> In this chapter you will notice the use of the `t()` and `st()` functions for translations. The `t()` function is the standard function to use for translatable text. The `st()` function should be used when some of the systems are not available. For example, in the tasks of the installer before the modules are installed. If there are functions that need to be called in both places and you need to discover which function to use, `get_t()` returns the name of the appropriate translation function to use.

After the task `store_create_content_types`, the task `store_configure_contact_form` is added. We provide this task with a `display_name` so it will show up as a step in the installer. The `type` is set to a form. Just like any other Drupal form, it will have access to `FORM_ID_validate` and `FORM_ID_submit` callbacks.

Once a profile has been selected in the first step of the installer, any additional task will be displayed using their `display_name` in the installer steps.

The form function will look a little different than a normal form function:

```
function store_configure_contact_form($form, &$form_state, &$install_
state) {

  drupal_set_title(t('Default site contact information'));

    $form['recipients'] = array(
     '#type' => 'textarea',
     '#title' => t('Recipients'),

     '#default_value' => '',
     '#description' => t("Example: 'webmaster@example.com' or 'sales@
example.com,support@example.com' . To specify multiple recipients,
separate each e-mail address with a comma."),
     '#required' => TRUE,
    );
  $form['reply'] = array(
     '#type' => 'textarea',
     '#title' => t('Auto-reply'),
     '#default_value' => '',
     '#description' => t('Optional auto-reply. Leave empty if you do
not want to send the user an auto-reply message.'),
    );
  $form['submit'] = array(
     '#type' => 'submit',
     '#value' => t('Save'),
    );
  return $form;
}
```

Notice that `$install_state` is passed in as a third variable into the form function. This is different from typical form functions in the Form API. It provides access to the state and information in the installer.

> **Setting the page title**
>
> Setting the `display_name` for a task only sets the title in the list of installer tasks. To set the page title, use `drupal_set_title()`. For full details on using `drupal_set_title()` see the API documentation at `http://api.drupal.org/api/function/drupal_set_title/7`.

Just like other Form API functions we have access to the `store_configure_contact_form_validate()` and `store_configure_contact_form_submit()` functions, as seen below:

```
function store_configure_contact_form_validate($form, &$form_state) {
  // Validate and each e-mail recipient.
  $recipients = explode(',', $form_state['values']['recipients']);
  foreach ($recipients as &$recipient) {
    $recipient = trim($recipient);
    if (!valid_email_address($recipient)) {
      form_set_error('recipients', t('%recipient is an invalid e-mail
address.', array('%recipient' => $recipient)));
    }
  }
  form_set_value($form['recipients'], implode(',', $recipients),
$form_state);
}

function store_configure_contact_form_submit($form, &$form_state) {
  $values = $form_state['values'];
  $values += array(
    'cid' => 1,
  );
  drupal_write_record('contact', $values, array('cid'));
  watchdog('contact', 'The default category has been updated.',
array(), WATCHDOG_NOTICE, l(t('Edit'), 'admin/structure/contact/edit/'
. $values['cid']));
}
```

There are some tasks which need to be run after a certain point in the process on every page load. An example of this is in the default install tasks. The installer initializes with a low-level Drupal bootstrap enabling very base level functionality. After the modules have been installed but before the site configuration part of the process, there is a point when the installer can do a full Drupal bootstrap with all the functionality of all the enabled modules. Once the installer reaches this point it runs a task on all subsequent page loads to perform a full Drupal bootstrap. The definition for this task looks like the following:

```
$tasks = array(
  ...
  'install_bootstrap_full' => array(
    'run' => INSTALL_TASK_RUN_IF_REACHED,
  ),
  ...
);
```

By setting `run` to `INSTALL_TASK_RUN_IF_REACHED`, the function `install_bootstrap_full()` is run on every page load after it is encountered in the install tasks.

Altering tasks

The installer provides a method to alter tasks in the installer. Where `hook_install_tasks()` provides a method to add tasks at the end of the install process, `hook_install_tasks_alter()` provides access to all the tasks in the installer (including the default tasks provided by the installer). This allows a profile to insert tasks earlier in the install process or alter the default tasks.

 Tasks performed before the `install_bootstrap_full()` task, which is before the modules are installed, only have access to a very base level of Drupal configuration, with access to the system module, user module, the PHP settings, and a site's `settings.php` file.

Let's look at an example of altering tasks before the modules are installed; only the base level system is available, which means your installation profile is not yet able to call `hook_form_alter` or `hook_form_FORM_ID_alter`. In this case we want to alter the step where the database is set up to add some additional instructions.

```
/**
 * Implements hook_install_tasks_alter().
 */
function store_install_tasks_alter(&$tasks, &$install_state) {
  $tasks['install_settings_form']['function'] = 'store_database_
settings_form';
}
```

Here, the task that sets up the database is altered, telling it to call a different function using the `function` key for the task.

```
function store_database_settings_form($form, &$form_state, &$install_
state) {
  // Retrieve the default form.
  $default_form = install_settings_form($form, &$form_state,
&$install_state);
  $default_form['basic_options']['database']['#description'] .= st('
If you choose use SQLite please provide an absolute path outside of
the webroot directory.');
  return $default_form;
}
```

In this task callback function, we retrieve the default form provided by Drupal, alter it, and use that form. Since we are using a different form callback, we need to provide `_validate` and `_submit` handlers to process the information submitted in the form. The following two functions wrap the `_validate` and `_submit` functions used for `install_settings_form()`:

```
/**
 * Form API validate for store_database_settings_form form.
 */
function store_database_settings_form_validate($form, &$form_state) {
  install_settings_form_validate($form, &$form_state);
}

/**
 * Form API submit for store_database_settings_form form.
 */
function store_database_settings_form_submit($form, &$form_state) {
  install_settings_form_submit($form, &$form_state);
}
```

Configuring blocks

Out of the box, Drupal does not have any blocks configured to be displayed. An installation profile will need to enable and configure any blocks it wants displayed. In this case we will use `hook_install()` in a `store.install` file as part of our install. When the modules for the profile are installed, the function `store_install()` will run, configuring the blocks. The following is a basic `store_install()` function enabling three blocks in the Bartik theme:

```
function store_install() {
  // Enable some standard blocks.
  $values = array(
    array(
```

```
        'module' => 'system',
        'delta' => 'main',
        'theme' => 'bartik',
        'status' => 1,
        'weight' => 0,
        'region' => 'content',
        'pages' => '',
        'cache' => DRUPAL_NO_CACHE,
      ),
      array(
        'module' => 'user',
        'delta' => 'login',
        'theme' => 'bartik',
        'status' => 1,
        'weight' => 0,
        'region' => 'sidebar_first',
        'pages' => '',
        'cache' => DRUPAL_NO_CACHE,
      ),
      array(
        'module' => 'system',
        'delta' => 'management',
        'theme' => 'bartik',
        'status' => 1,
        'weight' => 1,
        'region' => 'sidebar_first',
        'pages' => '',
        'cache' => DRUPAL_NO_CACHE,
      ),
    );
    $query = db_insert('block')->fields(array('module', 'delta',
'theme', 'status', 'weight', 'region', 'pages', 'cache'));
    foreach ($values as $record) {
      $query->values($record);
    }
    $query->execute();
}
```

There is no API function to enable blocks. Here we have to add rows to the block table for each block we want to configure. In this case we enable the main content, the login form, and the site management block.

Each row being added to the block table contains the following information about the block:

- `module`: The module that owns the block.
- `delta`: The name of the block within the module.
- `theme`: The theme the block will display within. Each theme has an individual block configuration.
- `status`: When set to 1, the module is displayed.
- `weight`: Used for ordering the block within a region. Larger weights are displayed below smaller weights.
- `region`: The region in the page that the block will be displayed within.
- `pages`: Any rules about the pages that the block will be displayed on.
- `cache`: How the block will be cached.

> In Drupal 7, the sidebars were renamed for better multi-lingual support. What used to be the left sidebar is now `sidebar_first` and what used to be the right sidebar is now `sidebar_second`.

Variable settings

Installation profiles will often want to set their own variable settings, which are out-of-the-box, separate from those provided by Drupal core. Drupal provides the `variable_set()` function which can be used in an install task or in `hook_install()` to set a variable. For example, adding the following lines to `store_install()` will set the `admin_theme` to the **Seven** theme:

```
function store_install() {
  ...
  // Set the admin theme to seven.
  variable_set('admin_theme', 'seven');
}
```

Text filters

Text filters, known as input formats in previous versions of Drupal, are created and configured by the installation profile. In order for a site to have text filters that users can choose from, the installation profile must set up the filter first. The simplest method for setting them up is in the `hook_install()` function inside the profile's `.install` file. Continuing our example, the following code at the top of `store_install()` would add Filtered HTML and Full HTML text filters, with the filtered one set as the default:

```
// Add text formats.
$filtered_html_format = array(
  'format' => 'filtered_html',
  'name' => 'Filtered HTML',
  'weight' => 0,
  'filters' => array(
    // URL filter.
    'filter_url' => array(
      'weight' => 0,
      'status' => 1,
    ),
    // HTML filter.
    'filter_html' => array(
      'weight' => 1,
      'status' => 1,
    ),
    // Line break filter.
    'filter_autop' => array(
      'weight' => 2,
      'status' => 1,
    ),
    // HTML corrector filter.
    'filter_htmlcorrector' => array(
      'weight' => 10,
      'status' => 1,
    ),
  ),
);
$filtered_html_format = (object) $filtered_html_format;
filter_format_save($filtered_html_format);

$full_html_format = array(
  'format' => 'full_html',
  'name' => 'Full HTML',
  'weight' => 1,
  'filters' => array(
```

```
    // URL filter.
    'filter_url' => array(
      'weight' => 0,
      'status' => 1,
    ),
    // Line break filter.
    'filter_autop' => array(
      'weight' => 1,
      'status' => 1,
    ),
    // HTML corrector filter.
    'filter_htmlcorrector' => array(
      'weight' => 10,
      'status' => 1,
    ),
  ),
);
$full_html_format = (object) $full_html_format;
filter_format_save($full_html_format);
```

Code placement

Code placed in the `.profile` file will be loaded on every page load. This means that after Drupal is installed, the install tasks contained in the `.profile` file for the installation will be loaded all the time. Since the install tasks will only be used during the installer, they do not need to be loaded after that.

The first step is to move the tasks to a different file that can be loaded only when needed. In this case let's create a file named `store.install.inc` in the installation profile and move the following install task functions into it:

```
store_configure_contact_form()
store_configure_contact_form_validate()
store_configure_contact_form_submit()
store_database_settings_form()
store_database_settings_form_validate()
store_database_settings_form_submit()
store_create_content_types()
```

The profile will need to load this file during the install process to have access to the tasks and forms. To do this update `store_install_tasks_alter()` needs to append a call to include this file as shown here:

```
/**
 * Implementation of hook_install_tasks_alter().
 */
function store_install_tasks_alter(&$tasks, &$install_state) {
  ...
  // Include store.install.inc containing the tasks and forms.
  include_once 'store.install.inc';
}
```

This could be appended to `hook_install_tasks()` as well.

Running the installer from the command line

The installer can be run from both, a browser as a wizard as well as a part of an external installation script. For example, the installer may be used as a part of a system that automatically builds new sites. This is useful for cases where the installation will be automated. By default the installer runs in an interactive mode where it runs as an interactive wizard. The installer is capable of running in a non-interactive mode where settings are passed in as an array which will fill in the detail for each step. For example, see the following script which installs the site using the default profile:

```
<?php

// The settings for the installer to use when installing Drupal
$settings = array(

  // This overrides the PHP array $_SERVER so we can tell
  // Drupal the path to the site. This is important for
  // multi-site support.
  'server' => array(
    'HTTP_HOST' => 'localhost',  // The domain name.
    'SCRIPT_NAME' => '', // The path to the site.
  ),

  // Select the profile and the locale.
  'parameters' => array(
    'profile' => 'minimal',
```

```
    'locale' => 'en',
  ),

  // The values to use in each of the forms.
  'forms' => array(
    'install_settings_form' => array(
      'driver' => 'sqlite',
      'database' => 'test',
      'username' => '',
      'password' => '',
      'host' => 'localhost',
      'port' => '',
      'db_prefix' => '',
    ),

    // The site configuration form.
    'install_configure_form' => array(
      'site_name' => 'Drupal Site',
      'site_mail' => 'email@example.com',
      'account' => array(
        'name' => 'admin',
        'mail' => 'email@example.com',
        'pass' => array(
          // On the form there are two password fields. The
          // installer is filling out the form so we need to
          // fill in both form fields.
          'pass1' => 'password',
          'pass2' => 'password',
        ),
      ),

      // The default country and timezone.
      'site_default_country' => 'US',
      'date_default_timezone' => 'America/Detroit',

      // Enable clean URLs.
      'clean_url' => TRUE,

      // Check for updates using the Update manager.
      // Possible values are:
      //   - array() = off,
      //   - array(1) = check for updates,
      //   - array(1, 2) = check for updates and notify by
      //      email
```

```
            'update_status_module' => array(1, 2),
        ),
    ),
);

/**
 * Root directory of Drupal installation.
 */
define('DRUPAL_ROOT', getcwd());

/**
 * Global flag to indicate that site is in installation mode.
 */
define('MAINTENANCE_MODE', 'install');
// Load the installer and initiate the install process using
// $settings.
require_once DRUPAL_ROOT . '/includes/install.core.inc';
install_drupal($settings);
```

This script starts by creating a $settings array that provides information for
the installer and the values for the forms within the installer. After the settings
are defined, the installer (includes/install.core.inc) is included and kicked
off by calling install_drupal() with the $settings being passed in.

Summary

We have now completed creating an installation profile. We started by looking at
where to store modules and themes associated with the profile. We then moved on
to creating the install profile, which included creating a new task and altering a task
bundled with Drupal core.

Along the way, we looked at how to create content types, enable blocks, and
set variables.

We closed the chapter by looking at how to optimize code placement and looked at
how to execute a Drupal installation outside the web-based install wizard.

A
Database Access

Although Drupal 7 has made major leaps forward in terms of the flexibility of its data storage in practice the vast majority of Drupal sites still rely on an SQL database for both their primary data and for most of the configuration. In the past Drupal has relied on a very thin database layer that provided only limited abstraction beyond PHP's native support for the MySQL and PostgreSQL databases, which was a serious limitation for complex or traffic-heavy sites.

Drupal 7, however, features a brand new database layer rewritten from the ground up to provide a wide range of robust features in the areas of security, scalability, and developer flexibility. Known somewhat tongue-in-cheek as "Databases: The Next Generation" or "DBTNG" during development, it offers support for many advanced SQL features as well as vastly improved portability between the leading SQL databases on the market. In fact, Drupal 7 now ships with support for the three leading open source databases (MySQL and variants such as Maria DB, PostgreSQL, and SQLite) out-of-the-box and as of this writing add-on drivers are available for both, Microsoft SQL Server and Oracle.

The database API is well documented, but this section will provide an overview of the major features of the database API and how to use them to ensure fast, robust code. We'll assume an existing knowledge of SQL. For more detailed information see `http://drupal.org/developing/api/database` and `http://api.drupal.org/api/group/database/7`.

Basic queries

Most **SELECT queries** are, in practice, fairly simple and do not change. Drupal calls these **static queries**, and they are very straightforward to use.

For example, to get a list of all enabled modules in the system, we could run the following query:

```
$result = db_query("SELECT name, filename FROM {system} WHERE type =
:type AND status = :status", array(':type' => 'module', ':status' =>
1));
```

 In practice, if we wanted to get that information we would simply call `module_list()` instead, but for the purposes of this example we'll do it the manual way.

The query looks very much like normal SQL that we would expect to see anywhere else, but there are a few important items to mention.

- All SQL table names are wrapped in curly braces. That identifies the string as a table name to the database layer and allows Drupal to easily add a configured prefix to all tables for a given Drupal instance.

- There is no MySQL-specific syntax (or any database-specific syntax) anywhere in the query.

- There are no literal values in the query. Instead, literal values are specified by placeholders. Values for placeholders are specified in an associative array as the second parameter to `db_query()`.

Those placeholders are significant. They allow us to separate the query from the values in the query and pass them to the database server separately. The database server can then assemble the query string and placeholder values as needed, with full knowledge of what data type makes sense in each case. That eliminates most (although not quite all) opportunities for SQL injection from unexpected data.

There are three other important things to remember about placeholders:

- Placeholders must be unique within a query, and must begin with a colon.

- Placeholders should never have quotation marks around them, regardless of the data type. The database server will handle that for us.

- Placeholders should be used for all literal data, even if it will not vary.

This third point is important for cross-database portability, as separating out literal values allows database drivers to make database-specific optimizations.

Result objects

The return value from a `db_query()` call is result object. In order to access the data returned by the database server, we need to iterate over the result set.

```
$list = array();
foreach ($result as $record) {
  $list[] = t('@name: @filename', array(
    '@name' => $record->name,
    '@filename' => $record->filename,
  ));
}
```

By default, each `$record` in the result set is a `stdClass` object. We can, however, get the record as an associative array by telling the `db_query()` call that we want arrays instead. Here's how it is done:

```
$result = db_query("SELECT name, filename FROM {system} WHERE type =
:type AND status = :status", array(':type' => 'module', ':status' =>
1), array('fetch' => PDO::FETCH_ASSOC));
```

Here, we specify a third parameter to `db_query()`, which is another associative array of options. We specify only one option, the fetch mode, which we set to `PDO::FETCH_ASSOC`. This tells the database layer we want associative arrays instead of `stdClass` objects.

We can also fetch a single record, or even just a single field:

```
// Fetch a single record as an object.
$record = $result->fetchObject();

// Fetch a single record as an array.
$record = $result->fetchAssoc();

// Fetch just the first field of the next record.
$field = $result->fetchField();

// Fetch the entire result set at once into an array.
$records = $result->fetchAll();
```

See the online documentation for more details about various ways to retrieve data from a result set.

Dynamic queries

Although most SELECT queries are static, at times we will need a more flexible query. That could be because the query itself may change depending on incoming user data, because we want to allow other modules to modify our query before it is executed, or we want to take advantage of some database feature that is implemented differently on different databases. For these cases, Drupal provides a mechanism for building dynamic queries using a robust query builder.

To start, we create a new query object with `db_select()`:

```
$query = db_select('node', 'n');
```

The first parameter is the name of the base table of the query and the second is the alias we want to use for it. We then call additional methods on the `$query` object in order to build up the query logic we want to create dynamically. For example:

```
$query = db_select('node', 'n');
$query->fields('n', array('nid, title'));
$u_alias = $query->innerJoin('users' ,'u', '%alias.uid = n.uid');
$query->addField($u_alias, 'name', 'username');
$query->condition("{$u_alias}.name", 'Bob');
$query->condition('n.created', REQUEST_TIME - 604800, '>=');
$query->orderBy('n.created', 'DESC');
$query->range(0, 5);
$query->addTag('node_access');
$result = $query->execute();
```

The `fields()` method tells the query to select the fields in the second parameter from the table in the first parameter. In this case, as of line 2, our query would effectively read:

```
SELECT n.nid AS nid, n.title AS title FROM {node} n
```

Note that the curly braces are added for us automatically. Also note that aliases are created for every field. If we want to specify an alternate alias, we need to use the `addField()` method for that one field. We'll see more on that shortly. We can also join against other tables using the `innerJoin()`, `leftJoin()`, and `rightJoin()` methods. There is also `join()`, which is an alias of `innerJoin()`. The `join()` methods take the table to join against, its alias, and the join conditions as parameters in the form of an SQL fragment. Note that in this case we are using the string `%alias` in the join clause. That's because while we are joining against the users table and asking for an alias of "u", we may end up with a different alias if that alias already exists in this query. Although we're quite sure that's not the case here, it could be the case in `query_alter()` hooks, so it's a good habit to get into.

The `join()` methods all return the alias for the table that was actually used, so we can use that in later method calls. In this case we will also select one field from the users table, the user's name, and alias it to "username". Again, since there's a slight chance the alias could already be used, `addField()` will return the alias that was actually used for that field.

Our effective query now looks like this:

```
SELECT n.nid AS nid, n.title AS title, u.name AS username FROM {node}
n INNER JOIN {users} u ON u.nid = n.nid
```

Now we need to restrict the query, that is, add the WHERE clauses. That is done with the `condition()` method, which takes a field name, the value to match against, and optionally a comparator. The default is equals. The above lines, therefore, add WHERE clauses for a username of 'Bob' and a node creation time within the past week (that is, where the creation timestamp is greater than or equal to the current time minus seven days' worth of seconds). For more complex conditionals there is also a where() method that takes an SQL fragment.

We then tell the query to order by creation time, in descending order (DESC) and to only return five results starting with record 0, that is, the five most recently created nodes. Our SQL query now looks something like this:

```
SELECT n.nid AS nid, n.title AS title, u.name AS username
FROM {node} n
  INNER JOIN {users} u ON u.nid = n.nid
WHERE (n.created >= 1286213869)
  AND (u.name = 'Bob')
ORDER BY n.created DESC
LIMIT 5 OFFSET 0
```

There's one more important method to call — `addTag()`. This method doesn't affect the query directly but does mark the type of query it is. If a query has been tagged then before it is turned into an SQL string it will be passed through `hook_query_alter()` and `hook_query_TAG_alter()`. That allows other modules an opportunity to change the query if they need to. The `node_access` tag, used here, is most important as it allows the node access system to alter the query, to filter out nodes that the current user should not have access to.

> When querying the node table, always us a dynamic query with the `node_access` tag. If you do not, then you have a security hole.

Finally we execute the query. `execute()` takes the information we have provided, runs the query through alter hooks if necessary, compiles the corresponding SQL string, and runs the query, returning a result object. The result object is the same as that returned from a static query.

Also note that most methods of the select builder return the select object itself and thus are chainable. The exceptions are the `addField()` and `join()` methods, as those need to return a generated alias instead. The above query could therefore also have been written as:

```
$query = db_select('node', 'n');
$u_alias = $query->innerJoin('users' ,'u', '%alias.uid = n.uid');
$query->addField($u_alias, 'name', 'username');
$result = $query
  ->fields('n', array('nid, title'));
  ->condition("{$u_alias}.name", 'Bob');
  ->condition('n.created', REQUEST_TIME - 604800, '>=');
  ->orderBy('n.created', 'DESC');
  ->range(0, 5);
  ->addTag('node_access')
  ->execute();
```

The query builder is capable of building far more complex queries, too, including subselects, complex AND and OR conditions, among others. See the online documentation for the full details.

Insert queries

While SELECT queries have both static and dynamic versions, INSERT, UPDATE, DELETE, and MERGE queries only support a dynamic version. That is necessary in order to support the full range of SQL databases in the wild, many of which require extra special handling for some field types. As a nice bonus, the dynamic version of these queries is often much easier to work with than the static version would be and makes it easy to add additional database-specific optimizations. We'll look at **Insert queries** first.

Just as with Select queries, Insert queries start with a constructor function and are chainable. In fact, all methods of Insert queries are chainable.

```
$id = db_insert('imports')
  ->fields(array(
    'name' => 'Groucho',
    'address' => '123 Casablanca Ave.',
    'phone' => '555-1212',
  ))
  ->execute();
```

The db_insert() method creates a new insert query object for the imports table. We then call the fields() method on that object. fields() takes an associative array of values to insert. In this case, we are adding a record for one of the world's great comedians. We then execute the query, causing it to be translated into the appropriate query string and executed. If there is an auto-increment or "serial" field in the imports table, the generated ID will be returned. That's all there is to it.

db_insert() can get fancier, too. For instance, it supports multi-insert statements. To do that, we must first call fields() with an indexed array to specify what fields we are going to use and then call the values() method repeatedly with an associative array for each record.

```
$values[] = array(
   'name' => 'Groucho',
   'address' => '123 Casablanca Ave.',
   'phone' => '555-1212',
);
$values[] = array(
   'name' => 'Chico',
   'address' => '456 Races St.',
   'phone' => '555-1234',
);
$values[] = array(
   'name' => 'Harpo',
   'address' => '789 Horn Ave.',
   'phone' => '555-1234',
);
$values[] = array(
   'name' => 'Zeppo',
   'address' => '22 University Way',
   'phone' => '555-3579',
);

$insert = db_insert('imports')->fields(array('name', 'address',
'phone' => '555-1212'));
foreach ($values as $value) {
   $insert->values($value);
}
$insert->execute();
```

On databases that support multi-insert statements, the preceding code will be run as a single query. For those that don't, they will run as separate queries within a single transaction. That makes them extremely powerful and efficient for mass import operations. Note that in a multi-insert query the return value from execute() is undefined and should be ignored.

Update queries

Update queries look like a hybrid of `Insert` and `Select` statements. They consist of both fields to set on a table and conditions to restrict the query.

```
db_update('imports')
  ->condition('name', 'Chico')
  ->fields(array('address' => 'Go West St.'))
  ->execute();
```

The `condition()` method works exactly like the `condition()` method of Select queries, and we can add multiple if we need to. `fields()` takes an associative array of values to set. The above query is therefore equivalent to:

```
UPDATE {imports} SET address = 'Go West St.' WHERE name = 'Chico';
```

We still always want to use the dynamic approach rather than just call `db_query()`, because on some databases (such as PostgreSQL or Oracle) there are cases where the above query would not work and we would need to run multiple queries with bound values and other odd edge cases. All of that handling is handled for us automatically by the database layer.

The return value from `execute()` for Update queries is the number of records that were changed by the query. Note that 'changed' does not mean 'matched'. If the `WHERE` portion of the query matches a record but if that record already has the values that it would be set to, it will not be changed and would not count towards the return value from `execute()`.

Delete queries

Delete queries should come as no surprise, as they consist of essentially just a `WHERE` clause:

```
db_delete('imports')
  ->condition('name' => 'Zeppo')
  ->execute();
```

The return value from `execute()` for Delete query is the number of records that were deleted by the query.

Merge queries

Merge queries are one of the oft-forgotten parts of SQL. In part, that's because the most popular open source databases do not support them directly even though they are part of the SQL specification.

A Merge query says, in essence, "If this record exists, update it with this query otherwise create it with this other query". The syntax for it is somewhat verbose, but it is a very powerful concept. It is most useful for setting records that may or may not exist yet, that is, merging data into the table. It can also be very useful for incrementing counters.

A true merge query is atomic, that is, we're guaranteed that it will run as a single uninterrupted operation or fail completely. Since most of the databases Drupal works with do not directly support Merge queries, Drupal emulates them with multiple queries and a transaction, which in most cases is close enough.

The syntax should be familiar based on the other queries we've looked at already. The following example is straight out of the variable system:

```
db_merge('variable')
  ->key(array('name' => $name))
  ->fields(array('value' => serialize($value)))
  ->execute();
```

The `key()` method takes an associative array of field/value pairs that are the pivot of the query. The `fields()` method is about the fields to set, and works the same as it does on `Update` or `Insert` queries. The above query can be read as "If there is a record where the field 'name' has the value `$name`, set the 'value' field. If not, insert a new record with name equal to `$name` and value equal to the given string." (Isn't the query above so much easier to say?)

We can also define more complex logic using the `insertFields()` and `updateFields()` methods. Those work exactly like `fields()` but, as we might expect, apply only when taking the insert or update branches.

```
db_merge('people')
  ->key(array('job' => 'Speaker'))
  ->insertFields(array(
    'age' => 31,
    'name' => 'Meredith',
  ))
  ->updateFields(array(
    'name' => 'Tiffany',
  ))
  ->execute();
```

In this case, if there is already a record whose job field is "Speaker" its name field will be updated to Tiffany. If not, a new record will be created with 'job' as Speaker and 'name' as Meredith. (Yes, this example is rather contrived.)

Advanced subjects

While the five basic types of queries cover the vast majority of our database needs, there are two other advanced subjects we should cover: Transactions and master/slave replication. We will just touch on each briefly.

Transactions

A transaction in a database is a way to wrap two or more queries together and declare that they should be atomic. That is, either all succeed or none succeed. That can be very useful when, say, saving a node; we don't want only some fields to get written and then an error to break the process halfway through. We saw an example of that in *Chapter 6*. In a nutshell, in Drupal we start a transaction by creating a transaction object. Everything we do to the database is then part of the transaction until that object is destroyed, at which point the entire query is committed at once. In most cases, we let PHP destroy the transaction object for us when a function ends.

```
function my_function() {
  $transaction = db_transaction();
  try {
    $id = db_insert('example')
      ->fields(array(
        'field1' => 'mystring',
        'field2' => 5,
      ))
      ->execute();
    my_other_function($id);
    return $id;
  }
  catch (Exception $e) {
    $transaction->rollback();
    watchdog_exception('type', $e);
  }
}
```

In most cases we don't need a transaction, and they have no effect on Select queries. They're most useful when we're going to be running a lot of data modification queries (Insert, Update, Delete, and Merge) together, and the system will be broken if only some of them run. Imports, rebuilds of lookup tables, and other modules allowed to run queries via hook in the middle of our process are good candidates.

Slave servers

Drupal also supports Master/slave database replication. Certain select queries can be run against a slave server to offload the work to separate servers, allowing the site to scale better. However, most sites do not have a slave server configured, so how do we write code that will work properly either way?

Drupal lets us do so by specifying "targets". The third parameter to `db_query()` or `db_select()` is an array of options that tweak the behavior of the query. We saw the `fetch` key earlier. The other key of interest is `target`, which specifies which database variant the system should try. Legal values are `default` (which is the default) and `slave`. If "slave" is specified, Drupal will try to run the query against a slave server. If one is not available, though, it will silently fall back to using the default server. Using our previous example:

```
$result = db_query("SELECT name, filename FROM {system} WHERE type =
:type AND status = :status", array(':type' => 'module', ':status' =>
1), array('fetch' => PDO::FETCH_ASSOC, 'target' => 'slave'));
```

The way we handle the query is otherwise identical.

So why don't all Select queries use the slave server? Data on a slave server is always a little behind the master server, by a fraction of a second or as much as a minute or two depending on the configuration and traffic. Not all `Select` queries can handle their data being slightly stale and there's no reliable way to detect automatically which are which, so by default all queries use the master server.

However, there is another trick up our sleeve which we can use. After writing data, we can call `db_ignore_slave()`. That will make a note in the active session to disable the slave server for the current user only for a configurable period of time. (The default is five minutes.) That way, `Select` queries run on subsequent page requests by that user will always get the most up-to-date data but other users will get the old data until the slave servers catch up. That can be very useful, for instance, when a user posts a comment. They want to see the comment immediately but it's OK if other users don't see it for 20-30 seconds.

Summary

Although in practice it's surprising how often we won't need to deal with the database directly, we do in some way or the other. In this appendix we've seen how to leverage Drupal's database layer to build powerful, cross-database queries that are, in many cases, easier to work with than SQL, while still mirroring actual SQL.

- We've seen how to portably and securely write arbitrary SQL queries.

- We've seen how to allow other modules to modify our queries before they're run.

- We've seen how to write complex queries that change based on user input in a portable way.

- We now know how to write data modification queries that will be automatically optimized for whatever database we happen to be using.

- We've seen how to use transactions to make our code more robust and fault-tolerant.

- We understand how to support master/slave replication to allow sites to scale to high levels of traffic.

B
Security

Throughout this book, we have repeatedly discussed the question of security. What makes good security practice? How do we make code more secure? How do we protect against common attacks? That's because security is not a feature to be bolted into a program. It is part and parcel of the development process itself.

Nonetheless, because it is such an important subject this appendix will give an overview of the tools Drupal offers to help make code more secure, and the sorts of things to think about when writing code to ensure that our code is as secure as possible. It is by no means exhaustive; many books have been written exclusively on the subject of security. However, it should lay a strong foundation for approaching code writing in a secure fashion.

Thinking securely

Security is a process. Specifically, it is a development process. The most important aspect of security is how we approach the code that we are going to write. We need to "think securely" in order to write robust code. Although there are many aspects to thinking securely, it can be summed up as "think paranoid".

The vast majority of input into our system is going to be sane and what we expect, not dangerous. However, there will always be that last 1% that is not at all what we expect. It could be someone deliberately trying to break into our website. It could be a spambot trying to find vulnerabilities so that it can turn our site into a billboard for fake proscription drugs. Alternatively, it could just be an honest user who entered input that we didn't anticipate and account for. All of these things will happen at some point during the life of a website or web application, and the best way to protect against them is to assume that any input is a suspected attack until we can verify otherwise.

Always assume that incoming data is insecure until and unless it's been processed to ensure that it is safe.

Most security vulnerabilities come from not properly checking whether a piece of data is what we expect it to be. Remember also that there are many of types of input.

- Any information coming from the user, either in the GET query or a POST request, is input and may be insecure.
- Any cookies the user sends are input, and may be faked.
- Any files read from disk are input, which may contain data we do not expect. Even if not malicious, unexpected data formats can pose a serious security risk.
- Any data stored in a database that we didn't write to may be insecure.
- Even data stored in Drupal's own database may be insecure, unless we know for certain that we cleaned it before saving it.

 Data does not have to be malicious in order to be a security threat.

Also remember that our website may not be the target of an attack. A very common tactic is to post comments on a website that contains JavaScript that, when viewed, will take over a user's web browser or trick them into visiting another site that will download malicious code to their computer. Although our site is not harmed, it is still used as a way to attack another user. We don't want that.

Filtering versus escaping

There are two ways of dealing with potentially insecure data, namely, filtering and escaping.

Filtering involves stripping out portions of the data that could be trouble, or forcing the data into a simpler, safer form. Common practice in PHP is to filter all input into the system unequivocally. Drupal takes a slightly different tactic, as for certain pieces of content, such as a node body, we may not know the proper format in advance. If a user changes a text format setting, for instance, we don't want the user's previous text to be lost, just filtered differently. Instead, we filter it on output.

Filtering

The following guidelines then should guide us as to how to properly screen incoming data:

- If we know in advance that a given piece of data is supposed to be numeric, and logically would not make sense otherwise, cast it to an integer or a float in order to filter out unsafe strings.

- If we know in advance that there are a fixed number of possible values a piece of data could hold, outrightly reject any values that are not one of those on the allowed list. In most cases, Drupal's form API does this for us.

- Do not filter out HTML tags when saving textual data to the database, as whether those tags are appropriate or not depends on where they get displayed later.

- Treat any textual data, even if it comes from our own database, as unsafe until filtered at display time.

Drupal provides a number of tools for filtering textual data. The most important are:

- `filter_xss()` will strip out all HTML tags except those in a specified list. The default list is reasonably safe.

- `filter_xss_admin()` is the same as `filter_xss()`, but with a very permissive tag list. It is best used for text that we know will only be entered by a trusted administrator.

- `check_markup()` will filter a piece of text according to a specified set of filter rules, which are configured through the administrative UI as text formats.

- `check_plain()` takes a more sledgehammer approach to a piece of text. Rather than removing untrustworthy HTML tags, it escapes all HTML tags so that they will appear literally in the browser. See below for more on escaping.

Escaping HTML

Escaping, by contrast, does not remove content from a piece of data but encodes it in a format that another system expects to avoid confusing that system. For instance, if we want to print HTML tags to the page such that the user can see them, we need to escape the < and > characters using HTML entity codes. The two most common systems that Drupal will be sending data to are an SQL database and the web browser, and both require different approaches.

For output to the browser, check_markup() may be configured to escape HTML or other content. The check_plain() function takes a somewhat more sledge-hammer approach, escaping all HTML in a string so that it displays verbatim on the page for the user to see.

SQL injection

For writing to the database, Drupal's database layer is built on the concept of prepared statements. Prepared statements, among other things, cleanly separate the SQL query from the variable data in it. That allows the database server itself to sanely construct a query while escaping input itself, avoiding the common attack known as "SQL injection". For example, a value that contains an apostrophe causes a syntax error in an SQL statement (since single quotes have meaning in SQL) at best, or allows an arbitrary extra SQL query to sneak into the command at worst.

To avoid that problem, never, ever put a variable into an SQL string directly. When writing a query against Drupal's database, always ensure that the query portion is a single string literal using placeholders and then provide values for the placeholders. Doing so will allow the database to separate the query template from the variable content and avoid SQL injection. If the query itself is variable, use the dynamic query builder, db_select().

 SQL injection from badly written queries is the most common, and the most easily avoidable, form of security vulnerability.

Node access control

A particularly Drupal-specific security question is how to control access to nodes. While Drupal's permission system handles the common use case of globally-readable nodes and limited access to edit or delete nodes, there are plenty of cases where we need more complex access control. Drupal's node access system handles those cases, but it requires that we tie into it every time we look up nodes, that is, any time we run a query that tries to find records in the node table.

Since there are so many varied situations where nodes could be used, such additional access checks can only be done at the database level, that is, in the query itself. Fortunately, Drupal allows modules to manipulate certain types of queries before they are executed to add any sort of filtering. In order to allow Drupal to modify our queries, we need to "tag" them appropriately.

First, whenever we write a query against the node table, we must use a dynamic query, built using db_select(). Second, we must call the addTag() method on the query object and give it a tag of node_access. For example:

```
$result = db_select('node')
  ->fields('node')
  ->condition('type', 'page')
  ->addTag('node_access')
  ->execute();
```

In the preceding code, we are selecting all the data in the node table for nodes of type "page". The extra tag, however, allows Drupal to alter the query before it is run and also to filter out nodes that the current user does not have access to view.

 Always use a dynamic query with a tag of node_access when querying the node table so that Drupal can apply additional security filters that are necessary.

See http://drupal.org/node/310077 for more details on how query tagging and query alteration work, and how some other common tags work.

Handling insecure code

Sooner or later, you will stumble across code that is insecure. It could be a module that you have written, or a contributed module that you have downloaded from Drupal.org, or possibly even Drupal core itself. No code is perfectly secure and no developer is perfect, either, so it will happen. It's just a question of when and what we do about it.

Regardless of whose code it is, the way to handle it is more or less the same:

- Don't panic.
- Investigate the module in question (whether ours or not) to determine exactly what the problem is. Sometimes it's a very simple bug that is easily fixed, and at other times it's very subtle. We need to figure out if it affects just one version of the module or multiple versions, or if it applies only to certain configurations (say, only on Apache web servers, only on Windows OS), among other things.
- If we are able to do so, put together a patch that fixes the issue but do *not* post it to the issue queue.
- Don't panic.

- Send a detailed description of the problem, along with a patch if you were able to make one, to the Drupal Security Team at `security@drupal.org`. They coordinate all security-related matters for code hosted on `drupal.org`. If it's not one of our modules, they will coordinate with the maintainer of the module.

- If it is one of our modules, let the security team review the problem and the patch. If they agree that it is a security hole, they will work with us to vet the patch or improve it and schedule a security release. It will be up to us to write a Security Advisory (SA) as well.

- Security releases almost always come out on Wednesdays, so we wait until we get a go-ahead from the security team. When they say its clear to do so, we apply the patch to all affected releases of the module and create a new release. The security team will then publish the SA.

- Did we mention don't panic?

Drupal operates on a principle of full disclosure. When a security issue is discovered, it is kept secret until a fix is made available. Once a fix is made available, the full details of the security issue, including the code to fix it and what releases are affected, is published for the whole world to see. This is a standard security best practice, as on the one hand it minimizes the chances of a ne'er-do-well learning of the vulnerability before there is a fix available but on the other, once a fix is available, we make it as easy as possible for people to know that they need to upgrade their code in order to stay secure before an attacker can take advantage of it.

For more information on how to handle security issues in Drupal, see:

```
http://drupal.org/security-team
```

Staying up to date

So how do we keep a site up-to-date with the latest security fixes? There are two key ways to stay on top of security needs, and any site administrator should make use of both of them.

First, all Drupal Security Advisories are announced on Drupal.org at the following site:

```
http://drupal.org/security
```

There are both RSS feeds to subscribe to and e-mail lists we can join to get notified any time an SA is issued. All Drupal site administrators and developers should subscribe to one or the other in order to be notified when there is a security-related release. Both are, fortunately, very low-traffic.

Second, Drupal itself includes a module called Update Status that will periodically connect to `drupal.org` to see if there is a new version of any module installed on our site. It is enabled by default but can be disabled. Don't disable it, though. In fact, it's best to keep the e-mail notification option enabled as well to remind us by e-mail when a module has a new security release. We can't keep a site secure if we don't know that it has a vulnerability to begin with.

Summary

Security is a large subject, and one that we could easily spend much more time discussing in greater detail. However, for the time being it is sufficient to focus on a secure approach to overall development.

- Security is a process
- All incoming data, from whatever source, should not be trusted until it has been verified and sanitized
- Filter all data, either on input or on output as appropriate
- Always filter or escape data sent to the browser in a way that makes sense, given where it will be used
- Protect against SQL injection using prepared statements, and never, ever put a variable directly into an SQL query
- When security vulnerabilities are discovered, don't panic, but follow established best practices to report and fix the problem
- Always stay on top of available security releases for Drupal or Drupal modules

Index

Symbols

Thank you for buying
Drupal 7 Module Development

About Packt Publishing

Packt, pronounced 'packed', published its first book "*Mastering phpMyAdmin for Effective MySQL Management*" in April 2004 and subsequently continued to specialize in publishing highly focused books on specific technologies and solutions.

Our books and publications share the experiences of your fellow IT professionals in adapting and customizing today's systems, applications, and frameworks. Our solution based books give you the knowledge and power to customize the software and technologies you're using to get the job done. Packt books are more specific and less general than the IT books you have seen in the past. Our unique business model allows us to bring you more focused information, giving you more of what you need to know, and less of what you don't.

Packt is a modern, yet unique publishing company, which focuses on producing quality, cutting-edge books for communities of developers, administrators, and newbies alike. For more information, please visit our website: www.packtpub.com.

About Packt Open Source

In 2010, Packt launched two new brands, Packt Open Source and Packt Enterprise, in order to continue its focus on specialization. This book is part of the Packt Open Source brand, home to books published on software built around Open Source licences, and offering information to anybody from advanced developers to budding web designers. The Open Source brand also runs Packt's Open Source Royalty Scheme, by which Packt gives a royalty to each Open Source project about whose software a book is sold.

Writing for Packt

We welcome all inquiries from people who are interested in authoring. Book proposals should be sent to author@packtpub.com. If your book idea is still at an early stage and you would like to discuss it first before writing a formal book proposal, contact us; one of our commissioning editors will get in touch with you.

We're not just looking for published authors; if you have strong technical skills but no writing experience, our experienced editors can help you develop a writing career, or simply get some additional reward for your expertise.

Drupal 7

ISBN: 978-1-84951-286-2   Paperback: 416 pages

A comprehensive beginner's guide to installing, configuring, and building a professional Drupal 7 website

1. Set up, configure, and deploy a Drupal 7 website

2. Easily add exciting and powerful features

3. Design and implement your website's look and feel

4. Promote, manage, and maintain your live website

Drupal 6 Panels Cookbook

ISBN: 978-1-849511-18-6   Paperback: 220 pages

Over 40 recipes to harness the power of Panels for building attractive Drupal websites

1. Build complex site layouts quickly with panels

2. Combine Panels with other Drupal modules to create dynamic social media websites

3. Get solutions to the most common 'Panels' problems

4. A practical approach packed with real-world examples to enrich understanding

5. Part of Packt's Cookbook series — each recipe is a carefully organized sequence of instructions to complete the task as efficiently as possible

[PACKT] open source ✲
PUBLISHING
community experience distilled

Drupal 6 Performance Tips

ISBN: 978-1-847195-84-5   Paperback: 240 pages

Learn how to maximize and optimize your Drupal framework using Drupal 6 best practice performance solutions and tools

1. Monitor the performance of your Drupal website and improve it

2. Configure a Drupal multisite environment for best performance

3. Lot of examples with clear explanations

4. Choose and use the best Drupal modules for improving your site's performance

Drupal E-commerce
with Ubercart 2.x

ISBN: 978-1-847199-20-1   Paperback: 300 pages

Build, administer, and customize an online store using Drupal with Ubercart

1. Create a powerful e-shop using the award-winning CMS Drupal and the robust e-commerce module Ubercart

2. Create and manage the product catalog and insert products in manual or batch mode

3. Apply SEO (search engine optimization) to your e-shop and adopt turn-key internet marketing techniques

4. Implement advanced techniques like cross-selling, product comparison, coupon codes, and segmented pricing

Please check **www.PacktPub.com** for information on our titles

LaVergne, TN USA
22 February 2011

217521LV00006B/51/P